Dear Pastor Berndt —

Please acc[ept] [this] [as a] token of my a[ppreciation for all] you have done & continue [to do] for myself and my family.

You have been an inspiration and a Rock in my spiritual walk with Christ Jesus.

I know how much you value missionary work, medicine and interesting spiritual stories! Dr Stevens weaves all three elements into a wonderful book to read.

I hope you enjoy it as much as I did...

In Christ, your brother,

Randy Fowler MD

2/2003

PRAISE FOR *Jesus, M.D.* BY DAVID STEVENS

Jesus, M.D. is irresistible. Drawing upon a global collection of fascinating medical stories, Dr. Stevens weaves life lessons that both challenge and inspire. This book contains something for everyone—just don't read it while eating a tuna sandwich!

RICHARD A. SWENSON, M.D.
PHYSICIAN, FUTURIST, AUTHOR OF FIVE BOOKS, INCLUDING
MARGIN AND *MORE THAN MEETS THE EYE*

A must-read not only for pre-med and medical students, teaching physicians and those in clinical practice, but also for every Christian who wants to think, feel, and react more like Jesus would in difficult life situations and thereby increase their power for living and impact on others.

HAROLD G. KOENIG, M.D.
ASSOCIATE PROFESSOR OF PSYCHIATRY AND MEDICINE
DUKE UNIVERSITY MEDICAL CENTER
AUTHOR OF *THE HEALING CONNECTION* (WORD PUBLISHERS) AND
THE HEALING POWER OF FAITH (SIMON & SCHUSTER)

Jesus, M.D. is one of the most exciting and inspiring books I have read in a long time. The applications drawn from the life of Christ are both insightful and compelling. It is an excellent book well worth reading. I found it hard to put down until I had read it all.

THOMAS H. HERMIZ
PRESIDENT, WORLD GOSPEL MISSION

When I was 16 years old, I dreamed of becoming a missionary physician. As the years went by, I felt God calling me into psychiatry instead, where I could be a "full-time missionary" to my patients. Now, 40 years after that dream, I see patients daily and ask myself the question, "What would Jesus, the Great Physician, do or say in this situation?" This book, *Jesus, M.D.*, was exciting for me to read. It reinforced the excitement I feel in serving the Great Physician. The book also gives countless lessons of life that we all benefit from by learning and applying them to our lives—no matter what career we find ourselves in.

PAUL MEIER, M.D., OF NEW LIFE CLINICS

What a privilege to be able to endorse *Jesus, M.D.* David Stevens is a man sold out to God and has written a book that is enlightening, challenging and convicting. I recommend this book highly.

RON BLUE
FOUNDER & PRESIDENT OF RONALD BLUE & CO., LLC

"Dr. Jesus never forgot his higher purpose. He didn't content himself with only temporary physical treatments; he was just as, and often, more concerned about offering spiritual healing and eternal life." Dr. Stevens reflects upon the ministry of Jesus Christ in applying those lessons to his years in medical service. For Christians the admonition is clear: "It's important to ask, what is God doing? And to then become a part of His plan."

JAMES N. THOMPSON, M.D.
VICE PRESIDENT/DEAN
WAKE FOREST UNIVERSITY SCHOOL OF MEDICINE

Jesus M.D.

A Doctor Examines
the Great Physician

DAVID STEVENS, M.D.
with GREGG LEWIS

ZondervanPublishingHouse
Grand Rapids, Michigan

A Division of HarperCollins*Publishers*

We want to hear from you. Please send your comments about this book to us in care of the address below. Thank you.

ZondervanPublishingHouse
Grand Rapids, Michigan 49530
http://www.zondervan.com

Jesus, M.D.
Copyright © 2001 by David Stevens
Requests for information should be addressed to:

Zondervan Publishing House

Grand Rapids, Michigan 49530

Library of Congress Cataloging-in-Publication Data

Stevens, David, 1951-
    Jesus, M.D., a doctor examines the Great Physician / David Stevens
    with Gregg Lewis.
       p.   cm.
    ISBN 0-310-23433-6
    1. Physicians—Religious life.   2. Missionaries, Medical—Religious life.
    3. Jesus Christ—Example.   I. Lewis, Gregg, 1951-   II. Title.
    BV4596.P5 S72 2001
    232.9'04—dc21
                                                      00-068669
                                                               CIP

This edition printed on acid-free paper.

Interior design by Melissa Elenbaas

Printed in the United States of America

---

02 03 04 05 06 07 08 /❖ DC/ 10 9 8 7 6 5 4 3 2

CONTENTS

To four people who shaped my life:

Dr. Maurice Stevens, evangelist, missionary, and dad—who showed me the greatest investment of a man's life is in the kingdom

Beverly Stevens, teacher, author, and godly mother—nothing is too daunting when you are praying for me

Dr. Ernie Steury, missionary doctor and mentor— you personify the Great Physician to me

Jody Stevens, loving wife, mother, and friend—the smartest thing I ever did was to marry you

FOREWORD

I MUST CONFESS THAT I HAD PLANNED TO LEAF through the manuscript of this book, picking up its message and the quality of its writing just enough for me to be able to recommend the book by an author whose life I already respected very highly. Within a chapter or two I found that the book took hold of me and held me in the grip of its fascination. I simply had to read every word. He had me sitting on the edge of my chair with Kleenex readily available.

There are now three reasons why I plan to give copies of this book to my friends as soon as it is published. The first is that it is an exciting storybook. Dr. Dave Stevens has had more than his share of dramatic life-and-death battles in which he has helped patients with every kind of near-fatal disease and accident in East Africa, often without the basic tools and medicines that every doctor needs. He is a great storyteller.

The title *Jesus, M.D.* tells us that Dave has studied and wants to share with us what he has learned about the great variety of healing work that Jesus accomplished on earth. The book alternates stories about Jesus healing in Palestine with stories from Kenya today. Now we see the spiritual principles that lay behind the physical healings at the hands of Jesus, M.D., and how they relate to the real needs of sick people today.

The third and dominant appeal is that it gradually becomes clear that the book is a challenge. It is for doctors and for all who share in a healing ministry for the sick. It reminds us that Jesus, M.D., is alive today and that His Spirit can take hold of any one of us and work through us for total healing—Spirit, Mind, and Body. We see that the acceptance of that challenge can transform our own lives as well as the lives of our patients, as our hands become the instruments of the living Christ today.

DR. PAUL BRAND
Department of Orthopedics at
University of Washington
Author, *Fearfully and Wonderfully Made,*
The Gift of Pain, and *In His Image*

WHAT KIND OF DOCTOR WAS JESUS?

JESUS, M.D. SOUNDS A LITTLE ODD, DOESN'T IT? BUT should it? The New Testament contains more than seventy-five references to the healing work and ministry of Christ. Down through the centuries, one of the names his followers have traditionally used to refer to Christ has been *the Great Physician*. The term is every bit as orthodox as *the Good Shepherd* or *King of Kings*. Indeed, the image of Jesus as *Great Physician* could be even more instructive for us today.

After all, how many of us, as we begin the twenty-first century, can personally relate to the ways and work of shepherds? Unlike the people of Jesus' day and for many following centuries, we have little practical experience with sheep and their everyday care. Come to think of it, few of us have any firsthand knowledge of royalty either. Kings are even more rare than shepherds in our day and age.

In contrast there are more M.D.'s today than at any point in human history. The United States alone boasts 800,000 licensed physicians. Most of us are personally acquainted with many doctors and have probably sat longer in more of their waiting rooms than we want to remember. So perhaps the time has come when anyone who wants to better understand and follow Jesus will benefit from a closer examination of the life and practice of *the Great Physician.*

Jesus Christ, M.D. It's still as hard to imagine that name on a sign in front of a modern medical building as it is to picture a hospital name tag reading "Dr. Jesus." Trying to envision him in a contemporary health-care setting raises all sorts of interesting images and questions— such as: What kind of physician would Jesus be?

I can almost hear the argument in the doctors' lounge now. There are representatives from numerous specialties—each one convinced, with scriptural references to bolster his or her argument, that they know for certain what kind of doctor Jesus would be, because he was clearly "one of us."

- The orthopedist knows Jesus was a fellow orthopod. After all, he made the lame walk and the "bowed" to stand straight (Luke 11:11–13).
- The internist notes that he healed people with heart failure (dropsy) (Luke 13:2–4).
- The ophthalmologist counters, "Don't forget he made the blind to see" (Luke 18:35–43).
- A neurologist points out that Jesus cured a man with palsy (Luke 5:18–25).
- Our ear-nose-throat specialist reminds us that he caused the deaf to hear (Luke 7:22).
- The infectious-disease specialist proudly declares, "He cured leprosy!" (Luke 5:12–14; 17:11–19).
- Then the pediatrician quotes Jesus himself, who said, "Let the little children come to me" (Luke 18:16).

- An elderly GP points out that great crowds came to Jesus for healing (Matt. 15:30), surely proving he must have been a general practitioner. A younger family practitioner thinks that Scripture and others imply that Jesus dealt with whole families, from young to old, and worked in the community.
- Nobody is surprised when the psychiatrist cites Jesus' treatment of the mentally ill (Luke 4:33–36).
- Of course, the gynecologist mentions the woman with the issue of blood (Luke 8:43–48).
- Everyone laughs with the colleague fresh from the OR who says: "Jesus must have had the heart of a surgeon. Note the boldness he showed in Luke 19:45–46, when he chased the moneychangers out of the temple with a whip. He rushed in where others feared to tread. He didn't carry a stethoscope. After reading Matthew 5:29–30, I'm sure he'd agree, 'When in doubt, cut it out.'"

I always try to respect the opinions of my learned colleagues in medicine, even as I appreciate their expertise and sense of pride in their chosen specialties. However, when it comes to deciding what kind of doctor Jesus was, I would have to disagree with all of the conclusions reached in this imagined scenario. It's obvious to me that Jesus was a missionary doctor.

You're probably thinking, *Wait a minute! Weren't you a missionary doctor? Your opinion is just as biased as any of those medical specialists!*

Maybe. Our personal experiences usually do color our perspective. So here in this book my observations and understanding of *Jesus, M.D.*, indeed will be shaped, not just by my own career as a medical professional, but by my years as a missionary doctor.

So humor me a little when I include some personal illustrations of the adventure and challenge faced by medical missionaries today as we carefully examine the Great Physician together. I know that by thoughtfully considering the life and example of the Great Physician,

I am repeatedly reminded as to what kind of physician my patients are looking for and what kind of doctor I want when I am a patient myself.

More important, by looking at both the practice and the person of Dr. Jesus, I have begun to see not only what kind of doctor, but what kind of person I want to be. Thus, you don't need a white coat or a stethoscope to keep reading.

This is not a book just for doctors and medical professionals. By looking to Jesus Christ as our model and personal mentor, I expect every reader (laypeople and medical folk alike) to identify practices, principles, and priorities in Jesus' life—specifically in his role as the Great Physician—from which we all need to learn. We'll do that by checking out his appointment schedule, accompanying him on rounds, and observing his bedside manner. We will watch Jesus, in his doctor role, as he examines, diagnoses, and heals. We will learn as medical students have learned for centuries—by observing, one on one, a masterful mentor superbly practicing his profession. We will compare and contrast his practice with mine and some of my colleagues, looking for applications in our personal and professional lives—sometimes even prescribing treatments that will benefit us all.

Together we will examine the Great Physician and look at him from a new perspective—through the eyes of a doctor. Hopefully, we will also let him examine us in the process.

Let's see what we all can learn about and from *Jesus, M.D.* There's no need to delay this divine appointment any longer.

PANGA SUNDAY

1

PANGA IS THE SWAHILI WORD FOR MACHETE. I KNEW that, and I knew other tribes used the same word, because my wife, Jody, and I had just recently fin-ished six months of Kipsigis (kip-suh-geez) language school and were serving our first term with World Gospel Mission at Tenwek Hospital in the beautiful highlands of the Kericho District in southwestern Kenya. At age thirty, after years of planning, praying, and preparing and after packing up my young fam-ily and moving eight thousand miles away from home, I felt excited to have finally begun my life's work as a missionary doctor.

I was still very much a rookie, but on this par-ticular Sunday, I happened to be the senior physician on duty at the hospital. The older doctors were gone. Thus, I would be expected to handle—on my own—any emergencies or medical crises that arose.

Since I had done my residency in family prac-tice, I felt capable of dealing with the vast majority

of routine cases I'd encountered since my arrival at Tenwek just months before. But I confess to feeling a little leery about what surgical emergencies might come in the door during the absence of my more experienced colleagues. That day my worst nightmare came true.

Sundays were always different from the normal daily routine. As the doctor on call, I had seen the sickest patients, examined new admissions, and checked the maternity ward for problems. I missed church and got home late for lunch, hoping to catch up on a little correspondence. It was about four o'clock on a sunny afternoon when the call came from the hospital saying we'd just received a trauma patient who needed immediate surgery—something about a *panga* wound.

I sprinted up the hill through the compound to the hospital, arriving at the OR short of breath from the high altitude and totally unprepared for what I saw in front of me. A forty-year-old Kipsigis man, covered in blood, was lying on the operating table. The blow from a machete had caught him across the bridge of his nose and sliced all the way across and through his face, down to the bottom of his jaw. His face had been literally cut in two, with the lower half peeled forward and lying on his chest.

The patient was in shock and struggling for breath. Amazed that the man hadn't bled out and died on his way to the hospital, I gave orders to mobilize what we at Tenwek referred to as our "walking blood bank." That is, we put out a call for any missionaries or hospital staff on the compound with matching blood type to quickly donate enough blood to save this patient.

Meantime, the nurse had started an IV and fluids were running wide open. I ordered a second IV in the other arm as I worked to secure his airway because the patient was in danger of choking to death from blood and his own secretions. The quickest and easiest thing would have been to intubate him, but that would have required placing an endotracheal tube into his throat—right through the middle of his gaping wound. I had no choice but to perform my second emergency tracheostomy ever—no small challenge without proper anesthesia or instruments. I breathed a big sigh of relief once I'd cut open his neck, placed the tube directly into the trachea, and saw the patient immediately begin breathing more easily.

As soon as we got the man stabilized, I literally ran from the OR to the doctors' "office," a closet-sized room where we kept the hospital's medical library. I didn't even know what to call this type of wound, but it probably wasn't in any index anyway. I grabbed our only orthopedic atlas and hurriedly thumbed through pictures and diagrams searching for something that looked like my patient's case. It was time to do what we often call on the mission field "a little cookbook surgery."

For some reason American medical texts don't contain much about machete wounds of the face. The closest thing I could find was in an orthopedic text showing a diagram for repairing different types of maxilla (upper jaw) fractures. Le Fort-type fractures are facial injuries that occur most often in automobile accidents where people are smashed into the dash so violently that the maxilla is fractured all the way across their cheekbones.

Actually, the textbook diagram I found only showed bones separated less than a quarter of an inch, so they didn't look much like my patient, whose entire face was lying open. The similarity was in the fact that these Le Fort fractures also resulted in a separation of facial bones and required literally pulling those bones (and the face) back together. Deciding this was probably as close an example as I was going to find, I started reading the text even as I rushed back to surgery.

By the time I walked into the OR, however, I realized I hadn't found the solution, but merely defined the problem. What good is a cookbook if you lack the ingredients?

The first step mentioned in the text was to wire the upper and lower teeth together with "arch bars." I had never seen a set of arch bars, let alone applied them. I showed the nurse the picture (she had never seen arch bars either) and sent her to the hospital storage room on the slim chance she could find a set—or at least uncover something else, anything, we might use to make do. Then I propped the text open on a stand beside the operating table and began looking back and forth between my patient and the pictures in the book to decide where and how to start putting this man's face back together. I knew if I didn't, he would certainly die.

About that time things went from bad to worse as the outpatient staff, almost in a panic, wheeled in a second victim. The same attacker had taken his *panga* to the twenty-some-year-old nephew of my first patient. The younger man's right arm had been almost completely severed just above the wrist, and another blow had chopped through the bone in the upper left arm—leaving it attached only by a bit of skin and muscle. He'd also suffered deep wounds to his back and three or four more blows to the head, blows that had gone through both tables (layers) of the skull. He was barely breathing and had no measurable blood pressure after being transported over who knows how many miles of rough roads.

Now I had two critical patients desperately needing emergency surgery in just one operating room—and I was the only doctor on duty.

Fortunately there was one other M.D. at the mission that day, so I sent for him. He arrived within minutes and immediately pitched in to help. Unfortunately, he was newer to the field than I was.

Never in my short professional life had I felt so aware of my own inadequacy as I did standing in that OR between those two patients. I had long dreamed of coming to Africa and perhaps earning a reputation as a modern-day David Livingstone. I naively envisioned becoming a medical superhero who could save his patients lives and their souls single-handedly—and simultaneously. I had worked and studied to become a missionary doctor for years. I had attended and graduated with honors from a Christian college with a widely respected premed program. I had been in the top 5 percent of my medical-school class. I chose one of the largest and best family-practice residency programs in the country to receive the breadth of experience I thought would be the most helpful when I got to Africa. My final year of residency, I even gained valuable administrative experience when I was named Chief Resident in our forty-resident program. By the time I left for the mission field I was prepared for anything—or so I thought.

But nothing in my training or experience had adequately prepared me for *Panga* Sunday.

I learned a lot about trusting God that day as I operated on those two men for the next eight hours. I used surgical procedures I'd never seen, let alone performed. Any stateside trauma center receiving patients like those would have mobilized more specialists than could have fit in our operating room. At Tenwek on *Panga* Sunday there was no one else to call.

We put in a central venous line and pumped both fluids and donated blood into the second patient to reestablish pressure. There was nothing to be done with his arms except to complete the amputations, carefully sew up the stumps and quickly control the bleeding in his other wounds. As my colleague worked on this fellow, I concentrated my attention on the first patient.

The nurse I had sent on a desperate scavenger hunt actually found a set of arch bars in our storage area. Whoever had donated them to our mission hospital never realized how desperately they would be needed. God had answered my prayer.

Using our limited dental and orthopedic instruments, I wired one bar to the upper teeth and one to the lower—one tooth at a time. I then wired the two arch bars together. By that time I was already worn out, but I wasn't half done. The more difficult part of the procedure lay ahead.

How could I elevate the lower face back into place when we lacked the instruments needed? "Necessity is the mother of invention" should be emblazoned on the operating room wall of every mission hospital.

The textbook showed what I needed to do was to wire the lower face to the bone above the eye (the superorbital ridge) in order to anchor everything in place. That required running a wire from the arch bars, up through the side of the face just under the skin, to where I could feed it into a small hole I would have to drill through the bone at the outside of each eye socket and tie the wire off. Sounds simple when you put it in one sentence, but I knew it was going to take hours for me to complete the procedure.

Problem number one: I lacked the surgical instrument needed to ream out a small tunnel in the subcutaneous tissue of the face, through which I could then thread the wire from the jaw up to the superorbital ridge.

How could I do that?

I thought of a surgical gadget we had called a Hemovac—a small cylindrical device used to suction blood during abdominal surgery. The Hemovac has a sharp metal attachment called a trocar—about six inches long and a quarter inch in diameter. It looks a little like a thick meat skewer. A trocar is typically used to make a hole through the abdominal wall and the surrounding tissue in order to insert a small drainage tube after intestinal trauma.

That trocar proved to be just what I needed. I tunneled it through the subcutaneous tissue of the cheek, up to the superorbital ridge, then threaded the wire through the resulting tunnel and tied into the bone where I had drilled a small hole. After finally approximating the bones and snugging the two halves of the man's face into place again, I began sewing the tissue back together—beginning deep inside and slowly closing the wound as I worked my way to the surface.

By the time I finished operating around midnight, I was totally exhausted. The physical strain was surpassed by the mental fatigue caused from having had to wear so many different medical hats. I'd started in the role of ER doc—resuscitating and stabilizing my patient. I then had to administer and monitor the anesthesia on my own patient while operating. I fulfilled the role of dentist and oral surgeon to reconstruct a workable jaw and align my patient's teeth. I performed my first maxo-facial surgery using orthopedic-surgery textbook photos and diagrams to repair and reposition the man's face. When I finally closed the man's wound, I used all the plastic surgery techniques I ever remembered studying in hopes of limiting the scarring.

But when I finished with Patient Number One, the second man remained comatose. Worried that he hadn't regained consciousness, I examined his pupils. One was more dilated than the other—indicating what I already feared—a subdural hemotoma. He was bleeding inside his skull and the accumulating blood was putting pressure on his brain. Unless that pressure was relieved, it would herniate his brain stem. If that happened, as the brain itself was forced down into the narrow opening at the base of the skull, the man's entire nervous system would be constricted to the point that everything, even the involuntary systems could shut off. His breathing would stop and the patient would die.

I knew the technique for relieving intercranial pressure, though I had never seen or performed the procedure. So after everything else I had done that day, I got my first experience in neurosurgery without a brain surgeon or even a CT scan to guide me.

Step one was to cut through the scalp and fold back a half-circular flap of skin to expose the skull over the spot of the suspected bleeding and blood clot. Next I had to drill my first-ever burr hole through the skull itself, using a hand-held surgical drill that looked more like a huge auger my grandfather might have used to do woodworking back in the days before Black & Decker power tools. The trick was to carefully apply just enough pressure for the very sharp, but rounded metal bit to bore slowly and steadily through bone, without also penetrating the dura (the covering of the brain) and sinking into the brain itself. There was no room for error.

When I successfully completed drilling the first hole, blood began to seep out. No longer in doubt about my diagnosis, I quickly drilled two more burr holes in a triangular pattern. Next I fed a Gilgli saw under the skull from one burr hole to another. After removing the protective plastic sheath from the Gilgli's wirelike blade, I gripped the ends of the wire and pulled it back and forth in a sawing motion while exerting a steady upward pressure against the underside of the skull. After sawing through one side of the triangle, I threaded one end of my wire saw to the third hole and began cutting out a second side. I had to be careful to saw at an outward angle so that once I had evacuated the clot, I could piece the skull back in place where it would fit perfectly with bone resting on bone. I had to make sure it could not be pushed inward and do more damage to the brain.

The emergency craniotomy my colleague and I performed worked. The triangular skull flap relieved the pressure. Once we evacuated the clot and stopped the bleeding, the patient stabilized. He awakened the next morning and spoke coherently to the staff and his family.

Only by the grace of God (certainly not by their neophyte surgeon's skill) both men survived. We had to tube-feed the first patient for a few weeks. He eventually healed with nothing more than a single, narrow, crease-like scar across the width his face, halfway down his nose.

The second man actually had the rougher road to recovery. His physical wounds healed just fine, but the prospect of facing life without hands and being unable to care for any of his own physical needs emotionally devastated him for a time. Fortunately, we were able to make a plaster mold of his right wrist stump, which we sent to a company back in the States that made and donated a prosthesis. Within months he had mastered the use of his hook and proudly demonstrated an encouraging measure of personal independence.

In the meantime I was called to testify in the prosecution of the young man who had attacked my two patients. Because it was such a serious case, his trial was held in a regional court in Nakuru, more than a three-hour drive away from Tenwek.

Kenya's justice system follows the British model. So I was sitting in the courtroom still trying to absorb the distinctives—the two witness boxes, the robed barristers, the long, startlingly white wig worn by the judge—when the accused was led into the courtroom. This troubled young man obviously hadn't fared well in prison. No sooner had he arrived than he collapsed to the floor and suffered a seizure unlike any I'd ever witnessed. I wasn't sure what was going on, but I knew this was not typical grand mal epilepsy.

Naturally the trial was postponed, so I had lots of time to think on the bumpy drive home. Back at Tenwek I sought out the two victims and asked them to tell me, again, exactly what had happened when they were assaulted. The young man who had almost killed them was a cousin. "We were just having tea in the hut," they told me. Their cousin got this odd, glazed look on his face, stood up, walked across the hut, picked up a *panga*, and suddenly began his violent attack without warning.

"There was no argument?" I asked.

"No."

"Has your cousin ever been violent before."

"Never."

"Did he have a bad temper?"

"No, not even that."

The entire incident seemed so strange.

Sometime later I was summoned back to Nakuru for the trial. In Kenyan courts a police prosecutor presents the case against the accused. If the defendant cannot afford, or does not want, a lawyer, he can act as his own defense. So when the prosecutor called me to the witness box, I summarized the written statement I had submitted, detailing the injuries I had seen and treated in the defendant's two victims. After I finished and had answered a few questions from the prosecutor, the defendant himself stood to cross-examine me. He spoke only Kipsigis, I was still far from proficient in the language, so his questions and my answers had to be translated from one language to another. He appeared nervous, flustered, and not at all articulate.

He asked me, "D-d-did you see me do these things I'm accused of?"

"No, I wasn't there when it happened. I never saw the victims until they were brought into the hospital at Tenwek."

Looking genuinely confused, he asked haltingly, "Then how ... can you say ... I did this thing ... when I didn't even see it with my own eyes?"

The moment he asked that question, I remembered his seizure and something clicked in my mind. I had only recently read a medical journal article about an unusual condition called a temporal lobe seizure (sometimes also referred to as a psychomotor seizure). The case I read involved a Vietnam combat veteran who acted normally until he suddenly exploded with violent behavior that he could never recall afterward. He was eventually diagnosed with temporal lobe seizures, which, unlike grand mal seizures (which totally incapacitate a person), allow victims to interact with their environment (carrying on conversation, for example) until suddenly something snaps and they erupt into violence. Afterward, they cannot recall anything about the incident or even what was happening for some time before it occurred.

"Your Honor," I asked, "could we have a short recess so I can speak to you in chambers?"

The magistrate stopped the proceedings. In private I told him, "I think it's possible this defendant is not responsible for his actions. He may have a medical condition for which he needs treatment."

"He's being treated for his seizures," the judge assured me.

"But he is probably being treated for grand mal seizures." I explained the difference and recommended the man be tested. When the magistrate expressed uncertainty about where such an evaluation could be conducted, I suggested he let me take the prisoner back and evaluate him at Tenwek. The judge thanked me for my testimony and said he would consider my medical recommendation. I went back to Tenwek, the trial continued, and the young man was convicted and sentenced to a three-year prison term. I never learned what happened to him after that. To my knowledge, he was never tested and never received proper treatment for his condition.

But as sad as I was for that young man, I was thrilled for the recovery of his victims. *Panga* Sunday itself became a memorable day in the history and lore of Tenwek Hospital, as well a personal memory that will forever epitomize for me the extent of the challenges I might face anytime I'm trying to do what I feel God has called me to do.

I must confess that few days in all my life as a doctor have provided such drama. Few cases have demanded so many different and untested skills in so little time. And few experiences have humbled me so much.

But *Panga* Sunday proved an invaluable lesson for a young missionary doctor still wet behind the ears. It convinced me that being a physician on the mission field, like being a Christian committed to serving Christ anywhere, would mean facing situations for which I could never be fully prepared. It would mean taking the risk of trusting God to use me despite my own inadequacies—in knowledge, skill, and experience. That experience also convinced me I had much to learn from the Great Physician—and I still do.

In fact, whenever I recall *Panga* Sunday, I am reminded that I have been called, not just as a doctor but as a follower of Christ, to do and be more than I am capable of doing or being on my own. We all are.

This is why we must consider the practice and the example of the Great Physician in the chapters that follow. So much of what we learn will apply not just to the practice of medicine but to the practice of our faith in everyday life.

2

THE GREAT PHYSICIAN ROUNDED WITH HIS ATTENDING

NO MATTER WHERE A PHYSICIAN RECEIVES HIS OR her training, one of the most common, most memorable, and most important aspects of that training is *rounds*. During medical school, also for internship, and even in residency, rounds are a big deal.

Rounds means the attending physician is coming—and you better be ready.

Imagine yourself as a doctor in training. You have probably been on call all night plus the whole day before that. You have another full twelve-hour day to go before you're off duty. You've gotten the histories and physical workups on all your patients— with the results not just written on the charts, but pretty well memorized. You've collected all the pertinent x-rays and lab results and made your best diagnosis. You've even decided on a treatment plan. Yet you have to be ready for what the attending is going to ask. Now is your turn to be examined. You know the attending is going to grill you on all of this, because he or she is your teacher, role model, and judge.

Teaching rounds—which is the time when your attending exercises all those roles—usually start early. Some of the best attendings come as early as 5:30–6:00 A.M. because they want to be there when things are relatively quiet. They want no distractions so they can have your full attention, teach and train you, and accomplish what they are supposed to do.

After your first two years of classroom work in medical school, rounding with the attending every day is one of the key ways you learn to practice medicine. Every doctor knows the importance of rounds.

Dr. Jesus was no exception.

MASTER ROUNDS

We read in Luke 5:15–16 (*The Message*): "Soon a large crowd had gathered to listen and to be healed of their ailments. And as often as possible, Jesus withdrew to an out of the way place to pray."

What was Jesus doing? He was having rounds with his Attending. He was talking to his Father about the situations he was facing, the people he was working with, and the most difficult issues and cases he had seen that day. This was such a priority for Jesus that he pulled aside to do it. Time and again throughout the Gospels we see Jesus slip away, withdrawing so he could focus and be alone with God. Since it is noted so often in the Scriptures, we can assume he rounded with the Attending every day.

Why? No doubt he wanted to set an example for his followers. But it was more than that. He *needed* to spend time with his Father, his Attending—and his Attending needed to speak to Jesus. Alone, and in an out-of-the-way place.

How important is that?

In an age when we feed our families with microwaveable meals prepared in seconds and we find our business principles in *The One-Minute*

Manager, it's no surprise that so many religion-on-the-run Christians have embraced the concept of sentence prayers while talking about experiencing and celebrating God in the midst of daily life. In and of itself that's fine. There is nothing wrong with 911 prayers. Jesus did that as well. But we must remember Jesus' other example—where he withdraws to an out-of-the-way place to talk to his Father.

If we really want to have a serious, meaningful conversation with a friend, our spouse, or our children, when do we do that? Shopping in the grocery store? Driving down the road with the radio blaring? No.

> *Doing that cost Jesus something. It also cost others. There were people not healed because he was rounding with his Attending.*

We find a quiet place, especially if it's important stuff, so that we won't have interruptions. That way we can really concentrate.

That is what Jesus did when he rounded with his Attending. Doing that cost Jesus something. It also cost others. There were people not healed because he was rounding with his Attending.

Mark 1 and Luke 4, for example, tell of the time when Jesus ministered all day in the synagogue. He had been to Peter's mother-in-law's house and healed her. Next the whole town showed up outside the door after supper with all their sick friends and relatives, and he was up half the night healing patients until he was exhausted.

What did Jesus do next? He got up early in the morning and went out to talk to his Father. It was that important. He missed sleep. He missed rest. He sacrificed something he truly needed. It meant he wasn't spending as much time with his disciples. This was clearly one of his top priorities.

In other words, if our time with God isn't costing us something, perhaps we are not doing it frequently enough or long enough. Maybe it's not important enough in our lives.

Not only did Jesus spend time with his Attending (God), but his disciples had time with their Attending—Jesus. He regularly took time apart to teach his students, to pray with his interns. He looked for and made use of those teachable moments. Something would happen and he would draw his followers aside to say, "Let me make clear what this means. Let me tell you what's really happening. You don't understand what's going on, so let me explain it to you."

We see a good example of this in Mark 4. After sharing several parables (including the one about the farmer sowing his seed) with a large crowd of listeners, Jesus elaborated on his teaching with a smaller group of followers. In other words, he pulled his interns (the disciples and a few others) aside for rounds with their Attending.

LESSONS FROM OUR ATTENDING

In a medical setting, rounds are where the attending, who has ultimate responsibility for all patients and their treatment as well as for teaching, holds the students, interns, and residents accountable. One reason you work so hard is because you know you are going to meet with the attending in the morning. It's not going to be a pleasant experience if you haven't done your job. Rounds, if you haven't done what's expected of you, serve as your reckoning day.

Because medicine, like life and faith, is a learn-as-you-go proposition, the more you know, the more an attending expects of you. He or she expects less of a student than of an intern, and less of an intern than of a resident. They are at different places in their training. This is why he expects better decisions out of residents—he spends more time with them. There's a spiritual analogy there for us as well.

ONE DANGEROUS MISTAKE

No doctor is perfect. Doctors-in-training are less so. I remember all too well one encounter with my attending that I would rather forget. But I will tell you about it anyway, because it illustrates how even the reckoning-day aspect of rounds is not only corrective but instructive.

It took place during one of my rotations as a fourth-year student at the University of Louisville Medical School. I don't recall exactly what the patient's complaint was. But we wanted some sort of neurological workup to rule out meningitis, which required a spinal tap on this man. I had had an exhausting, pressure-filled night after working the day before. It was just before the attending was to come, so I was in a hurry to do the procedure, send the sample to the lab, and get the results back in order to be ready to present this and a half-dozen other cases when the attending arrived.

> *I turned to leave the room and suddenly realized I had just done a spinal tap without using any antiseptic.*

I took the patient into the treatment room to do the spinal tap. I got in on the first stick and collected the sample I needed. Everything seemed to go great—until I turned to leave the room and suddenly realized I hadn't prepped the patient's back. I had just done a spinal tap without using any antiseptic. By poking a needle through his skin I could have transferred staphylococci or any other of a number of bacteria on the man's skin right into his cerebral spinal fluid. If he didn't have meningitis before, the chances of my giving this patient a life-threatening infection was high.

And the attending was coming!

The first thing I did was go and tell the resident. I was almost in tears at that point. I couldn't believe I'd done something so stupid. I knew being tired and rushed was no excuse. I also knew when the attending came, I had to tell him. I could see my future medical career, all the work I had done, going down the tubes. At the very least, I expected the attending to have me for breakfast.

But guess what. He didn't. He could see how upset I was. I was already punishing myself, so he said, "You know, Mr. Stevens, this is a great opportunity to teach you some important lessons. First, don't *ever* do that again! Second, learn to think even when you're tired. Third, here's what you need to do in a situation like this." He went on to tell me what antibiotics to administer to protect the patient. Finally, he thanked me for confessing what I had done.

He held me accountable. He disciplined me. But he didn't destroy me.

Isn't that a good example of what happens when we come to God? When we meet with him, he wants to hold us accountable. It shouldn't just be a friendly visit—as if we're sitting down with someone and chatting. This should be a time when the Lord can really deal with us regarding the critical issues in our lives. About our most difficult cases. About our failures, our mess-ups. About all the things we've done that don't please him. That's the time he holds us accountable.

I want to draw a distinction here between our Bible study and our prayer time. Bible study is definitely a time of learning—of checking the text for help and direction. But during our prayer time, if it's the right kind of prayer time, we are held accountable for our words, our thoughts, our actions, and our plans.

The Lord, like a good Attending, reveals things to us. He convicts us and encourages us to correct a problem right away. Rounding with the Great Physician needs to be a two-way conversation.

When I went on rounds, do you think I expected my attending to sit there in silence after I had given my reports on my patients? Of course not. I knew that after I had spelled out the information I had gathered, the attending was going to respond. He was going to talk to me and ask me questions. He would suggest possibilities I hadn't considered and thus instruct me.

In the same way, it's not just because we ought to talk *to God* that we come to him in prayer. It's also for him to talk *to us*. Are you making that time to listen and learn from your Attending in prayer?

We come with our nice little formulas, useful acronyms, such as:

A-doration
C-onfession
T-hanksgiving
S-upplication

We give our report—put it all in the right format, just as we have been taught, similar to what a medical student does when he or she starts with the chief complaint and then covers the history, the physical, and the labs—all in order. We offer our own diagnosis and sometimes spell out our treatment plan for his okay and blessing. Do we then walk out, ready to go about our daily business, in a rush to finish our shift before we give God the opportunity to really teach us?

> *The most teachable moments in the learning of medicine don't happen in the classroom but at the bedside, where you face the problems firsthand.*

What an opportunity lost!

Any good doctor will tell you that rounds are where the real teaching takes place and where you can learn the most. The most teachable moments in the learning of medicine don't happen in the classroom but at the bedside, where you face the problems firsthand.

In fact, during my first two years of medical school the professors were dumping out such floods of information I couldn't possibly remember it all. It seemed a lot like drinking from a fire hydrant—there was so much gushing out no one could hope to swallow it all. Nor do you know what is really important for patient care.

Then in my third year I began clinical rounds. That's when I really learned medicine. Everything that came before was just information and facts I furiously crammed into my brain. Now, all of a sudden I was learning how to take care of patients. I finally got to apply some of that knowledge. I did everything I knew to do, and then the attending came in and asked, "Did you do this? Did you think of that? Why are you giving this treatment instead of that treatment?"

I remember one time a lady came into the Louisville hospital where I was assigned as a med student. She was pregnant and extremely anemic. I tried to recall everything I had learned from my classes and textbooks about anemia. Was she getting enough iron in her diet? Had she been bleeding anywhere? Had she been taking a folate supplement and enough vitamins and minerals during her pregnancy? I went through a whole differential diagnosis—did lab tests that would tell me the size of the blood cells, the amount of hemoglobin present, and so on. Nothing made sense. The case didn't fit anything I knew about or anything I could remember reading.

And the attending was coming.

Finally I concluded the problem had to be iron-deficiency anemia. True, the lab results didn't really fit. But since the patient hadn't been taking iron throughout pregnancy, I decided it must be iron deficiency. So that's what I presented.

My attending just listened. When I finished, he said, "Let's go talk to the patient."

We went into her room and he sat down to ask the woman, "Have you been having any unusual food cravings during your pregnancy?"

I remember thinking, *Food cravings? Where is this guy going with a question like that?* But I leaned forward to hear the response.

She said, "Not really."

"Are you sure?" he pressed. "Are you maybe eating some things you weren't eating before you got pregnant?"

The patient suddenly got this funny look on her face and said, "I'm a little embarrassed to admit this. But I have had this craving for Argo starch."

I said, "Argo starch? How much Argo starch do you eat, ma'am?"

She shrugged, "Maybe two or three boxes a day."

I couldn't believe what I was hearing. Have you ever tasted plain starch? It's the blandest, most awful stuff you can imagine trying to swallow.

But what this woman had, which the attending turned around and began to teach me, was something we call pica—a craving during pregnancy for an unusual food. Because she was eating so much starch, she was leaching iron out through her digestive system and was causing a profound anemia.

I had never heard of pica. I must have been asleep the day we covered that in class—if they taught it at all. But let me tell you something. In all the years since, I have *never* forgotten what pica is. Anytime I see a pregnant woman with anemia, I always ask the question my attending asked. After all these years I can still see that woman in my mind. I can even remember her blood count. I can see everything about her because my attending used that teachable moment to really instruct me.

That's just what God wants to do. He wants to take us aside in the midst of our busy schedules with so much impacting us, such as the challenges at work, our kids acting up, the tension in our marriage, our worry about the future—from the most common cases to the most unusual issues—and he wants to use them. He wants to meet with us and say, "Okay, let me teach you something about this. You haven't seen this before. You haven't thought about this. You haven't been here. But I want to take you aside and teach you about this today."

Those times with our Attending are the most teachable moments for all of us, because that's when God takes what we have learned in Bible study, listening to sermons, or memorizing Scripture and shows us how to apply it to the situations we face. You see, the Attending has more than knowledge; he has wisdom to teach us how to apply his principles to every case and situation we encounter in ways we will never forget.

AT THE BEDSIDE

Another thing I have learned about rounds is that often the best teaching is not done in the room off to the side of the ward. Traditionally in rounds you go into the staff lounge or some other meeting room and sit down with the attending to present your cases, away from patients.

That's fine and good. But when you have finished presenting your case, the best attendings will often say, "Okay. Let's go see the patient—

together." They realize that a lot of teaching can take place at the bedside—when you get to see the attending work. He or she asks questions, as in the case of the woman with pica, examines the patient, then turns to say, "Listen right here to detect the heart murmur you missed," and so on.

Here is where we learn those critical little tidbits we used to refer to in med school as *the pearls of medicine.* These things almost seem to drip off a good attending—ways to remember something, subtle signs and symptoms that the attending points out in a way you will forever remember.

I recall another troublesome case soon after I arrived in Kenya. I could, of course, recount any number of difficult cases, for every doctor spends a lifetime encountering and trying to get a handle on difficult cases. That is one reason why it's called the *practice* of medicine. If practice doesn't make perfect, it does at least improve your skills.

A nine-year-old girl came in to our hospital at Tenwek with persistent vomiting. She hadn't kept anything down for a couple days—not even water. I thought it sounded as if she might have a bowel obstruction. And sure enough, when I examined her, I felt this mass in her abdomen. And I remember thinking, *What could this be in a nine-year-old girl's belly?* It would be unusual to find cancer of the colon at that age. She didn't seem to have a fever. I found no indication of appendicitis. I couldn't imagine what was going on.

So I took an x-ray and I could see the mass. Still I thought, *What can that be?* I palpated the abdomen again. It didn't feel real hard, but it wasn't exactly soft either. It was different from anything I'd ever felt before. *Maybe we're just going to have to do exploratory surgery to find out,* I thought.

Finally I went to Dr. Ernie Steury, the senior physician on our Tenwek staff, and asked him to examine the patient. "Feel this abdomen, Ernie," I said. "I don't know what in the world this is. Have you got an idea?"

Ernie walked over with me and began to palpate this little girl's stomach. When you palpate anyone's abdomen, you always start where it doesn't hurt, or where the mass isn't, and begin to work in closer and closer to the problem. I could tell Ernie was using his fingertips when he said, "Right here, Dave. Feel this. Put your fingers right here, rub them over the mass, and tell me what you feel."

"It almost feels like a ball of string," I said, "like heavy cords."

"That's good. You're right," Ernie said. "What do you think that is?"

"I don't know."

"Feel it again," he insisted. "You think she swallowed a great big ball of string?"

"No," I grinned. "I don't think that's it."

"She has a bowel obstruction, all right," Ernie said, "From roundworms. There's a big ball of parasites in her small intestines. You haven't felt that before, have you?"

"No," I admitted. It was something a doctor in the States would probably never see.

"Well, we have a lot of it out here," Ernie said. "And you'll need to remember what it feels like, because that's typical of roundworms."

The reason Ernie knew that was because he had experience I did not. He knew what to do when I didn't have a clue. That reminds me of another reason why it's important for all of us to have rounds with our Attending—because God has had experience we have never had; he knows everything, he has all knowledge and all understanding. He's been there and done that. So it's important that we get together with him on a regular basis, for whenever we don't know what to do, he does.

We may see the symptoms. We may think we know a little about the situation. But when we come to him in prayer, as we talk with and listen to him, he can reveal to us what is really going on and what we should do.

Not long ago I talked with a doctor whose sixteen-year-old daughter had run away twice. The oldest of five children, she was in total rebellion—promiscuous, into drugs. This doctor and his wife cried as they talked about the girl and about not knowing what to do.

I had no easy answers for them. But I knew someone who could give them help—a loving Father, who has grieved over countless rebellious children.

What about that boss who's unfair? How do you deal with an aging parent or some other elderly relative suffering dementia? Maybe you have a problem in a marriage that you have struggled with for years. Maybe you are facing difficult situations where there seem to be no solutions and no clear path out.

In Matthew 11:28–29 Jesus says, "Come to me, all you who are weary and burdened, and I will give you rest.... Learn from me ... and you will find rest for your souls." The Great Physician is telling us, "I've got the experience. I know just what's going on here. I understand the situation. You can learn from me. You will find rest for your soul. Come on rounds with your Attending. Come, spend some time with me."

> *The Great Physician is telling us, "I've got the experience. You can learn from me. Come on rounds with me."*

Yet sometimes even after we learn what the problem is, we don't know what to do about it. Fortunately, the attending can usually do what his or her students, interns, and even residents don't yet know how to do.

After Ernie taught me what was causing the bowel obstruction in that little girl with worms, I still did not know how to treat her. Should I give her regular antiparasitics? Ernie told me we needed to operate on her right away. He knew exactly what to do.

We wheeled her into surgery. Ernie put in an nasogastric tube to decompress her stomach, got an IV started, prepped her abdomen, and gave her a spinal block. Then he opened her abdomen by cutting with a scalpel very gently, layer by layer. When he got through the fascia, the dilated intestines proximal to the obstruction popped out. Sure enough! You could see this big ball of moving worms!

What do we do now? I thought to myself.

The first thing Ernie did was to pack it off to protect the rest of the abdomen from any spillage that might occur when he opened the intestines. The outside of the intestines was sterile, but what was inside there was not.

Next he gently placed a special clamp on the intestines below the ball of worms to keep them from going on down. Then he placed a couple clamps called Babcocks, which don't crush the intestines, on either side of the mass and lifted it up to where he had it isolated. That's where he made a very small incision, controlled the bleeders, and then took a pair of ring forceps and started pulling those things out. By the time he finished we had collected a large basin of those worms. (This was not the kind of case you want to do right after lunch.) Then he sewed the intestine back up, gently removed the clamps, and began to close. Finally, Ernie worked his way out of the abdomen, closing it up level by level, until the whole procedure was done. The patient made a complete recovery.

The important thing to note is that at that stage of my career and medical experience, I had had no idea what to do. But Ernie did. Similarly, when we take our cases to our heavenly Attending, he knows what to do. It's what the Great Physician himself found when he went to his Attending Father.

In our self-sufficient American society too many of us believe we can handle everything, or at least we think we need to try. Those who are a little further along in their walk—believers who may consider themselves past the student stage, perhaps even into the Christian resident stage—are sometimes the most likely to feel this way. But I want to remind you that we can't. There is always going to be something that in our own might, our own power, our own wisdom, and our own experience we cannot do. There will always be those impossible situations—when we have done all we can and God says, "Allow me. I can do what you can't do."

Maybe you have tried to bring an unsaved person to Christ—a parent, a spouse, or another loved one. Only he can help reconcile a broken relationship or help you love and forgive an unfaithful spouse. When we have been hurt so badly, we think we can never trust or love someone again. Christ says, "I can do what you can't do." In Mark 10:27 the Great Physician reminds his interns, "With man this is impossible, but not with God; all things are possible with God."

I'm so glad for that. The more impossible the situation, the more I have to trust that the God who does impossible things can handle it. That's what he specializes in. Impossible cases are what my Attending does best.

That's what he specializes in. Impossible cases are what my Attending does best.

We can go to him in prayer and say, "Listen, God, I can't handle this. It's beyond me. It's above and beyond anything I have experience with." God will reply, "That's fine. Just give it to me. I'll handle this one." Isn't it good to know that we can have rounds with our Attending every day?

But that privilege does not come without responsibility. Whenever we come before an attending, there are expectations of us as well.

OUR RIGHT APPROACH

It's always important to come to rounds with the proper attitude. I remember my first night ever on call at the beginning of my third year in medical school. I didn't know what to expect. I was doing a rotation in internal medicine at a Veterans Administration hospital. After two years of classroom work in gross anatomy, histology, physiology, biochemistry, pharmacology, and physical diagnosis, I was finally going to be responsible for real patients.

As in any other kind of schooling, students in med school always talk about professors—how easy or how hard they are. I remember when I got my internal-medicine rotation, one of my friends said, "Oh boy! Are you in trouble! That attending is really a bear!"

So I had an inkling that this was not going to be easy. The more I asked questions, the more concerned I became because this attending had a reputation for being extremely bright—one of the top researchers in our school—but also for being very, very demanding. Indeed, when I got on the service, my intern and my resident warned me and two other students about our attending and all he required in their orientation briefing. They said that when he arrived for rounds each morning promptly at 7 A.M., he required full histories, physicals done, and tests concluded (including all lab reports and all x-rays in) for any and every patient admitted before 5 A.M.

That could be a challenge because things didn't always run efficiently at this VA hospital. In other words, students might have to personally chase down lab reports, collect x-rays from radiology, and make sure they had the interpretation on any EKGs and anything else they ordered. Not only did you need to have these in hand, along with a diagnosis and a treatment plan, but you had to present all this information on each of your patients—completely from memory! Every scrap of patient information had to be memorized when you gave it to him, or woe be unto you.

That first night I had only one or two new patients. But it seemed like a lot of information to memorize on top of everything else I was doing with the patients. So when morning rolled around and I approached my first experience with the attending, I admit being a little scared, though not as scared as I should have been.

There were actually three of us third-year med students on that rotation. One of the other guys got called on to make his presentation first. He stumbled a bit in his presentation and failed to remember a couple of lab results, but for his first time doing this with an attending, I really thought he had done pretty well. I wasn't sure I could do any better.

When he finished, the attending turned to the intern and asked, "What do you think about that presentation?"

The intern, trying to be kind and encouraging said, "Well . . . he had some of the same problems I had when I started doing this. But for his first time I think he did pretty well."

Then the attending turned to the resident on the service and in a more threatening tone asked, "Well, what did you think?" The resident replied, "He should have gotten more history. He forgot a couple of his lab reports. And I'm not sure he's considered all the possibilities on this diagnosis, but for the first time he didn't do that badly."

Then the attending turned around to the student and said, "You know what I think? I think that stunk. That was one of the worst histories and physicals I've ever heard, and I can't believe you would meet me on your first morning so ill-prepared and . . ." He went on and on, tearing into the poor guy in what became a verbal massacre. He not only attacked what he had done, but he attacked him as a person. It got so vicious that this medical student sat there in stunned silence. The next day he quit medical school, saying, "If this is the way I'm going to be treated, I don't want to be a doctor." So after two whole years of incredible effort and sacrifice, he just walked away.

In the meantime, after he'd finished tearing apart the first student, the attending turned to me and said, "All right, Mr. Stevens, what cases do you have to present?"

And I thought, *Dear God, help me!* Talk about fear and trembling! Somehow the Lord got me through it. I'm still not sure if I really did a better job than the first fellow or if the attending decided he had made his point. But I do remember that for the rest of that rotation, which lasted two months, you never saw anyone more prepared than I was. Every time I knew I was going to meet the attending, I went into the encounter with a healthy measure of fear as motivation.

I learned this attending only slept two hours a night and didn't think anyone else needed more than that. So he really pushed us. As a result, I will say I learned a lot from that guy. While I wouldn't recommend his teaching technique, going in with a proper sense of respect and measure of fear certainly did help motivate me.

You know what? I think we need to come before God, our heavenly Attending, with a lot more respect and, yes, some fear and trembling. Of course, he's more understanding and forgiving than my attending was. Yet I think we miss so much of what he wants to teach us because we approach him as if we were just buddies. We aren't totally focused on who he is. We are altogether too casual about it. We see our encounters with God as a little like we're meeting someone on the sidewalk, where we instinctively say "Hello" and "Some weather, huh?" or "How's the family?" and off we go.

That's not what God wants from our meetings with him. He's looking for an attitude different from the one we have in the morning as we trudge out to get the daily paper. It's not supposed to be routine, something we do every day simply because it's a habit we've fallen into.

When we have rounds with our spiritual Attending, we would be much better off with an attitude like the one I developed back in medical school—an attitude of total concentration, motivated by just the right amount of healthy awe and fear. Yes, God loves us, but at the same time this is not your average attending we're talking about here. This is the Lord of Lords, the King of Kings, the Creator of the universe, who holds the entire world in his hands. Since we have the privilege of rounding with the greatest Attending of all, we need to be focused and come to him without distraction so we can better hear and remember what he says when he speaks.

> *When we have rounds with our spiritual Attending, we would be much better off with an attitude of total concentration, motivated by just the right amount of healthy awe and fear.*

Of course, we should always remember he loves us and cares for us. But our time with God should not be all warm and fuzzy. He will need to get on our case sometimes to let us know where we need to change our lives. If we don't come to him with the right attitude, that is not going to happen. Proverbs 1:7 says, "The fear of the LORD is the beginning of knowledge, but fools despise wisdom and discipline."

Thus, a fear of God and a humility of spirit are really where knowledge begins. If we truly want to learn from the Great Physician, that's how we must come before him. In Psalm 86:11 we read: "Teach me your way O LORD, and I will walk in your truth; give me an undivided heart, that I may fear your name."

This really speaks to the idea of no distractions—nothing else pulling me away and not thinking about or doing other things. If we are really going to learn from him, we need to fear his name and him—which will give us an undivided heart so that he can teach us his ways.

ARE WE READY?

To come before our Attending the right way, we also need to be coming prepared. I hinted at this in the story about my first attending—how important it was to have all the right information. It wasn't enough to have the history, the physical, the labs, and the x-rays. I always felt it necessary to go back and check the text again to make certain what it said about whatever I thought was going on—to be absolutely sure I was considering all the options.

In the same way, whenever we are going to meet with Christ, we must first get into his textbook and compare it with our own heart and mind and with what's going on in our lives. We must see how what he is saying fits in with how we are living. Are we coming to the right diagnosis and the right prognosis about what we are doing in our lives?

Just as in med school, it's so easy to look at a case and think you've considered all the possibilities, until you read the text and discover that you are off track on a couple critical signs or symptoms crucial for making the right diagnosis and for choosing a proper course of treatment. Or perhaps you find a lab result that doesn't fit with what you are thinking is the real issue and you have to change course and start looking in another direction.

That's what the Great Physician's textbook does for us. We can think we are heading down the right path and doing the right things; we've got it all together. Only when we hold ourselves up against the Scripture

> *Whenever we are going to meet with Christ, we must first get into his textbook and compare it with our own heart and mind. Are we coming to the right diagnosis and the right prognosis about what we are doing in our lives?*

do we see that's not the case. We spot our mistake and begin to understand the direction we need to go. Thus, whenever we meet with our Attending, Bible study and even memorization prepare us to get the most from our time together.

If we do come before the Attending prepared, that gives us a more effective time of interaction and learning, in order that we can become more like him. This is the real reason we spend time with the Attending, so that we begin to model ourselves and our lives after him. We want to become more like the Great Physician.

ARE WE TEACHABLE?

The last attitude that is important when we go to the Attending is an eagerness to learn—to take it to the next level and to know him better.

I remember at Tenwek that when we had medical students visit and I was their attending, the ones I loved best were those who wanted to pick up everything they could while they were with us, to have as many experiences as possible. Those students would say, "Dr. Stevens, I'd really like to have the opportunity to deliver some babies while I'm here. So if you get some interesting cases, can you call me? I don't care if I'm on duty or not, whether it's during a meal, day or night. Just call me. I want a chance to deliver a set of twins or help on a breech delivery." They were so eager to learn that they made themselves totally available to learn from me. Such students were a joy.

Occasionally, however, we had students who were not so eager to learn. I remember one fellow (I'll call him John) who came with the attitude that he already knew everything. He was just as good a doctor as any of us, we just didn't know it yet. In fact, he gave an air that we could probably learn a few things from him.

This guy had just finished his third year and thought he could do anything even without being taught. His wife had come with him. She was having some back pain, so without asking permission he took her to our small physical-therapy area to treat her himself. Unfortunately, he had no training on any of the equipment, which was all precious to us because we didn't have much.

We had just gotten a new shipment of equipment and supplies from the States—which we were excited about—including a diathermy machine to provide deep heat for people suffering muscle spasms. John talked one of the guards into opening a locked room and decided his wife needed a diathermy treatment. He had no instructions but assumed since he was a smart guy, he could just read the directions on this new piece of equipment and make it happen. The first thing he did was plug this 110-volt machine into our hospital's standard 220 outlet and completely fried the wiring and all the internal electronics. Sparks flew. Smoke filled the room.

That would have been enough to stop most people and prompt an immediate apology and offer to make things right. But not John. He went directly to another machine used to provide electrical stimulation to muscle tissue. When he hooked his poor wife up and turned that machine on, he shocked her with so much voltage it nearly stopped her heart—at which point she belatedly decided she didn't need any more physical therapy from her husband. They promptly left without John ever voluntarily coming forward to confess what he had done.

When the damage to the diathermy machine was discovered, we ended up with a serious disciplinary situation—all because this med student came to Tenwek with a wrong attitude, an arrogance that said to everyone he didn't need to learn anything.

Sometimes, maybe not even consciously, we do that with God. We don't really come to meet him as our Attending with an attitude that says, "Lord, teach me something." We don't bring an eagerness to learn, a humility of spirit, or a focus of attention. Maybe we come simply out of habit—or we don't come at all.

The Great Physician himself knew he needed to be most disciplined about his time with his Father if he was going to be spiritually healthy. Despite the fact that he had so much to do while he was here on earth, despite realizing his time here was so limited, despite knowing he would have eternity with his Father, he still made regular time with his Attending. If the Great Physician himself needed that, how much more do we need rounds with our Attending. Without it we may become spiritual fatalities or emergency cases ourselves.

Only when we go on rounds regularly and approach them with the proper attitude will we be able to learn the most important lessons our Attending has for us. Then he will find us to be the kind of students who are a joy to teach. He will be able to take us to a new level of competence in the practice of our faith.

This is also what I hope will happen as we examine the Great Physician by rounding with him throughout the remainder of this book.

THE GREAT
PHYSICIAN ESTABLISHED HIS
OWN RESIDENCY PROGRAM

I'VE ALREADY MENTIONED DR. ERNIE STEURY AS A colleague, a veteran missionary doctor who functioned countless times as my attending at Tenwek. But Ernie was more than that; he was my mentor.

As a junior premed student at Asbury College, I already felt a call to go into medical missions. During that school year I had been spending time praying and talking with my dad about the direction God might be leading me.

One day Dad said, "You know, Dave, I think it would be great if you could go to Kenya this summer and spend some time with Dr. Ernie Steury. I have known Ernie for fifteen years. Your mom and I have supported him since the beginning of his ministry. Of all the mission hospitals I've visited in the world, of all the missionary doctors I've seen, I think Ernie is the best." This was high praise coming

from Dad, who was an evangelist and led short-term mission teams all over the world.

So in June of 1972 I naively and excitedly got on a plane and headed to Africa. For much of that summer I lived in Ernie's home. The Steurys' house contained maybe twelve hundred square feet, and they had four children. So Ernie asked two of their kids to sleep on the living-room couch for a number of weeks in order for me to have a room to myself.

I ate breakfast with Ernie every morning and went up to the hospital with him each day. I didn't know a thing about medicine. But he let me pass him instruments, taught me how to scrub, took me into surgery, explained things, and answered questions—naive questions, stupid questions. He answered all of them with infinite patience.

We would go up to the hospital to do surgery in the morning. Then we would come down the hill and climb under one of the nurse's cars to make some repairs.

Suddenly we would get called up to do an emergency C-section and after that maybe we'd try to repair an old water heater in the house of one of the less mechanically gifted missionaries. Then back to the hospital to see another fifty to seventy-five more patients in the afternoon. Sometimes we wouldn't get back to the house for supper until 8:30 or 9:00 P.M.

Since Ernie was the only doctor on call, in the middle of the night I often awakened to see a glow come around the corner of the house. I knew one of the hospital guards was coming down to knock on the window: "Dr. Steury, come quickly!"

We would rush up to the OR for an emergency to save someone's life or to see a seriously ill patient who had just arrived. Or Ernie would check on a critically ill patient the nurses weren't sure would make it through the night.

When I came home at the end of that summer, I knew a great deal about what it was like to be a missionary doctor, because I had had a mentor. And I remember thinking to myself, *I want to be just like him!*

After I graduated from med school and completed my residency, I went back to Kenya and spent eleven years working with Ernie. I have more respect for him now than I did as a student. I have learned so much of what I know about medicine today from that man as I watched the Great Physician work through him to minister to other people.

Medicine's Model

Until the 1800s, if you wanted to become a doctor, you had no choice but to find a practicing physician who agreed to take you on as an apprentice. Some doctors charged a fee, others did it simply because they wanted to. The physician would give you some of his own books to read and then allow you to work beside him for a number of years before you were considered qualified to be a doctor. At the time, this procedure didn't seem at all odd because apprenticeships were the norm in many professions.

The world has changed a lot since those days. So has the practice of medicine. But medical training has maintained more of the old apprenticeship feel than most other professions.

The study of medical science is far more structured today than in the days a would-be doctor had to teach himself the fundamentals from what books he found on the shelves in his mentor's study. Now we enroll in medical school, where it takes at least two years just to learn the basic sciences that underlie all medicine. Traditionally you take anatomy, physiology, embryology, biochemistry, and all those other first-year courses that help you understand the human body and how it works. During the second year you learn the basics of pathology, pharmacology, physical diagnosis, and other skills that help you identify and know how to treat disease.

Then in your third year an apprenticeship of sorts begins as you finally work on the wards. You do rotations for a month or two at a time—in internal medicine, surgery, pediatrics, obstetrics—until you've gotten time and exposure in each of the major areas of medicine. In your fourth year you have a few more required rotations, but you also have more electives that allow you to gain experience in one or more specialties you may be considering for your career. In the fall of your fourth year you apply to residency programs.

In the United States, where you actually do your residency is ultimately determined by a process referred to as "the Match." This routinely starts with med-school students deciding which specialties they want to pursue and beginning to learn everything they can about residency programs in their targeted specialties. Library and Internet research provide valuable information, but the real scoop on the strengths and weaknesses of a program comes through a personal visit. The program interviews you, and you check them out as well. It's a critical process because you are essentially apprenticing yourself to them for at least the next three years, and they are taking on the responsibility of training you.

Once med students apply and rank their top choices, the residency programs look at their list of qualified and interested students to rank their choices of possible residents. The two lists are then combined, and your highest choice is matched against the program that rated you highest. That's how it's decided where you will spend the next few years of your life.

On Match Day in March of 1977 I got my first choice. Jody and I headed to Columbus, Georgia, for my final three years of training. I couldn't have been happier. My family-practice residency met my own goals of having both quality and quantity of education, a good balance between teaching and experience, enough patients with a variety of medical problems, good supervision, great residents to work with, and even reasonable night-call demands by 1970s standards—every third night my first year and every fourth night in year two.

What excited me most was the breadth of experience my residency would give me. I was going to be able to do at least a little bit of everything and a lot of many things I knew would serve me well when I finally got to Kenya.

I manned ICUs (intensive care units) and NICUs (neonatal intensive care units). I worked on burn patients, dealt with all manner of trauma, performed many surgical procedures, and delivered a ton of babies—all of which the Lord knew would be required of me when I got to Tenwek.

MASTER MATCH

The Great Physician had a pretty rigorous match system for the residency program he headed almost two thousand years ago. He could have selected any number of people. We read in the Gospels that there were often hundreds, sometimes thousands, of people following him around the countryside. Yet he carefully picked only twelve for his match.

That's not a big number. Thus, we may safely conclude that Dr. Jesus had some stiff requirements for acceptance into his residency program, not because the task was so small but because he knew it was so big.

But Jesus also knew what many of us have had to learn for ourselves: If you want to be a mentor who deeply affects somebody's life, you must have the opportunity to really know that person and spend time with him or her as an individual. If you have too many people, it becomes a congregation rather than a mentoring relationship. Jesus realized that the time invested in deeply affecting the lives of those few people would ultimately have more impact on the world than all his preaching to the multitudes.

Christians refer to what Jesus did with his twelve residents as *discipling*. Unfortunately, I think that term has come to seem imposing. When we think of discipling someone in terms of faith, we often feel a little concerned

> *Dr. Jesus carefully picked only twelve for his match. We may safely conclude that he had some stiff requirements for acceptance into his residency program, not because the task was so small but because he knew it was so big.*

that we don't really have what it takes to do that. To do the job right we assume we need to be this wonderful Christian, some sort of saint walking on earth who knows the Bible from cover to cover and has a comprehensive understanding of theology and philosophy; only then can we impart all this holy truth to the next generation. At the very least we assume real discipling takes a lot of education, training, and skill. Thus, we are not personally involved in it.

But the Great Physician's expectations were different. His discipling method was much like what happens in residency. His basic mentoring strategy can be seen from the start of his ministry with the disciples. He as much as told them the heart of his residency requirement when he first called them. The accounts of those initial encounters are scattered throughout the Gospels. Mark 2:13–14 is typical of most: "Once again Jesus went out beside the lake. A large crowd came to him, and he began to teach them. As he walked along, he saw Levi son of Alphaeus sitting at the tax collector's booth. 'Follow me,' Jesus told him, and Levi got up and followed him."

How did Dr. Jesus do his mentoring? Let's look at five principles that are obvious in his residency program.

The *first*, most basic element of Jesus' mentoring style was simply this: **He expected his disciples to follow him around.**

What Jesus said to Levi was pretty much the same thing he told Peter, Andrew, James, John, and all the rest: "Follow me. Come along and spend time walking and talking and watching what I do."

Mark 3:14–15 summarizes his whole residency idea in a nutshell: "He appointed twelve—designating them apostles—*that they might be with him* and that he might send them out to preach and to have authority." The whole idea was for these men to follow Jesus around for three years, to be with him, so that they could then go out themselves and do what he did. That's not only a pretty good description of medical residency; it defines all kinds of mentoring.

This is exactly what I did with my mentor, Ernie Steury. I don't think Ernie and I ever had a one-on-one Bible study together. We never met for prayer at 5:00 A.M., though there is nothing wrong with such things. But the primary way Ernie mentored me was *by letting me spend time with him.*

It started that summer I lived in his home as a college student. I ate meals with him. I watched how he disciplined his children and how he treated his wife, Sue. I participated in family devotions. I saw how he interacted with the nationals who were in his home or working with him at the hospital. I witnessed him in surgery, where he prayed before each case. I noticed the way he put his arm around a patient or held the hand of someone who was hurting. I listened to him supervise the construction staff working on a new building.

Mentoring is neither a special gift we are born with or a task we need expert training for. It's simply saying, "Come along with me. Let's spend some time together doing what I normally do."

Sometimes I asked him questions. Other times he questioned me. But mostly I just spent time with Ernie.

I went back to Kenya to spend part of another summer with Ernie when I was a junior in medical school and for another month during residency. Then for the eleven years I worked at Tenwek, Ernie Steury continued to have an incredible impact on my personal and professional life as my mentor.

What the Great Physician understood, what my experience with Ernie illustrates, is this: Mentoring is neither a special gift we are born with or a task we need expert training for. It's simply saying, "Come along with me. Let's spend some time together doing what I normally do." It's like a lot of parenting; our kids learn more by watching and doing than they ever learn from what we tell them.

A *second* component of Jesus' mentoring strategy also has its parallel in medical training: **He taught through the natural flow of daily events.**

In medicine, when both learning it and teaching it, I have noticed that the best educational opportunities come when you are dealing with real-life issues. That's when you have people's focus and attention.

Let me cite one example. In medical school I had read about Burkitt's lymphoma, a rare cancer seldom found outside of East Africa. It's a cancer of the lymph glands in which a history of malaria is a cofactor. There was even a picture on a textbook page. I read what it said and promptly forgot it, because I knew I wouldn't be seeing Burkitt's lymphoma in clinic that afternoon.

But I will never forget the first case I did see. A child came in to Tenwek with massive swelling of the face. The boy's head had swollen nearly to the size and shape of a basketball. I didn't have the slightest clue what was going on. I looked in the child's mouth to examine his teeth. Instead of sticking up and down, they were lying flat and all pointing straight in—pressured by the tumor mass.

It was a massive deformity that looked as if it had taken months to develop. But when I took the history from the mother, she insisted this had started only a month before. Her son's condition had been getting noticeably worse each day. Just recently he was having difficulty breathing.

I was totally bumfoozled; I had no clue what was going on. I called Ernie, who took one look at the child and knew immediately what was wrong, since he had treated dozens of such cases during his years in Kenya.

Yet instead of announcing his diagnosis, Ernie began asking me questions about what I saw, questions that helped me eliminate various possibilities, until I came close to the right answer. Then Ernie began telling me about Burkitt's lymphoma and its key signs, pointing out the symptoms and the clinical course, and finally explaining how we could treat it.

I may have forgotten the textbook information I had seen, but after encountering this one case I have never forgotten what I learned about Burkitt's lymphoma. I certainly never forgot this patient's response to treatment, because this is one of the most rapidly responsive tumors in the world to chemotherapy. The tumor practically dissolves before your eyes. It seemed almost miraculous that within a few days, after a couple doses of Cytoxan, this child's face was almost back to normal.

Not all the valuable lessons doctors learn from a mentor during the course of daily events have to do with disease and treatment. Dan Cabanis, the medical director of my residency program, was another mentor. When I did my cardiology rotation with him, he taught me a lot about treating the heart. But the most memorable and most valuable thing I learned from him was something I noticed in our time together, something I saw and caught without it ever actually being taught.

> *When I look people in the eye, nod my head as they explain something to me, and assure them "I understand," I'm halfway there in providing for their needs.*

Whenever Dan questioned his patients and they described a symptom or related a detail of their medical history, he listened and then responded by saying to them, "I understand." They would go on and tell him more, and at an appropriate time he would again tell them, "I understand." As I followed him from room to room, from patient to patient, I couldn't help noting this litany he went through with almost every patient.

Finally I asked him about it: "Why do you always say, 'I understand'?"

"Because, Dave," he replied, "I've learned what people want more than anything else is someone who understands their problem. Everyone is looking for understanding. I've found tremendous therapeutic effect just in that phrase. When I look people in the eye, nod my head as they explain something to me, and assure them 'I understand,' I'm halfway there in providing for their needs. They know they have a doctor who is caring, who has heard them, and who, because he understands, is going to do something about it."

That lesson has served me well over the years. I have noticed that even in some cases where there was no effective medical care or physical healing I could provide, the offer of this gift of understanding still helps. And I have used it not only with patients but with employees and in interpersonal relationships with colleagues, friends, and loved ones.

I learned it from a mentor by seeing it used again and again in the natural course of daily activities.

The *third* dimension of Jesus' mentoring style was this: **Jesus made effective use of questions.**

Questioning is also an essential part of any medical residency program. It's a major part of how attendings teach on rounds. It makes students and interns, and even residents, a little afraid, or at least uncomfortable, to know they will be asked questions they may not know the answers to. They don't want to be embarrassed. Thus they prepare harder, think better, and develop reasoning skills. It pushes them to a new level of understanding. That little bit of fear often heightens awareness and concentration because they know they are going to be accountable whenever questions are asked and answers are given.

Christ did this all the time. Just read through the Gospels and count all the "what's" and "why's" and "who's" he used to push and pull and prod his disciples toward the truth.

Note how in Mark 8:1–30 Jesus asks a raft of questions:

How many loaves do you have?
Why does this generation ask for a miraculous sign?
Why are you talking about having no bread?
Do you still not see or understand?
Are your hearts hardened?
Do you have eyes but fail to see, and ears but fail to hear?
And don't you remember?
When I broke the five loaves for the five thousand, how many basketfuls of pieces did you pick up?
When I broke the seven loaves for the four thousand, how many basketfuls of pieces did you pick up?
Do you still not understand?
Do you see anything?
Who do people say I am?
But what about you?
Who do you say I am?

All these questions are from the first thirty verses of one chapter of one Gospel account of Jesus' life and teaching. Any quick read of the New Testament will find hundreds more.

The Great Physician continually asked his disciples questions, in order to force them to think, to decide what they believed, and to work through difficult issues and concepts.

As far as the *fourth* principle is concerned, **Jesus knew the best mentoring is long-term.**

He spent three years, the same length as my medical residency, with his disciples. But he clearly did not consider his responsibility and relationship over even then, because one of the last promises he made to his disciples at the end of his earthly ministry was this one: "Surely I am with you always, to the very end of the age" (Matt. 28:20). Then he sent the Holy Spirit to spend more teaching time with them after he was gone (see John 14:26).

In our day and age many attending physicians keep tabs on former students. A lot of doctors throughout their medical careers stay in touch with influential professors and attendings they know and appreciate from residency days.

I have been particularly blessed with the fact that I worked alongside my most influential mentor on a daily basis for so many years. While he's retired from the mission field now and we haven't worked together for ten years, he still checks up on me regularly through notes, e-mail, and occasional phone calls—still asking questions and wanting to know what cases I'm struggling with so he can pray for and affirm me. He continues to give me advice and encouragement that make me more effective in what I do.

Ernie Steury has been my mentor for almost thirty years now. It has definitely been a long-term commitment for *both* of us.

The *final* key to Jesus' mentoring, and another parallel to medical residency, is this: **Jesus believed in the "See One, Do One, Teach One" concept.**

Every doctor has heard and experienced this principle. Let me illustrate with another personal experience. I was at Tenwek as a resident when a man came in looking six months pregnant. He could hardly move because his distended abdomen hurt so much. He'd been vomiting for a couple of days and had had no bowel movements.

I wasn't sure what was wrong, but the exam revealed a grossly distended abdomen that sounded tympanic—meaning it sounded like a hollow timpani drum when you tapped on it. I took an x-ray on which you could see a huge loop of bowel I had never seen before. So I called Dr. Steury, who immediately recognized what was an all-too-common problem in the Kipsigis culture.

Like people in much of Africa, the tribes in our region eat a diet in which the staple is corn. Every meal and for a lot of snacks in between, the Kipsigis eat *gimet* (pronounced gim-ee-yet), a thick, heavy, and bland cornmeal mush. It's such a central part of their diet that the word they use for it in Kipsigis is the same word they use for food.

Patients in the hospital often told me they had been there for two weeks and hadn't had any food the whole time. Yet we fed them more nutritionally balanced meals than they got at home. What they meant was only that they hadn't yet felt well enough to eat *gimet*.

They eat so much of this roughage—several pounds a day—that there is rarely colon cancer among the Kipsigis. But the problem with this diet is that their sigmoid (the looped portion of the colon on the left side of their abdomen), which isn't attached firmly to the abdominal wall, can get very long and distended from the weight of a heavy corn diet. I have operated on people in Kenya whose long sigmoid colon could have been stretched almost over their head—whereas in the United States a normal colon can hardly be stretched to the top of the abdomen. Because this floppy piece of colon gets so big, it can actually twist on its mesentery, the thin tissue that connects the colon to the back of the abdominal wall. This is called a sigmoid volvulus.

The arteries and veins of the colon come through this mesentery to provide the blood the colon needs to digest food, carry away waste products, and be nourished itself. So when the colon twists, it pinches off some of the blood vessels. If that happens, the life-sustaining blood cannot get to the bowel, nor can the bowel contents move up or down because it is twisted shut. As a result the bacteria in the colon multiply and create gas, and if the blood supply is completely shut off, the tissue itself actually begins to die.

We rushed this fellow to the OR and prepped him for surgery. The moment we carefully opened his abdominal wall, the bowel popped out—not pink and normal, but black and necrotic. The twisted section of bowel had actually died and was life-threatening—it could create peritonitis, a generalized infection in the abdomen, and seed bacteria into the bloodstream, which could kill the patient through over-whelming sepsis.

In situations like this a doctor must clamp above and below the twist and the dead tissue, then resect—cut out the piece and reconnect the bowel. In this case the man already had abdominal infection, so we closed the distal colon and did a temporary colostomy, bringing his colon out of the abdominal wall to allow the bowel to function. We treated him in the ward with antibiotics until the infection was con-trolled, waited for the swelling and inflammation to subside (sometimes that can take weeks or months), and then went back with a second operation to reconnect the ends of the colon.

When I saw another man two weeks later with the same prob-lem, I knew what it was. After I called Ernie to tell him my diagno-sis, he said, "Do you want to do this one?" I had never done it before. But since I had seen the other case, we opened this second man up and discovered his case was not as serious. "What do you think you should do?" Ernie asked. I told him, "Since this bowel still looks viable, maybe we can just untwist it and not have to resect the bowel." Ernie then explained how and where such bowels normally twist and taught me the trick to untwisting them when you can't see which way they are twisted.

I followed his instructions. After a turn and a half, sure enough, the blockage was relieved, and the bowel began to pink up and look better immediately. We watched it to make sure none of it was necrotic, then irrigated the abdominal cavity to decrease the contamination there. We closed the patient up and continued his antibiotics, and he did great.

A couple weeks later a third case came in. This time the bowel was necrotic. "What should we do?" Ernie asked me.

"I think we need to resect and do a colostomy on this one."

"Okay," Ernie said. "You learned to destrangulate last time." He handed me the tools and said, "Now let's see how you resect this one. Here's what you do first. . . ." I was slow, but I did it. Before long I didn't need to call Ernie for help on those cases at all. If there had been anyone around with less experience than I had, I would even have been ready to teach him or her how to do one.

> "See One, Do One, Teach One" is a strategy used in learning any procedure in medicine. It's another one of the reasons our profession is called the practice of medicine.

"See One, Do One, Teach One" is a strategy used in learning any procedure in medicine. It's another one of the reasons our profession is called the *practice* of medicine.

Of course you have to understand and master the basics—the anatomy, the pathology, the fundamental surgical principles. You need to know how to handle instruments, control bleeding, do suturing. But especially as you get into surgery—and one reason surgery takes longer than many other specialties—you learn by seeing, then doing. By the time you are a resident, you are helping teach—interns and less experienced residents. And of course that is also instructional; you may learn the most at this stage because you have to verbalize and demonstrate the steps and procedures that make you better at what you are doing.

This is true not just of surgery but of all aspects of medicine. You cannot learn what you need to know simply from books and lectures. You have to get in there and actually do it. You have to be in the game.

Medicine is not a spectator sport.

Neither is the Christian life.

Jesus made this clear to his disciples in his regular application of the "See One, Do One, Teach One" principle. Clearly the Great Physician could have done anything and everything better than his followers. But he knew it wasn't enough for them just to watch what he did every day. So he got them involved. Asking questions and giving or receiving feedback was only part of it. He also got them doing what he was doing.

> *The Great Physician could have done anything and everything better than his followers. But he knew it wasn't enough for them just to watch what he did every day. He also got them doing what he was doing.*

This is obvious in the story of the feeding of the five thousand in Mark 6:30–44. After Jesus' disciples have finished their own teaching responsibilities, they think Jesus has taught enough and suggest he stop and send the crowd away so that the hungry people can buy something to eat.

Isn't it interesting that the interns are telling their attending what to do? Let me tell you from experience, that's usually not a good idea. But Jesus handles it very well by turning it right around on them, saying, "You do it. You handle the food problem."

Shocked, they want to know, "Are you serious?" In offering them the chance to "do one," he is willing to give them a chance to fail. He knows that in failure we sometimes learn the most. To "do one" always requires taking a risk.

M & M ROUNDS

We see this same principle also at work in Luke 10, where Jesus sends out the seventy-two—two at a time—in thirty-six short-term missions teams. He gives them careful instructions about what to do and not do in various situations. He gives them good, detailed, and practical training. Then he sends them out to preach and to heal.

Imagine how they feel: *Of course, we've seen Jesus do it, but we don't really know how.*

Jesus puts them out on a limb of faith—they have seen one, now he is going to let them do one, because he knows before long, after he leaves them, they are going to have to teach one.

So what happens when his followers return? That's when Jesus conducted a postmortem—what we call in medicine M & M Rounds ("morbidity and mortality rounds"). After a difficult case is over, you hold a meeting with all the doctors, interns, and residents. Someone presents the case, and everyone else critiques how it was taken care of, what should have been done, what should have been done differently, how we could have avoided such a long course of treatment, or what we could have done to prevent certain complications or even death.

After a patient dies it's an especially valuable learning experience to go back and review the autopsy report, to see if you missed something or if you might have taken a different approach. How did the autopsy findings relate to the signs, symptoms, and lab work the patient had? Were you on track? You may learn as much when things don't go well as when they do.

In this case the seventy-two return in joy. They have done it. They realize they have learned from what they have seen Jesus do and can now actually minister themselves. We can learn from them—and from Jesus' reaction. Luke 10:21 says the Great Physician was full of joy.

I can tell you from experience working with students and interns that there is no greater joy or satisfaction than when you know they finally get it. Those *aha* moments mean every bit as much to the mentor as the mentee.

What Jesus' mentoring method means, then, is this: We who see the Great Physician as our Master Model for living need to be mentored by him and become mentors to others.

It's never hard to find people who want or need to be mentored. We have student Christian Medical Association chapters on 172 medical- and dental-school campuses across the country. So I speak to many students who tell me that what they want most, what they feel is missing in the course of their training, is the chance to spend time one-on-one with a Christian doctor. Not that they aren't learning the science of medicine—they are. But they also want to learn the art of medicine—how to deal with a dying patient, counsel someone, treat their staff, collect their bills, manage their time, balance family needs, and so on. They want to see how their Christian faith can be applied to their daily life as a doctor.

At the Christian Medical Association we are starting a mentoring program that connects Christian med-school students with local Christian graduate docs who are willing to act as mentors and let these young doctors follow them around in their office and at the hospital, and even see them in their daily lives at home.

While working on this book I received a letter from Al Weir, then president-elect of the Christian Medical Association, an oncologist from Memphis. Though Al is a wonderful Christian, he would never consider himself a Bible scholar or a great speaker. But after we talked about mentoring and what that meant—just letting people spend time with you—Al wrote me and stapled to the letterhead the note a medical student had sent him.

"Dave," Al's letter explained, "I let this student come into my office for just three or four days. I don't know that I even witnessed to a patient while she was here. I just let her follow me around. This is the note she sent me."

Attached was a brief handwritten thank-you in which this student told Al what had impressed her—how gentle he was with patients, how he looked in people's eyes, how he treated his staff, and how he prayed with a couple patients. She was amazed and excited and encouraged just to see what a Christian doctor could be like. Because of what she had seen in those few days, she said she wanted to be just like Al Weir in her own practice of medicine.

"Dave," Al concluded, "you were right. This is what it's all about!" Al had never before realized the impact that a small amount of time could have on a medical student or resident. That's what the powerful secret of mentoring can do.

Called to Mentor

Doctors aren't the only ones who can be influential mentors. No matter what our profession, we can develop a powerful ministry in the lives of others if we apply Jesus' mentoring style to our younger colleagues at work. At church we can easily find newer Christians to mentor. Or Jesus' mentoring model may work best of all at home, with our own children. Parenting, after all, is in effect an eighteen- or twenty-one-year residency program.

I recently took my college-age son with me to Africa for two weeks on a medical mission trip. We didn't have a Bible study together the entire time. I never sat him down for a formal lecture or tried to teach him things. I just took him with me to watch and work beside me. I let him ask me questions, and I asked him questions and used those teachable moments to impact his life.

But you don't have to let a child follow you to Africa to impact a young life. You don't even need to be a parent. There are countless children today, many in your own community, without parental models. What they desperately need is a mentor—someone who says, "Spend some time with me today. Follow me around. We'll have some encounters, some cases that come along that will be good learning opportunities. I'll ask you questions, you ask me questions, and we'll see what we learn."

Effective parenting, like mentoring, is becoming a lost art in our culture. Surveys tell us most parents spend only a few minutes a week actually interacting or talking with their kids. At work we have jobs that bind us to a desk, a phone, or a computer and isolate us from contact with real human beings.

Yet I think it's still possible in our day to focus on a few whom God has entrusted to us. I challenge you to do that. At work or school, at church, out in the community, or in your own home—look for those you can mentor. Find someone and just let him or her spend time with you. You will be amazed at the impact you can have. Like my friend Al Weir, you may discover that one of the greatest satisfactions and rewards you can have in life is reproducing yourself in the lives of other people. That's just what Jesus did.

I've told you about my most important medical mentor, Ernie Steury, whom the Kipsigis people called Mosonik. After deciding before I ever started my own career that I wanted to be a missionary doctor just like Ernie, I considered it one of the greatest honors of my life when the Kipsigis people gave me the name Arap Mosonik—son of Mosonik. Why? Because I had become a lot like him.

Yet the greatest mentor any of us can ever have is the One who is perfect, who never made a mistake, who always gave a perfect example. That's Jesus Christ, the Great Physician.

The same principle applies to us as to his first twelve followers. He wants us to see what he does, do it ourselves, and then teach someone else. That was the basis of his residency program two thousand years ago. It's the secret of mentoring today. Christ expects nothing less of all of us who bear his name.

THE GREAT PHYSICIAN WAS A PREFERRED PROVIDER

THE GREAT PHYSICIAN WAS NEVER AFFILIATED WITH any HMO. No PPO ever included him on their list of approved medical providers. He wasn't associated with any medical group and did not become a part of a coverage plan. Yet he became a preferred provider for everyone he encountered.

Young Dr. Jesus opened up a small solo "practice" in what seemed like a remote, out-of-the-way location. Where many new physicians starting out must work hard for years before their practices begin to get busy, Jesus' reputation as a healer rapidly "spread all over Syria, and people brought to him all who were ill with various diseases" (Matt. 4:24). He hung out his shingle in Capernaum, and on the first day "the whole town gathered at the door" (Mark 1:33). The demand was so great he soon had to leave the city and begin practicing in wide-open spaces to accommodate the crowds.

People from all over the country traveled for days just hoping he would treat their sick loved one. Every day was a mob scene. No waiting room with Muzak and magazines, no orderly lines taking turns. No, he "healed many, so that those with diseases were pushing forward to touch him" (Mark 3:10). Such numbers of sick and suffering people soon came flocking to Jesus for help that there was not enough time in the day for even the Great Physician to heal them all.

Like Jesus, most missionary doctors see and treat everything. In fact, if you could have simply picked a day, any day, to follow me around at Tenwek Hospital, the truth of that statement would be driven home for you as it was time and again for me.

A DAY IN THE LIFE OF A MISSIONARY DOC

The patient is shaking and shivering so violently with chills from his 105-degree fever that our staff has tied him into a bed vibrating steadily across the floor with every tremor and twitch.

When I walked up the hill from our house to the hospital each morning on that mission compound in Kenya, there was never any way to anticipate what my day would be like. Every day was so different that *different* became the norm.

Take an imaginary flight back in time to Kenya and join me as I start my morning rounds in the men's ward because I am especially concerned about a semicomatose malaria patient I admitted yesterday. The man's kidneys have already been damaged to the point that hemoglobin is passing into his urine, turning it almost black with the byproducts of blood—hence the old and most descriptive name of this critical stage of the common tropical disease—*black water fever.* The patient has somehow survived the night. But the sweat pouring off of him has soaked his sheets. He is shaking and shivering so violently with chills from his 105-degree fever that our staff has tied him into a bed vibrating steadily across the floor with every tremor and twitch.

The man would undoubtedly be in ICU if he were in the States. All we have for him at Tenwek is a 1950s bed in a forty-man ward. Of course, in most U.S. hospitals he would be the first critically ill malaria victim his doctors would have seen in their entire careers. At Tenwek we successfully treat more malaria patients than you can shake a stick of mosquito repellant at every year. I am concerned that this father of eight may be on the less fortunate side of the statistical ledger as I order a cocktail of backup drugs for resistant malaria and a blood transfusion.

No sooner do I scribble my name illegibly for the first of a hundred items I will write today than one of the national staff informs me of a pediatric emergency. I rush to the outpatient area, where they have just admitted a one-year-old girl with a severe case of dehydration from gastroenteritis—probably acquired by drinking contaminated river water. Not that the cause matters right now, because after two days of vomiting and diarrhea this child is obviously so weak she is going to die unless we can get her rehydrated soon. The nurses have tried to start an IV, but the baby is so dry she is in shock. The veins in her arms and legs, where we normally put an IV, have collapsed. I have no choice but to perform a veinous cutdown on her leg.

With our one operating room already occupied, I decide to do the procedure on an outside veranda where the light is better anyway. Cutting into the leg, finding a collapsed vein, nicking it without slicing all the way through, and then slipping in a tiny plastic cannula can take anywhere from a few minutes to an hour. God answers my quick prayer and I'm signing a raft of orders ten minutes later. Practice makes perfect, and I have regrettably had to do more cutdowns in an average year at Tenwek than most doctors will do in a lifetime.

Another urgent case keeps me from rounding on the other thirty-nine patients in the men's ward. An eight-year-old boy has fallen out of a tree, and the x-ray reveals a broken arm above the right elbow.

One of the other missionary docs has just finished shelling out an enlarged prostate gland the size of a navel orange, which had completely obstructed the bladder of an elderly man. So there is a short break in the OR schedule; if I hurry, we may be able to fit my patient in.

I ask the mother when the boy last ate as I draw up a dose of Ketamine, an injectable anesthetic. I get to be anesthesiologist and orthopedist at the same time since we have neither in this remote corner of Kenya. I pray with the mother and the child as I give the injection. With the boy asleep and breathing well, I get one of the national OR staff to stabilize the upper arm while I pull with one hand and work to manipulate the fractured piece of the humerus back in place. I wouldn't touch a supercondylar injury like this in the United States because of the vascular and neurological risk but would refer it to the best orthopedist I knew. At Tenwek I have no options.

I feel the bone move back into place, splint the boy's arm in flexion, and send him for a quick x-ray. It shows the angle is still a little off, but my second attempt is right on the money. I call an attendant up from the ward where the boy will go in order to reemphasize my written orders. The boy's pulse and neurological status has to be checked frequently for any sign of compromise from the swelling that will follow.

The boy is only half awake as I carry him out and put him in his mother's arms. There are no fancy recovery rooms here, so I emphasize to the mother to not try and give him anything to eat or drink till he is fully awake. Like most African mothers, she has her hands full. She now has her groggy eight-year-old in her lap, a four-year-old girl standing at her side, and a six-month-old baby tied in a bright piece of printed cloth on her back.

I explain that when the swelling goes down in a day or two, she will be able to take her son home. Then in a few weeks we'll take the splint off, and the boy's arm should soon be as good as new. She smiles and thanks me.

Another nurse pulls me aside. She needs me right away to examine a two-year-old who has just been admitted to the pediatric ward. One look and I'm virtually certain of my diagnosis. The mother says her daughter was running a fever and her neck became stiff and sore.

The little girl's head is actually arched backward, and she cries out in pain when I attempt to turn it.

I need a spinal tap to confirm my suspicions. The nurse knows the routine; without any instructions from me she leans over the exam table in the tiny room off the ward, wraps one arm around the child's head and the other behind the child's knees, and pulls toward herself, bowing the back out in my direction. The poor child screams and tries to squirm, but the nurse has her pinned. I quickly run my finger down the spine until I find the correct vertebrae, swab on the antiseptic, and carefully insert my needle right between the bones of the spinal column.

During epidemics of meningococcal meningitis, we may see ten or a dozen cases a day. Timing of treatment is so critical that hours, even minutes, can make the difference between life and death.

Extracting a few drops of telltale cloudy spinal fluid into each of three test tubes clinches it. The child definitely has meningitis. The specimens head to the lab so I will know the cause, even as the nurse gets an IV started and I order antibiotics stat. That's all we can do except pray to see if we caught it in time. If we have, the child should recover completely. If not, she may suffer permanent brain damage or even die. During epidemics of meningococcal meningitis, which is terribly contagious, we may see ten or a dozen cases a day. Timing of treatment is so critical that hours, even minutes, can make the difference between life and death.

From pediatrics I head for maternity to check on two women who had C-sections yesterday. I find both mothers and their babies doing well in a ward so crowded that many of our beds contain two women—their heads at opposite ends of the bed.

There are over 10,000 births a year in the area of Kenya that Tenwek services. Fortunately, three out of four women give birth without any problems at home in a hut, attended by a mother-in-law. But that means the 2,500 deliveries we see each year at Tenwek include a much higher percentage of complications. Add to that the fact that the Kipsigis people have a one in twenty-eight rate of twins (one of the highest multiple births rates in the world), and you see why the OB services at our small hospital are often taxed beyond our limits.

Today when the OB nurse learns I have arrived in maternity, she summons me to the delivery area, where a young woman is in labor with her first child. The nurse explains that everything was proceeding normally until a few minutes ago. The baby's head, which is past the midline of the pelvis, has stopped advancing, despite good contractions and vigorous pushing.

My exam reveals that the opening in this young woman's pelvis is not quite big enough for her baby's head to pass through. Putting on a set of forceps is not going to solve the problem. Normally in the States with any sort of outlet obstruction like this, an OB automatically performs a C-section. Then with the next pregnancy there's a chance for a normal vaginal birth or, if need be, a scheduled C-section. An outlet obstruction assures, unless the baby is a lot smaller, that every pregnancy will require the same operation.

In African tribes like the Kispsigis, where a healthy young woman might be expected to have six, eight, or even more babies, a uterine scar from a C-section may weaken a bit with each pregnancy until it eventually ruptures. That usually results in a dead baby and a dead mother.

So at Tenwek, to avoid this problem in young mothers, we use a procedure seldom seen any longer in North America. It's called a synphysisotomy. After putting on a pair of sterile gloves and prepping the skin, I take a needle and inject a local anesthetic into the heavy cartilaginous tissue at the synphysis of the pubic bones in the front of the pelvis. Then I take a heavy scalpel, the old-fashioned kind without a removable blade, and begin a stab incision, carefully transecting the connective tissue that holds the pelvic bones together in front. I proceed carefully, millimeter by millimeter, guided only by touch. The danger is suddenly cutting through the tough tissue and plunging the blade into the bladder or urethra. When the cartilage is finally severed, the pelvis actually pops apart in front—a quarter to maybe a half inch. That small change in diameter is a much larger change in potential volume. Usually that little bit of margin provides just enough room for the baby's head to pop out after one or two more contractions and some *"Tigiii-iiil inne!"* ("Push really hard!") vocal encouragement.

Moments later a healthy eight-pound baby is lying snugly in his smiling mama's arms and I'm sewing up the cut I'd made, with a few quick stitches. This mother will be up and walking tomorrow. When she completely heals, the chances are that her pelvic opening now will have enlarged enough that she'll have a better chance of delivering vaginally with any subsequent pregnancies.

From delivery I return to maternity to find two staff people trying to calm an obviously agitated woman. The patient, who has just been admitted, is clutching an infant to her chest and talking so fast I can't follow her Kipsigis. When she notices me, she stops talking and gently lifts a corner of the blanket covering her child.

One look at that day-old baby's face and I immediately realize why this mother came to the hospital so upset. The first time anyone sees a meningomylocele can be a shock; to see one on your own newborn baby has to be downright horrifying.

Let me explain. While meningomyloceles can occur anywhere in the brain or neural-cord system, this congenital defect is usually found in the lower back. But in this child's case, the bones at the front of the head haven't closed properly, and a portion of the brain is bulging out through the forehead above and between the eyes. This baby has a translucent, rounded balloon hanging out—a fluid-filled membrane so thin I can see actual brain tissue inside.

As alarming as it looks, as serious as it would be if the membrane broke and exposed the brain to infection, I can honestly reassure the mother that our surgeon should be able to fix the problem the following morning. She probably can take her baby home a couple of days later.

We will have to excise the protruding tissue. Chances are it's not a functioning part of the brain. Even if it is, an infant's brain tissue is so adaptable that other cells will likely take over those functions. Once it's removed, we will make sure the rest of the brain stays tucked back inside and out of the way until the skull bones can grow together properly. We will also sew up the hole in the skin, and if there is no infection, the baby should do well.

Finally I get back to the men's ward. The remaining morning and afternoon hours are filled treating old and new patients with a continuing diversity of medical complaints. By the end of the day I realize I haven't encountered many distinctly African cases today—nary a hippo bite, lion mauling, or even an arrow wound.

But the day isn't over yet because at five or six every evening, after we have seen to all the inpatients, there is outpatient duty. All day long our nurses and other staff who run our outpatient clinic have handled the vast majority of routine complaints they've encountered—from wounds needing sutures to infected ears and throats calling for a round of antibiotics. But when our outpatient clinic closes each afternoon, there are always at least twenty or thirty more complicated cases left— patients the staff thinks need to see a doctor. Today that's my job since the only other doctor is tied up in the operating room.

It's almost seven o'clock in the evening when I finally finish with the last outpatient and head back down the hill from the hospital to share a late supper at home with my wife and kids.

A NIGHT IN THE LIFE OF A MISSIONARY DOC

After we eat, the family plays table games until the children go off to bed. I work for a time on the regular news-and-prayer letter to our supporters. By lantern light I outline the sermon I've been asked to preach this Sunday. Then, sometime around eleven, Jody and I fall asleep.

It seems I've just closed my eyes when an incessant knocking drags me out of deep sleep. An instinctive glance at the fluorescent hands of my windup alarm clock indicates a few minutes before midnight. The night watchman has come from the hospital. My day isn't over yet after all. Our outpatient area (it wouldn't begin to qualify in the States as an actual emergency room) has just received the first victims of a terrible accident.

> *As the truck careened down the steep hillside, it had flung kids in every direction— onto rocks and into trees. Some had been pitched free only to be rolled over moments later by the truck itself.*

A dump truck transporting forty to fifty kids home from a school soccer match in a distant town has slid off a slick and muddy road—tumbling and spilling its passengers down a deep ravine about twelve kilometers away from Tenwek. The first couple of victims have already arrived for treatment, and the lorry driver who delivered them says we should expect another thirty victims as soon as enough private vehicles can be commandeered to bring them all in.

We immediately mobilize the entire hospital staff—not just those on duty, but everyone we can summon in from the mission compound and the countryside around it. By the time I dress and hurry up to the hospital again, the second wave of victims has arrived, along with added details of the accident.

Rescuers at the scene are evidently having difficulty finding all the victims in the dark. As the truck careened down the steep hillside, it had flung kids in every direction—onto rocks and into trees. Some had been pitched free only to be rolled over moments later by the truck itself.

We have victims with multiple broken bones, internal injuries, head trauma. Some have suffered such severe cuts and lacerations they bled out on the way to the hospital. We have more patients coming in than we have room to treat in our small outpatient area, so they are on the veranda on stretchers, on the cement, and wherever else we can put them.

The schoolchildren are being transported as they are found in the dark and loaded into a vehicle, not in the order of seriousness of their injuries. So we set up a triage outside on the hospital patio, where I and other staff quickly examine one victim after another by lamplight to determine which ones require immediate treatment and who is next in line for our one and only OR.

The frantic nightmare lasts all night long for our medical staff, the victims, and the distraught parents, who have heard the news and begin streaming into the hospital after walking and running many miles over dark trails. Emotions run high as anxious, weeping mothers and fathers are reunited with their frightened, injured children.

It's nearly dawn when I begin the long downhill walk through the compound to my house, knowing I have less than an hour to sleep before I will need to get up and face another morning. I hope this new day won't be as long, though it's sure to be just as full, just as varied, and just as unpredictable.

A missionary doctor faces a never-ending variety of overwhelming need.

ONE WITH US

If such a wide spectrum of medical challenges typifies a missionary doctor's work, then Dr. Jesus clearly had to be one of us. The imagined doctor's lounge debate in the introduction of this book merely hinted at the diversity of cases the Great Physician encountered. The more than seventy-five references of Jesus' healing ministry in the four Gospels specifically mentions many diseases or conditions he treated. From what we read in the New Testament, we can only assume there must have been countless more. In other words, whenever I'm feeling whipsawed by such a diverse and demanding onslaught of seemingly incongruous problems in my own work and life, I know Jesus has been there and certainly understands what I am going through.

AGAINST THE ODDS

In the United States there is one doctor for every four hundred people. When I arrived in Kenya for my first term in 1981, I was just the third M.D. on staff at Tenwek Hospital—the only hospital serving a region of 300,000 people. The other two doctors and I used to joke that it wasn't as bad as it seemed. Ernie Steury, the first physician to arrive at Tenwek back in 1959, would take his 100,000 patients. Dick Morse, a family-practice doc who had come to Kenya in the late 1960s could take another 100,000. I said I would just be responsible for the 100,000 who were left over.

What wasn't so funny and could seem pretty overwhelming at times was just how many of our 300,000 patients showed up at once. When I arrived, Tenwek was a 120-bed hospital averaging between 180 and 200 percent occupancy. You're probably thinking, *Wait a minute! Those numbers have to be wrong! That kind of occupancy rate is impossible!* Not when you have two or more patients per bed!

The medical needs were staggering—almost constantly. Yet when I remember the devastating demands I saw at Tenwek Hospital in Kenya, when I hear about the physical suffering and crushing needs other missionary doctors encounter around the world today, I am reminded that the Great Physician was faced with an even bigger challenge. His mission agency didn't send him out to meet the needs of only 100,000 potential patients. Jesus spells out his even more ambitious mission assignment in John 3:16–17. The Great Physician's challenge was to save the entire world.

Though we believe the Great Physician had the advantage of being fully God, we also know he was fully human. A number of Scriptures make it clear that his human nature was regularly, physically exhausted by the enormity of his assignment. Thus, we can be assured that he relates to the stress you and I feel whenever and wherever we encounter overwhelming need.

Hardship Duty

But there are other ways Dr. Jesus can relate to and share with us. Every missionary doctor in history has accepted the risk of the unknown, walked into an unfamiliar world, and found what seems at times to be strange, disturbing, almost unfathomable conditions. I had an advantage over a lot of first-term missionary docs when I arrived at Tenwek. I had spent a summer visiting the hospital during my college premed days, then two months with my wife, Jody, after my third year of med school, and yet another rotation there during my residency. So I thought I knew what to expect; I wasn't walking into a totally unknown situation.

But after training in American med schools and hospitals and living my entire life with North American expectations, I still had some major adjustments to make practicing medicine as a missionary doctor. I had to make do with limited drugs, outdated or unavailable equipment, and a tremendous shortage of adequately trained staff. We used to instruct visiting doctors, "Tell us what you need, and we will tell you how we've learned to get along without it."

One of the greatest frustrations for me, and a serious hardship for our patients, was the fact that Tenwek only had electricity from seven to eleven hours a day. There were no public utilities or private power companies in our part of Kenya. The hospital generated its own power—fifty kilowatts of it.

You could hear that generator hum all over the hospital and living compound. It kicked on around six each morning, but was off a good part of every afternoon. In the evening it was turned on until five minutes before nine, when the lights blinked. That was the signal to turn on a battery light or find matches to light a candle or lantern.

The fuel to run the generator cost so much to truck in that it consumed 25 percent of our limited hospital budget each year. We simply couldn't afford to run it any more. Whenever oil prices went up, we would have to cut the hours back even farther.

It's easy to imagine some of the limitations this placed on the medical care we could offer. We couldn't operate a true ICU without power. We couldn't run respirators or electrically monitor critically ill patients through the night.

What's harder to imagine is what it was like (before we got our phone system) to be roused from sleep in the middle of the night by the sound of tapping on your window and the glow of a lantern held high outside by a night watchman, sent to summon you for some sort of medical emergency. Then you walk by flashlight back up the hill and into a darkened building, where each ward is only dimly illuminated by the flickering flames of one or two kerosene lanterns hanging from the ceiling.

Because most of our patients must walk a long way to get to our hospital, many of their relatives stay right with sick loved ones, sleeping all over the floors between and under the patients' beds, with a single blanket pulled over their heads to ward off the evening chill you can experience even in the tropics at Tenwek's seven-thousand-foot elevation.

> *I can't count the number of times— long after the light of morning stirred the crowd—that someone would realize the lump under that blanket hadn't moved, and we would find a patient who had died unnoticed during the night.*

Our hospital staff found it difficult even to wade through the dark sea of humanity on the wards at night, let alone provide adequate around-the-clock medical care for our patients by lantern light. I can't count the number of times—long after the light of morning stirred the crowd—that someone would realize the lump under that blanket hadn't moved, and we would find a patient who had died unnoticed during the night. What we wouldn't have given to have the electricity needed for constant monitoring, for alarms that buzzed, for suction machines—or even for a single incandescent light bulb in each room to dispel the darkness.

Patients were literally dying for the lack of electricity. I remember the sad case of a young child on whom we had had to perform a tracheotomy. Because we didn't have electricity at night to run automatic suction and didn't have enough nursing staff to man the wards twenty-four hours a day, I taught this girl's mother how to use a foot pump to suction the tube periodically throughout the night, until we turned the generator on the next morning. But when morning brought enough daylight and we could blow out the single kerosene lantern hanging from the ceiling in the middle of the ward, we found the mother asleep. The little four-year-old girl's trachea had gotten clogged, she had been unable to breathe, and she was dead—simply because her mother had fallen asleep (though ultimately because we didn't have the electricity to run the equipment that would have kept the child alive).

However, before I overemphasize the twentieth-century hardships we underwent at Tenwek back in the early 1980s, I must realize my experience doesn't compare to that of the Great Physician. Yes, I took my family with me to practice medicine in a foreign land. However, I flew to Nairobi on a 747 and even drove the rest of the way over rough roads in an old Volkswagen van. The actual risk I took in doing that was pretty small.

Yes, I encountered strange customs and endured limitations and conditions that are almost unimaginable in the United States. But earlier missionaries endured much more, and my patients lived with many fewer luxuries than I enjoyed. So my family's adaptations were nothing like the adjustment the Son of God, the Creator of the universe, must have experienced when he began his first years of a thirty-three-year medical missionary term as a helpless human baby.

The hardships God shouldered with the Incarnation dwarf even those taken by courageous medical-missionary pioneers. David Livingstone, for example, destroyed his own health during years of trekking by foot and canoe from one coast of the continent to the other along previously uncharted routes to carry healing and the hope of the Gospel to the interior of what was called in his day "the Dark Continent." But the comparative darkness Christ found on earth must have seemed unbearable to a Great Physician who was also "the light of the world" (John 8:12). Obviously Jesus knew what it was like to live and work in a different culture and under the most trying conditions. That says to me he can relate to my experience, whatever hardships or stressful situations I must face here on earth.

A PRICE TO PAY

When Jody and I left for Africa, we felt the stress and the cost of leaving home and family—to be separated from our loved ones by eight thousand miles and one very deep and wide ocean. I remember the tearful good-bye scene at the airport. As we stood there with our families, I think each of us realized the price to be paid—a lot of Christmases, a lot of Thanksgivings, and even more birthdays missed. Our three-year-old son and one-year-old daughter were leaving loving grandparents and doting aunts and uncles. My dad looked at me and said, "Dave, this is tough. But I want you to follow God's will for your life. And I'm so proud of you." With tears in his eyes he went on, "You know, Dave, this separation is just for a moment in light of the eternity we will have together." Believing that made it easier, though it didn't reduce the cost of that separation.

I'll be forever grateful for Dad's attitude. It was so different from many other families. A dear friend of mine, a young physician, once confided to me that God was also calling him to the mission field. "But I can't do that," he said sadly. "It would just kill my mother for me to go overseas." So he never did. For some the cost is greater than they are willing to pay.

Before I feel too smug about the price I paid, before I wrench a shoulder patting myself on the back as some sort of medical martyr, I need to stop and realize that I have sacrificed embarrassingly little in comparison to the price paid by the Great Physician. When he left the presence of his Father and the glory of his home in heaven to journey to our broken and troubled world, the Son of God surrendered power over all creation to subject himself to the rule and law of sinful humankind and the limits of his humanity.

True, the Lord of the universe was the Great Physician, but he lived a life of poverty rather than privilege. Note the summary of his chosen lifestyle in Matthew 8:20: "Foxes have holes and birds of the air have nests, but the Son of Man has no place to lay his head." The price Dr. Jesus paid to practice here on earth was far higher than any other missionary doctor I know.

FIRST CALL

To become a missionary doctor requires a true sense of call. But I sometimes think we make this into something more mystical, more mysterious, than it needs to be. In my current position as executive director of the Christian Medical Association, I regularly speak on medical-school campuses, where I meet many students who tell me they are open to a call to missions. While they say they have no clear sense of direction, they seem to be waiting for a bolt of lightning to strike them as they stroll across campus, a loud authoritative voice in the night, or maybe some handwriting on a dorm or apartment wall.

I have no doubt God could speak that way if he wanted to. He has used similar methods in the past. But this is what I say to both med students and graduate docs who tell me they are willing but waiting to see where God is going to call them: "You know, even God has a hard time steering parked cars. If we will just start moving forward, it will be so much easier for him to begin steering us in the right direction."

I say that because it fits with my own personal experience and definition of a call—whether to the mission field or in any other area of service in our lives. A call is nothing more or less than seeing a need and realizing that God has specially equipped you to meet that need.

That's what happened with me. I didn't make the decision to become a missionary doctor because a Bible verse jumped off the

> *Even God has a hard time steering parked cars. If we will just start moving forward, it will be so much easier for him to begin steering us in the right direction.*

page or because some song spoke to me. I didn't feel my heart tugged toward Africa because a sermon convicted me or I responded to an altar call. Though I have heard testimonies from people who have experienced a call in each of those ways, what happened in my life was far different.

I got my first up-close look at the need for medical missionaries when I went with my father on a two-week short-term mission trip to Haiti as a fourteen-year-old high school freshman. It was some of the best money Mom and Dad ever invested. They wanted each of their children to know that all of the world wasn't like the United States. They wanted us to see that children suffer and die from lack of food, shelter, or a simple immunization. I saw all that, plus a lot of other desperate needs, in poverty-stricken Haiti.

But what will stick in my mind forever from that trip was the afternoon I spent observing at a clinic out in the Haitian countryside. From a distance I had seen this little building with a line of people outside— a line so long it wrapped around the entire place twice. So I walked down to see what was going on. Some of the people waiting there obviously needed serious medical help. When I got close enough to look in the door, there was one nurse, all by herself, diagnosing, treating patients, writing orders, and even doing minor procedures—things I knew a doctor normally did. This little clinic had no doctor; they couldn't find anyone willing to come.

That nurse really impressed me. I noticed the way she took care of people. She seemed so concerned and so compassionate, despite the overwhelming crowd. Every once in a while she would get up and walk into a little side room with a patient. I wondered what that was about, but I didn't want to ask. Finally after the third or fourth time it happened, I worked up the nerve to lean around and peek through the crack in the door. I saw her kneeling there on the floor, praying and leading a patient to the Lord. That made a tremendous impact on me, providing me a vivid and unforgettable image of what it meant to be a medical missionary.

God used that image a few years later during my senior year of high school as I began to pray about what I would major in during college. What did God want me to be? How did he want me to serve him? I had seen the need for missionary doctors and began to think maybe God could use me and my strengths in science to meet that need. I made the decision to declare a premed major as I started Asbury College, a Christian liberal arts college in Kentucky.

My call was a growing realization that God had specially equipped me to be a medical missionary. I wasn't absolutely sure as a senior in high school, but I put the "car" in motion. As I continued my training, God slowly steered me toward a clearer confirmation of his call in my life. I spent twelve years of long and difficult preparation answering that call before I stepped off the plane with my little family as a career missionary in Kenya. I envisioned a lifetime spent ministering physically and spiritually to the Kenyan people, but God had other plans.

NEW CALL

Years later, I experienced a new call when I made the most difficult decision of my life—to leave Africa and come back to the United States to head up World Medical Missions, the medical relief ministry of Samaritan's Purse. A few years later a change happened again, when I saw the needs at the Christian Medical Association and realized God could use me, with my strengths and experience, to meet those needs.

One reason I feel comfortable with my definition of a call is because this is pretty much what happened with Jesus himself. God saw the need for the world to be redeemed. His Son, Jesus, had all the right qualifications to meet that need. Indeed while he was on earth, the Great Physician spelled out his ultimate calling to his disciples with these words: "I am the way and the truth and the life. No one comes to the Father except through me" (John 14:6). Jesus was the *only* One whom God could use to meet that need. That was his call in a nutshell, and it's the primary reason I would argue that Jesus was indeed a missionary doctor with the most difficult task anyone could have—to be the Healer and Savior of the world.

What motivates a missionary doctor to tackle overwhelming needs, to risk facing so many unknowns, to endure hardship, and to answer the call is a clear sense of a higher purpose. In fact, I would go so far as to say you cannot be a good missionary doctor without a constant awareness of that higher purpose.

I speak from experience, for I have to confess that at times I didn't always stay focused on, or even remember, my higher purpose as a medical missionary. Let me cite one quick and life-changing example.

A Higher Call

Near the end of my first term at Tenwek, the physical needs seemed so great, and there were so few of us to meet those never-ending demands. I know I was fast approaching the point of burnout. I was working constantly from early morning until seven or eight o'clock each evening and in addition had to take night call every third day.

To cope with the pressure of the workload I had become more and more efficient; that is, I became faster and more focused on the most essential steps of an exam or a treatment. Thus, I became much more mechanistic and a lot less people-oriented in how I practiced medicine.

At no time was this more true than when it was my turn to see outpatients at the end of the day. I actually came to resent our outpatient clinic.

We saw between sixty and seventy thousand people as outpatients every year. Many of them walked for miles and waited all day long to receive medical care, for Tenwek was the only place they could get it. Fortunately, our outpatient nursing staff could handle most of their cases. But there were always a couple of dozen patients, sometimes more, who would be instructed to stay and see a doctor at the end of the day. Some of them had waited since early morning, but we could seldom see them until five or six o'clock—after we had completed our rounds, cared for the needs of all our hospitalized patients, dealt with many emergencies and urgencies, and finished the day's scheduled surgery.

Dr. Steury was our primary surgeon, so he was usually tied up in the OR. Dr. Morse had a never-ending assignment with the pediatric ward, so the backlog of outpatients usually defaulted to me. Thus, my primary goal each day was to see outpatients as quickly as possible so I could finally get down the hill and eat with my family.

The prospect of seeing more patients after five o'clock than most doctors see in their office in an entire day was not something I looked forward to every afternoon. I handled the stress by becoming an extremely efficient medical provider. I even felt a little proud of it, telling myself the patients needed efficient care so they could go home.

I was a machine. I found myself able to whip quickly through a line of outpatients. Two, maybe five minutes per patient (unless a procedure was required), and I was out of there! No long conversations asking about their family and kids. I only wanted to know their main issue so I could solve it in record time.

That's what I was doing on this particular afternoon. I had already made short work of the first half of the line when an elderly Kipsigis gentleman named Arap Towet walked into the examination room.

One look at this patient was enough for me to make a certain diagnosis. Arap Towet had what is called a retropharyngeal carcinoma. This is an extremely aggressive cancerous tumor that starts in the upper throat, behind the soft palate near the base of the brain, and quickly spreads. In this case the malignancy had already invaded the lymph nodes along the neck and the side of the cheek. Pus oozed from the ugly growth bulging out at the side of what otherwise struck me as a very serene and dignified face.

As much as I hate to admit it, as terrible as it sounds, my very first thought when Arap Towet walked in the room was, *This one will be easy. There will be no procedure to do—no need for a biopsy. No chemotherapy will help this obviously dying man. I will write a quick prescription for pain meds and give him some vitamins. Then I can go on to the next patient.*

In that moment God convicted me. It wasn't an audible voice, but it was a strong feeling that clearly said, *You have got to do more than that. I knew when I brought this man here that you couldn't help him medically, but what about his spiritual cancer?*

As I examined the growth by feeling along the man's neck, I began to weigh carefully my words. In the Kipsigis culture it isn't considered proper to speak directly about death. So, knowing I had to be honest with him, I looked my patient right in the eye. Using the best euphemism I could think of, I said to him, "Arap Towet, this tumor is likely to finish you."

"I know that, Daktari," he replied. He told me he would not have even made the two-day walk from his village, which was near the Masai (a neighboring tribe whose territory borders the Kipsigis), except that his son insisted he come.

Impressed by what seemed a calm acceptance of his imminent death, I asked a more pointed question. "Arap Towet, if this illness does finish you, do you know what will become of you?"

He nodded and simply said, "My son will bury me."

"What I meant was," I told him, "what will happen to your spirit—your soul?"

"I don't know," he answered softly.

"Have you heard the story of Jesus Christ?" I said. He shook his grotesquely marred head from side to side. Surprised, I gave a quick glance at the chart and noted he was from a remote area. Then I simply and briefly explained God's plan of salvation—how by believing in Jesus he could know in his heart that he would spend eternity in heaven. I took no more than two or three minutes, but the entire time I talked, Arap Towet's eyes were riveted on mine. He was hanging on every word.

When I finished, I asked if he would like to invite Jesus into his heart so that his spirit could live with God forever in heaven. I will never forget his words, for when I asked if he wanted to accept Jesus, Arap Towet looked at me and simply said, "Of course."

It hit me that this old Kipsigis gentleman had lived his entire life without ever hearing the good news of salvation in the name of Jesus. When someone finally shared it with him, it seemed so simple, so appealing, so obvious to him that when asked if he wanted to respond and accept it, he couldn't imagine any answer but "Of course."

So Arap Towet and I got down on our knees right there in that outpatient examination room, I put my hand on his shoulder and prayed with him as he accepted Jesus Christ as his Savior. When we stood up, his face had been absolutely transformed. Oh, the carcinoma was still there. But even more obvious now was the joy and peace that radiated from his countenance.

When I finished, I asked Arap Towet if he would like to invite Jesus into his heart. I will never forget his words, for he looked at me and simply said, "Of course."

I knew I had to see my next patient. But before I let Arap Towet go, I called for our hospital's national chaplain, who I knew would counsel him, give him a Kipsigis Bible, and arrange for a local pastor to come and visit his home.

I never saw Arap Towet again. It was too far for him to come back to the hospital. But I believe some day he and I will meet in heaven. In the meantime I can say in all honesty—though I had seen thousands of patients before him and have seen thousands more since—I don't think I'll ever forget the face of Arap Towet—the outpatient who reminded me of the higher purpose every missionary doctor, and every believer for that matter, needs to have.

No matter how good and efficient a doctor I am, no matter how well I perform in surgery, no matter how many lives I save in dire emergencies, every patient I treat is going to die, sooner or later. As a physician, I can only delay the inevitable. My skills cannot make people live forever; only the Great Physician can do that. Only as I refer people to him can they find eternal life.

My skills cannot make people live forever; only the Great Physician can do that. Only as I refer people to him can they find eternal life.

To his credit, and unlike some of us who endeavor to follow him, Dr. Jesus never forgot his higher purpose. He didn't content himself with only temporary physical treatments; he was just as, and often more, concerned about offering spiritual healing and eternal life. He always kept in mind, and often reminded his followers of, his higher purpose: "I have come that they may have life, and have it to the full" (John 10:10).

Jesus wasn't just *a* missionary doctor. He was *the perfect* missionary doctor. He never faced a need—physical or spiritual—that he couldn't meet. Yet he never forgot which was most important—as we see in his healing of the paralytic man whose friends brought him to see the Great Physician (Mark 2:1–12).

Though he was never part of any insurance-coverage plan, Jesus was the preferred provider of everyone who came to him. He still is. He can meet our every need. No matter what our profession, he knows the hardship and stress we face. He understands. He knows what it's like to feel overwhelmed by the demands of life. He knows what it will cost to fulfill our higher calling as Christians. He can teach us so much more about how to practice and live our faith as we continue our rounds with him.

5

THE GREAT PHYSICIAN UNDERSTOOD THE POWER OF TOUCH

I REMEMBER WHEN ELIZABETH, OUR FIRST AIDS patient, came to us at Tenwek in the early 1980s. She had been exposed to HIV through no fault of her own. Her husband had gone into the city to work and contracted the virus from a prostitute. When he returned home, he infected his wife, who developed a full-blown case of clinical AIDS. Not much was known about AIDS at the time—especially in Africa. People were frightened. So when Elizabeth was admitted, she was automatically taken to our isolation ward.

When I was making rounds the next day, I walked into the room to find this poor woman all alone, sitting on the edge of the bed in a pool of her own diarrhea, drooling profusely. She had such a serious case of thrush—a fungal infection of the mouth—that she couldn't swallow. The saliva was just streaming down her chin, from which long strands of spittle dripped into a rag she held on her lap. If ever I had seen an image of misery, this poor skeleton of a woman was it.

Had you walked into that room with me that day, you would have had every reason to ask, "Dr. Stevens, what in the world is going on here? Doesn't your hospital staff know how to take care of patients? This woman is a mess! You are the medical superintendent here, so tell me, What kind of a hospital are you running?" I knew exactly what the problem was. The ward attendants were scared to death they were going to catch AIDS, so they avoided going into the room to take care of this patient.

What I saw in that isolation ward upset me. I knew I could call in the staff and bawl them out, order them to take care of this woman, and they would do it. Reluctantly and fearfully perhaps, but they would do it.

> *One of the reasons touching is so important in medicine is because it says we care.*

Instead, I called an attendant and asked her to bring the things needed to clean the patient up. Then I started doing it myself. I learned a long time ago that the best way to make an example was to do something myself. I cleaned up Elizabeth's diarrhea, washed her where she was contaminated, and began changing the sheets on her bed. Before I'd gotten very far in the process, three staff members were helping me, embarrassed that the doctor was doing their job.

Yet what I remember best about that experience wasn't my staff's reaction, but that of Elizabeth. The care she received had an incredible and immediate therapeutic effect on her—to have me as the doctor actually touch her and take care of her. A new peace came over her face, and you could hear added strength in her voice—though all she could manage to say when I got her tucked back in bed was *"Koingoi mising! Koingoi mising!"* ("Thank you! Thank you!").

One of the reasons touching is so important in medicine is because it says we care.

Touch Matters

The Great Physician knew about the importance of touch. One of my favorite passages is Mark 5:24–34, the story of a woman who had been hemorrhaging for twelve years. Slipping up behind Jesus as he worked his way through a huge crowd, she was evidently thinking, *If I can just touch him, I will get well.* Indeed, the second she managed to grasp the corner of his robe, the flow of blood stopped. But the next moment Christ stopped, turned around, and demanded to know, "Who touched me?"

His disciples thought that a strange question. And it was. Jesus was pressing his way through a throng of people, being bumped and brushed and reached out to from every side. Yet he somehow sensed a different kind of touch had taken place.

Perhaps he recognized the sensation of healing power leaving him. That would have been a familiar feeling because touch played such an important role in so many of the recorded stories from Jesus' healing ministry. With his own hands he put mud on a blind man's eyes. He held the children in his lap. He reached out to help a paralytic man to his feet.

But to truly understand the full significance of touch in this story of the woman who touched his robe, we need to understand the cultural context. In Jesus' day Jewish women could not go to synagogue, prepare food, touch cooking or serving utensils, or sleep with their husbands during their menstrual period. They were considered unclean and made anything they touched unclean. So women became socially isolated eleven to fourteen days every month (they were considered unclean until seven days after their period ended)—virtual outcasts in their own homes.

The woman in our story hadn't experienced such ostracism for only a few days a month but for twelve long years. She had been unable to worship in the synagogue and probably could not even do simple daily tasks because of weakness associated with anemia. Even if she could have mustered the strength, she would not have been allowed to do anything for anyone other than herself. Other people didn't want to be around her because she was unclean.

What little she had in the way of financial resources, this woman had already spent on doctors, but to no avail. She must have had a poor, miserable, and lonely existence. Somehow she managed to survive day to day, but she undoubtedly had little hope for the future. She was almost certainly depressed.

So when Jesus sensed what had happened and turned around to confront her, she must have been terrified—in part because he was her last resort. But she also had dared to touch a rabbi, and it was a serious offense to contaminate a holy man. Jesus had every right to be angry, to demand punishment, perhaps even to imprison her for making him unclean.

But Jesus didn't do that. When he turned around, it wasn't to explode in anger but to reach out to her in compassion and forgiveness. I cannot help but think that he touched her in the process. Perhaps he placed his hand on her shoulder or her back. Maybe he held her hand while he talked with her. Whatever he did certainly would have shocked the onlookers overhearing what the woman's problem was. Yet here was this rabbi, a holy person, who had been touched by and was now touching an unclean woman. What a message that sight must have conveyed to everyone who witnessed it!

As we round with the Great Physician, we see for ourselves the powerful impact of touch.

HIGH TECH VERSUS HIGH TOUCH

I began thinking a lot about the role of touch in medicine when we started a nursing school at Tenwek in the late 1980s. Our hospital had always used an American philosophy of nursing simply because we had started the hospital with American nurses. But to have our new nursing school conform to Kenyan government regulations, we were required to adopt the British style of nursing, which has been the standard in Kenya since colonial days.

American nursing today tends to be high tech because we have developed the best medical technology in the world over the last half of the twentieth century. An American nurse working in an ICU, watching maybe a dozen or fifteen EKGs and other monitors from as many patients in as many different rooms all at once, can pick up on a problem in a split second and run to take care of it instantly. Many ICUs even have a TV camera focused on each patient and banks of TV screens at the nurses' station. So in America we teach nurses how to use IV pumps, BP monitors, oxygen sensors, and a host of other equipment to provide the most effective and efficient modern medical care in the world.

They have much the same technology in England, of course. Yet in the British system of nursing the emphasis has remained more *high touch* than *high tech*. The transition between systems at Tenwek required us to change everything from how we charted to how we dispensed medicines.

At Tenwek, for example, following the American system, a nurse took each of her patients' pills out of a bottle and put them in a little marked disposable cup, which was then placed on a tray. Then the nurse walked around the ward with the tray, handing each patient his or her meds. You don't do that in the British system because they feel it increases the risk you may give a patient the wrong medicine. Instead, British nurses are required to carry the original pill container around the ward and dispense each dose of meds to patients directly from the marked container.

British nursing also places a higher emphasis on basic nursing skills—how you give a bed bath, how you turn a patient, even how you fluff the pillows. In other words, the British style is concerned with how you make patients physically comfortable in every way possible.

To be honest, if you were a patient, the kind of nursing you would want is the British style. They spend more time with their patients, directly seeing to your comfort and care. That's not to indict American nurses, for a lot of them do that very well. But if you contrast the two systems, the British clearly place greater emphasis on providing personal care to patients.

When we made the switch at Tenwek, we found that patients appreciated higher-touch nursing care. It helped them feel more cared for. This shouldn't be too surprising because touch is such a crucial part of our lives as human beings. Much research has proven how important it is for people's emotional and physical health.

FOR LACK OF TOUCH

This principle is especially true of newborn babies. Touch is essential to the bonding process, to one's normal physical, emotional, and intellectual development—even to one's survival.

This hasn't always been understood. In the opening decades of the 1900s the supreme household authority on child rearing was a book called *The Care and Feeding of Children* by Luther Emmett Holt, a professor of pediatrics at New York Polyclinic and Columbia University. Holt recommended abolishing rocking, not picking up crying babies, feeding by the clock, and not spoiling babies with too much handling. Not only families, but many hospitals and foundling homes religiously followed Holt's advice.

During this time a surprisingly high percentage of infants died of a condition called *marasmus*, a Greek word meaning "wasting away." In a 1915 study conducted in ten different U.S. cities, in all but one children's institution surveyed every child under the age of two had died. In one New York City hospital the pediatric mortality rate was so close to 100 percent that it was common practice to list the condition of any infant as "hopeless" on every admission card.

Many doctors were, of course, concerned with the death rate. A few even questioned or changed the prevailing child-care practices in their institutions. After New York's Bellevue Hospital made it a rule that every baby should be picked up, carried around, and "mothered" every day, their mortality rates for infants dropped to less than 10 percent. Nevertheless, it still took some time for "tender loving care" to be seen as the most significant factor in combating marasmus and assuring the healthy development of small children. It took even longer to prove what had actually been happening to these kids: They were failing to suck/eat and thus starving themselves to death, all because of a lack of touch and the necessary stimulus it provides.

One of the major criticisms leveled at the developers of a child-rearing program popular with American Christians in the 1990s makes me think we didn't learn as much as we should have during the twentieth century. This best-selling parenting program (like Luther Holt's) attacked on-demand feeding and, in the interest of "discipline," warned against picking up and comforting crying babies; it also cautioned about spoiling babies with too much physical attention. The authors ignored much literature and research to belittle the concept of bonding and to downplay the significance of the emotionally reassuring and therapeutic benefits found in the comfort of human touch.

I would go so far as to say if you regularly withhold physical comfort in favor of leaving a fussy baby in a crib or a playpen, you are more apt to have a child who grows up to be a person you don't want to live around. Babies need to be touched to develop socially as well as physically and emotionally.

There's plenty of evidence—both clinical and anecdotal—to warrant concern about any system of child rearing that suggests babies today need less physical contact than they are getting. And there's more than enough scriptural evidence to indicate that the Great Physician's way was definitely high touch.

TOUCH AS A PARENTING TOOL

The requirement for touching doesn't end in childhood. My mother taught me a lot of things over the years. But I will never forget what she told me one day as we were reminiscing about my childhood and discussing parenting issues I was then experiencing with my three young kids. As we were talking about parental affection Mom said, "You know, Dave, as your children enter their teen years, your affection is going to become more and more important. The natural tendency as kids reach the often challenging adolescent years is to touch them less. But their need to be touched doesn't really change."

Now that my two older kids have grown out of their teens, I understand what my mother was saying. I think we dads especially start to feel awkward about demonstrating affection when our little girls begin turning into young women. We can't afford to let that stop us from hugging and kissing or giving them a shoulder rub. If they don't get the affection they need from us along with the sense of acceptance and self-worth it so powerfully conveys, they may begin looking for their daily dose of loving touch elsewhere—sooner rather than later.

Teenage sons need to be touched as well, even if hugs pose a serious threat to their budding macho image. Horsing around with boys, massaging their backs, giving them playful punches in the arm, or just reaching out and giving their shoulder a squeeze every time you pass by their seat when they're studying or watching TV can be a more acceptable, yet effective means of providing them with their recommended daily allowance of affection.

People never outgrow their need for human touch. Elderly folks today are often among the neediest when it comes to physical contact with others. If they are confined in a nursing home or live alone after their spouse has died and their children live too far away to visit, some older folks may go weeks or months without meaningful physical contact with another human being.

Low-Touch Culture

Whether it's a natural by-product of a mobile culture, fallout from our technological age, or something else, it seems all of society is less in touch physically than ever before.

We don't even shake hands as much anymore. I realized this when I came home from Kenya for the first time and noticed that people were taken aback by my habit of shaking hands with everyone I encountered. In Kenyan society you wouldn't think of starting any conversation without first exchanging handshakes, then greeting the other person and even asking about their family. You always made this sort of high-touch approach before you got down to business. But when I carried this custom home, even in church settings where I'd been invited to speak, I noticed people looking at me as if I was a little strange.

Unfortunately our society's deemphasis on touch has often transferred over into medical and hospital situations. When that happens both medical professionals and their patients lose out. As a doctor who has dealt with tens of thousands of sick people, I have learned that there is tremendous therapeutic benefit to touch. In fact, in the special training the Christian Medical Association offers at our Saline Solution conferences to help teach our members what it means to be a Christian physician and live out one's faith in one's practice, we talk a lot about the importance of touch.

The truth is, when people come for a doctor's appointment and they aren't touched, they usually aren't satisfied.

We encourage docs, when they go in a patient's room, to sit down at the edge of the bed, to hold the patient's hand, or to place a hand on a shoulder. The truth is, when people come for a doctor's appointment and they aren't touched, they usually aren't satisfied. I have had patients complain to me, "I went to see Dr. What's-his-name and he didn't even examine me. He just took my history and gave me a prescription." He may have made a perfectly good diagnosis and prescribed the very drug they needed. But the patients were unhappy with their treatment because they weren't touched.

In other words, I learned a long time ago that even if the problem is obvious and routine, I always touch the patient in some way during the appointment. I don't just do it for their benefit, but also for mine, for touch can often confirm or discount my diagnosis. In med school doctors learn how to touch appropriately, preserving the patient's modesty while getting the necessary information to make the diagnosis or to evaluate the response to a previous treatment.

DIAGNOSTIC TOUCH

As a doctor you quickly discover there is tremendous sensitivity in the tips of your fingers—they are some of the most sensitive parts of the human body. I can often suspect a patient is hypothyroid or hyperthyroid—depending on whether the skin texture feels coarse or as smooth as a baby's bottom. I can learn much from what a skin lesion or a bowel obstruction feels like. If someone comes in with a lump on his or her back, I touch it. I can often tell by the feel whether it's a lipoma (a benign fatty tumor that's harmless) or a possible sarcoma (a cancer of the fibrous muscle and connective tissue of the body), in which case something needs to be done immediately.

I can feel a lymph node and tell if it feels rubbery and may indicate tuberculosis, or if it feels hard, which may indicate the presence of cancer. All these things, and a whole lot more, can be discovered with the simple touch of a doctor's fingers.

Usually when a patient comes in with an infection, the doctor needs to touch it. If it's fluctuent, that means there's infection inside and an abscess is unlikely to heal until you open it up and drain the pus out. If that isn't done, the infection will usually fester and open up itself with much more pain (or worse). But touch will indicate what needs to be done.

Diagnostic touch is something a doctor has to learn. This skill increases over time—with practice, as a more experienced medical person says to you, "Come over here and feel this."

I have often felt what we call fremitus. I would place my hands on the patient's back and ask him to say "ninety-nine" several times in order to feel the voice vibrating the chest wall. A tumor or pneumonia causes the vibration to be greater over the affected area of the chest.

Another form of touch we use is percussion. If someone comes in with a consolidated area in his or her lungs filled up with fluid or with an effusion (a build-up of fluid around the lung), you can percuss (tap) the back using your fingertips. There will be a duller sort of response where the fluid is as opposed to a more hollow sensation from something filled with air. But you don't actually *hear* the dullness as much as you *feel* it through the tips of your fingers.

We also do what is called a percussion splash when we are trying to detect fluid in the abdominal cavity. We will place a hand on one side of the abdomen and then tap the other side; what we're actually trying to do is create a fluid wave. If there is fluid present, there will be a little delay and then you'll feel the splash on the other side.

Touching the Heart

Yet physical diagnosis is hardly the only use a doctor has for touch. Equally important is the touch of the human heart and soul.

The Great Physician knew people with emotional hurts needed to be touched. That's one lesson that has been driven home for me as I've led Christian Medical Association short-term medical mission teams (cosponsored by Prison Fellowship International) into African and South American prisons to minister to both physical and spiritual needs. During orientation sessions for those trips I always explain to team members that many of the inmates we encounter in prisons throughout the developing world have not been touched by another human being, except maybe to be beaten by a guard, in years. They are so hungry for a caring, gentle, compassionate touch that warmly shaking hands with them or simply placing a hand on their arm as they tell us about their medical problem may be the most powerful and helpful treatment we can offer.

This was beautifully demonstrated for me not long ago on a visit to a prison in Zambia. One of the four hundred and some prisoners we saw that day was in the last stages of AIDS. Medically I could do nothing more for the man than to hand him some vitamins and prescribe two weeks worth of pain medicine from our limited pharmaceutical supplies. But since I knew this prisoner was facing soon and certain death, I wanted to make sure we dealt with his spiritual and emotional needs. So before I went on to my next patient I called over George, one of the national Prison Fellowship staff who had helped arrange our mission, told him the situation, and suggested he counsel this inmate.

George asked the man what it was that had prompted such a sudden change of heart. This dying AIDS victim looked up and smiled through grateful tears as he said, "I never expected you to touch me."

It wasn't until we had left the prison and were eating supper at the guest house where our team spent the night that I learned what had happened. George told us he had shared the Gospel with this man, explaining how God offers eternal life to all those who confess their sins and accept Jesus as their Savior. The man had listened politely without making any sort of commitment or response. But when they finished talking, George asked the man's permission to pray with him. The man nodded and as they began praying together, George reached out and gently placed his hand on the inmate's head. The prisoner trembled, suddenly began to sob, then broke down completely and wept as he asked God to forgive his sins and accepted Christ right in that prison courtyard.

When George and his brand-new Christian brother finished praying, they talked some more. George gave the man a Bible and promised that a Prison Fellowship volunteer would be back to visit him every week. Then George asked the man what it was that had prompted such a sudden change of heart. This dying AIDS victim looked up at George and smiled through the grateful tears in his eyes as he said, "I never expected you to touch me."

He had heard everything that George said about God's love. He had understood the words. But it was a simple touch that broke down the barrier of suffering and pain to allow Christ to transform his heart and life.

WE NEED TO TOUCH

When someone is grieving, he or she often needs to be touched. I remember when my daughter Jessica broke up with her first boyfriend. She came into the house just sobbing. I put my arms around her, and she cried for fifteen minutes without saying a word. Even after she could talk, we didn't have much of a conversation. But I realized there had been a tremendous amount of therapy in that long hug.

What all hurting people need is to be appropriately touched—physically and emotionally. What the Great Physician's example says to all of us who claim to be his followers is that we are to be like him—high touch. That means that whoever, whenever, wherever we encounter people in suffering and pain, we must be reaching out and touching them—not just physically but emotionally as well.

Whoever, whenever, wherever we encounter people in suffering and pain, we must be reaching out and touching them—not just physically but emotionally as well.

We must begin by using emotional touch in a diagnostic way. We need to be looking for where the hurts are in other people, where the real pathology is brought on by sin and despair.

It doesn't take a medical examination room to do this. It can take place with our neighbors over a backyard fence or over a cup of coffee with our coworkers. When we do this, we must do it gently and carefully. Like a doctor palpating a sore abdomen, we have to start probing away from the painful area and work toward it slowly and gently until we finally get to the source of the problem and the pain.

Sometimes in medicine we may get what is called rebound. This happens when there is peritonitis in the abdomen. You gently push down and then release quickly. If the peritoneum is infected, it's not the pressure but the release of pressure that causes severe pain and may indicate the need for surgery.

If we expect to minister to hurting people when we're trying to get in touch with their pain, we too may experience a sort of rebound effect. People may cry, pull away, or even lash out at us. But that shouldn't keep us from trying to gently touch them, because we have to know where the pain is in people's lives before we can offer care and healing.

Let's say you know someone who is going through a painful divorce. You could think, *That's too bad! What a shame!* and keep your distance. Or you can go to them, talk with them, and gently feel out where their emotional hurts are, how you might help, where you can minister, and what you could pray about.

On far too many occasions we tend to avoid getting involved. We think getting in touch with someone's deepest pain may take more time than we want to commit. We don't know what words to use. Perhaps we feel as if we have enough pain of our own to deal with, or we don't feel qualified to get involved. But remember that touching is a learned skill. Like a doctor using percussion or feeling for fremitus to diagnose pneumonia, we get better with practice. The most important thing is to make a start.

Jesus teaches us by example as we round with him. What God is asking us to do is to move in and do as he, the Great Physician, would do—touching the needy people we encounter where they hurt so that we can then begin dealing with the pathology and help them work through it—to pray for them, support them, and encourage them back to health.

I know there are times when the last thing in the world we want to do is deal with this person or that particular problem. The toughest thing for me to deal with throughout all my time in medicine was those sigmoid volvulus cases I talked about in chapter 3. When these bowel obstructions went on for so many days that the bowel became necrotic and we then opened up the abdomen of those patients, the stench became so overpowering that the only way we could stay in the room was to have the nurse place a few drops of oil of wintergreen, which is almost as powerful a smell, on our upper lip just under the nose.

It Costs to Touch

Touching people at their point of pain can be unpleasant at times. There may even be risk involved. The medical example most people best understand is the AIDS patient. In North America we now use what is called universal precautions, meaning we treat everyone as if they have AIDS. We have developed an entire protocol for maintaining sterility, gloving, and dealing with needles and other sharp instruments. It is why your dentist wears a mask, eye shield, and gloves. It places a tremendous burden on society as we spend billions of dollars protecting ourselves by treating everyone as if they have AIDS.

But in Africa, where the incidence of AIDS is many times higher (as I write this, more than 25 percent of the adult population in some African countries are HIV positive), we couldn't afford to do that. In my early days at Tenwek a pair of surgical gloves would cost as much as some of our staff's daily salary. Thus, we took our gloves and resterilized them. We used a new pair for major surgery, but then washed, dried, and repowdered them, sterilized them, and packed them in sterile cloth inside a sterile canister. Then when we needed a pair of gloves for some minor procedure, we would open the canister and use sterile tongs to take out a pair of gloves to use a second, third, or fourth time.

When we operated or dealt with open wounds or abscesses, of course, we needed gloves. But we didn't have the luxury of using them every time we touched an AIDS patient. This took a little getting used to for some of our staff.

In the early 1980s we had a visiting doctor at Tenwek who was almost phobic about getting AIDS. She walked up the hill to the hospital her first day with two boxes of gloves, masks with a face screen, and a surgeon's cap on—planning to take every precaution she could to avoid contracting AIDS while she was with us.

I heard about this quickly because she created quite a stir walking around the hospital and seeing every patient with all this paraphernalia on. I had to pull her aside and tell her she couldn't do that. I explained to her that every national staff member at the hospital was going to be scared to take care of patients and begin demanding all these precautions for themselves. We simply couldn't afford either of those things to happen. She really struggled with our policy, but she survived her tour just fine.

Because of the prevalence of AIDS in Africa and our own financial limitations, we learned that we had to simply do the best we could to use reasonable precautions. But we also had to be willing to touch and deal with those people and trust the Lord for his protection.

I remember a South American surgeon who came to work with us for a time. One day during surgery Juan (not his real name) stuck himself with a needle—a deep stick. So we followed our usual routine, drawing blood for an AIDS test on the patient. This one came back positive.

Juan knew he was seronegative, so after waiting the mandatory six to eight weeks it usually takes to convert positive for HIV after exposure, he tested himself. The lab report came back positive. As you can imagine, Juan was absolutely devastated. He was only in his thirties. He and his wife had two small children, and now he was HIV positive. He couldn't believe it and was crying out to God, asking "Why?"

We had all been praying about the situation for weeks after the stick. We intensified those prayers after his positive test, and a week later we decided to reconfirm the test. This second test came back negative. We tested again—and he was negative again. Juan was clean. I can still see the joy on Juan's face when he told us the good news. The widow whose only son Christ raised from the dead (Luke 7:11–15) couldn't have been happier!

I cannot explain what happened. Perhaps the first test was a false positive. Or God may have healed Juan. I don't know. But I remember that during the time Juan thought he was HIV positive, he and I talked a lot about what this meant for his life. Juan had come to a peace about it saying, "I did the right thing. I'm doing what God wants me to do. If I didn't take care of people with AIDS, who would? I took reasonable precautions. What happened couldn't be helped. If this is God's will, it's God's will." Juan accepted the fact that following the Great Physician meant that he had been willing, and had to be again, to put himself in danger to help other people.

The Great Physician wants us to overcome our fears and our reluctance to become high touch and be willing to endure painful experiences for the ultimate good and even to put ourselves at risk to touch others. We know this because that's what Jesus did.

Leprosy was the AIDS of New Testament times. Everyone thought if you touched a leper, you would be contaminated and catch the disease. We know now that is not the case, but that's what people thought in that day. Yet Jesus touched lepers. He touched other "untouchables" as well—not just the woman with the issue of blood but prostitutes, tax collectors, insane people, and other outcasts. He had a huge impact on the lives of these people by bringing many of them into a relationship with his Father. But first he had to be willing to touch them.

Certainly we must be reasonable and cautious. But we have taken precaution to the extreme in our culture. If you walk into an AIDS patient's room looking as if you have just come from Mars, you will send a message that shouts you are afraid and that they are "unclean," just as loudly as the lepers shouted in Jesus day.

If we always approach our unsaved friends and neighbors and coworkers with our emotional defenses up, we won't be able to communicate the love and the acceptance that our touch is meant to convey. Sometimes we have to make ourselves vulnerable, to accept a certain degree of risk, to mix with the crowd. In order to achieve the kind of open, therapeutic interaction in which we can touch and help others, we also have to first allow ourselves to be touched.

Reluctant Touch

I am reminded of a nonmedical story from Kenya, which still has a few remote areas in which the people have seldom seen white children. We had taken a family outing to Masai country to see some big game. On the way back to Tenwek, miles from nowhere on some tiny back-country dirt road, we ended up stuck in a mud hole up to the doorframes. A crowd from a nearby village soon gathered to watch and help out.

To begin with, we left all three of our kids sitting in the backseat of the car because we were surrounded by mud. But soon we had a small flock of Kipsigis youngsters surrounding the car, gaping in the open windows, and even reaching into the backseat to touch our children—especially Jessica, who had light hair at the time, and Stacy, who was just a baby. They wanted to feel and see if the kids were real. Did the white rub off? At first our children didn't know what to think and complained about all these "people touching me, Daddy!"

Finally we decided to get our kids out of the car and carried them beyond the mud to the side of the road, where they were to stay while we continued trying to get the car out of the mud hole. As other curious children quickly gathered around, I laughingly suggested to my three kids, "If they want to touch you, why don't you touch them back?" So Jason, Jessica, and Stacy began touching the other kids' hair and faces. Before we knew it, they were all having a wonderful time running and playing with these kids. This whole delightful interchange started with a willingness to touch and be touched.

This brings me to an aspect of this subject I haven't looked at yet: If you are unwilling to be touched, the doctor may not be able to help you much. That's true of our own spiritual relationship with the Great Physician too. If we are unwilling to let him touch us, delve into our lives, and minister to us where our real pain is, it's almost impossible for healing to take place.

We tend to put up barriers between us and God and between us and other people. We are reluctant to reveal who we really are, what really concerns us. So a lot of facade building goes on, making it more difficult to connect with others—to touch or be touched.

This is why doctors ask patients to undress. I cannot feel what I need to feel through jackets, pants, shirts, bras, and all the rest of it to really tell what's going on. I must be in contact with the tissue. That kind of touching requires trust and faith that the person doing the touching has your best interests at heart.

TOUCHING DEEP

Probably the most intrusive type of touching anyone experiences is during surgery. That's not just being touched on the outside; it means the exposure and touching of your innermost being, which definitely calls for real trust.

Touching requires trust and faith that the person doing the touching has your best interests at heart.

An experienced surgeon who knows what he or she is doing can actually locate and feel a perforated ulcer through the intestinal wall. When you have opened the abdomen, you feel the duodenum and the pylorus, the area where the intestine comes out of the stomach, and if you gently take your time to palpate the region, you can often feel where that ulcer is, even where the perforation has occurred.

Or we actually "run the bowel" through our fingers when we are feeling for problems there. As surgeons we not only see but also feel for abnormalities in each of the patient's organs. We touch patients intimately, on the inside, in ways most people have never done and never will. But people let us do this because they trust us as doctors. They have faith that only by doing this surgery are we going to be able to take care of the problem and make them better.

In the same way, if we are going to allow the Great Physician to work in our lives, we must have faith in him. We must realize what needs to be done may be painful—nobody wants to have surgery, physical or spiritual. But if God is going to restore us to health, we must let him into our most inner parts, our deepest being, where the real pathology is, so he can take care of it.

Sometimes as a surgeon doing an operation, you cannot see what's going on. You have to do it by touch. Perhaps there's a lot of blood in the surgical field, or you're working way down in the body cavity and there are organs in the way. This is especially true in pelvic surgery, when you are working on the uterus or the ovaries and tubes. Sometimes you can only feel the anatomy to know where to clamp or whatever. You have no choice but to rely on touch.

There may be times when we have to work that way with other people. Especially when we are not really sure what's going on in their lives, we have to feel our way carefully, relying on the sensitivity we have seen in and learned from the Great Physician and trusting him to help us know just where to go and what to do.

TOUCHING TRIBUTE

Let me close with one final story that always comes to mind when I think of the Great Physician's touch. This too occurred when our family encountered travel trouble on the backcountry roads, an all-too-common occurrence in Kenya. We had gotten word that Jody's mom had metastatic breast cancer and didn't have long to live. So we used our meager savings to purchase airline tickets home for a visit. When we left Tenwek, we were running late and still had a five- or six-hour drive to Nairobi to catch our evening flight. The muddy roads remained passable despite recent rain—until we came to a ravine where the track at the bottom disappeared into a brown, roiling stream.

A bridge had been built there, but the approaches to the medium-size concrete box that made up the bridge had been washed away. There must have been a big thunderstorm upstream to create such a flash flood. The prospects didn't look good, but I got out, pulled on a pair of boots, and waded into the stream, praying I could find a way across. I knew we would miss our flight if we had to turn around and take a longer route to Nairobi. But when the water went over my boots within a couple steps of the bank, I was forced to retreat in frustration. As I sloshed back toward the car, I saw an elderly man walk out of the bush and greet Jody in typical Kipsigis fashion.

"Chamege?" (Cha-muh-gay means "Hello," literally, "Do you love yourself?")

Jody replied, *"Chamege mising."* (Cha-muh-gay me-sing: "I love myself very much.")

The conversation progressed as I approached the car.

"How are you?" the man asked.

Jody said, "Fine!" (despite our obvious dilemma).

"Iweni ano?" ("Where are you going?")

"Kibendi Nairobi," Jody told him.

By this time I was on the other side of the car, sitting sideways in the driver's seat, pulling off my wet and useless boots.

The man's next question was predictable. "Where do you live?"

When Jody told him we lived at Tenwek Hospital, he suddenly became more animated. "Do you know Mosonik?" he asked, using the Kipsigis name for Ernie Steury.

"Yes, we do," Jody assured him. "In fact, they call my husband Arap Mosonik [son of Mosonik]! He isn't really Mosonik's son, but is like a son because he is the young doctor following in Mosonik's footsteps at the hospital."

A huge smile filled the face of the old man. Then strangely he turned and at a half-trot he headed back into the bush, yelling at the top of his lungs. He was still shouting, his Kipsigis too rapid for me to understand, as he disappeared over a nearby ridge.

Within minutes we realized what was happening as people began streaming onto the road. Each one carried rocks. They waded out into the stream to wedge in their load before running back into the bush for more.

They were building us an on-ramp to the bridge. I started down to the river to help, but the old man returned and insisted I relax as he issued more rapid-fire instructions to his crew. Within minutes they began adding logs and rough-hewn boards to the top of the rocks.

Satisfied that everything was progressing as he wanted, the old gentleman turned to continue the conversation after Jody introduced me more formally. He told us, "When my wife was sick, Mosonik came to her bed many times, even in the middle of the night. I don't think that man ever sleeps. My wife would have died, but Mosonik cut her belly open to make her well. Then my daughter, when she had her first baby, it wouldn't come. So we took her to Tenwek, and somehow Mosonik got my first grandson out. He lived and is growing well. We Kipsigis know, if we get sick and go to the hospital and just touch Mosonik, we will get better."

> *His compassionate touch had made such an impression that people for miles and miles around had come to a conclusion much like the sick woman who grasped the edge of Jesus' robe: "If we just touch him, we will get better."*

By this time, the crude but lovingly provided ramp was complete. So I drove my car up onto the concrete bridge in the middle of the river and stopped. There I waited as our personal road crew disassembled the wood and stones to construct an off-ramp to the other side. Within minutes we pulled onto the other bank and got out of the car to thank our rescuers and shake hands all around.

Watching the waving crowd in the rearview mirror as we headed off again for Nairobi, I laughed as I thought, *Even in Africa, it isn't what you know so much as it is who you know.*

The rest of the way into Nairobi that day I couldn't help replaying that man's words in my mind again and again. "We know, if we just touch Mosonik, we will get better." What a powerful tribute to the sacrificial service of Ernie Steury! What an impact he has made on people throughout this entire region of Kenya!

Ernie's patients noticed, as I had noticed countless times, how he would put an arm on their shoulder or hold their hand as he cared for their hurts, their wounds, and their sicknesses. They noted how gently he probed and palpated. His compassionate touch had made such an impression that people for miles and miles around had come to a conclusion much like the sick woman who grasped the edge of Jesus' robe: "If we just touch him, we will get better."

Can people say as much about you and me?

Maybe they would if we really understood, as the Great Physician did, the healing power of touch.

THE GREAT PHYSICIAN VOLUNTEERED TO BE ON CALL

MANY JOBS REQUIRE PEOPLE TO BE ON CALL—TO step in and solve a problem, deal with an emergency, or fill in for someone else. Whether you are a police officer, a flight attendant, a factory foreman, a business owner, or a corporate executive, the chances are your job description (at least unofficially) requires you to be on call whenever your authority, your expertise, or just your presence is required—even if you're not scheduled to be on duty. Given that definition, parents are on call twenty-four hours a day for as long as their kids are at home—and sometimes even longer.

So doctors certainly aren't the only ones familiar with the concept of being on call. However, I cannot think of another profession in which being on call is considered such an expected part of the job that this experience is made an integral part of formal training.

When I was in medical school, it was not unusual for a surgical resident in demanding training programs to be on duty for thirty-six hours and off twelve, on thirty-six and off twelve, for his or her entire first year of residency. That meant kissing your family and any semblance of a normal life good-bye for the duration. Fortunately, my own family-practice residency required me to take night call only once every third night my first year. But even then I found that being on duty all night between two full days of work could be a terribly draining experience. The night I describe in the next section was not unusual.

It Happened One Night

As the resident on call for internal medicine, I took Mr. Adam's case when he showed up in the ER early one evening. An elderly man who had smoked all his life, he had chronic pulmonary disease and manifested a low oxygen saturation in his arterial blood gas. I increased his oxygen level, but when he failed to improve, I sent him to the ICU. Even with a number of medications and respiratory therapy, his condition continued to deteriorate.

Eventually I had to intubate him and put him on a respirator, leaving orders for the nurses to contact me if his condition changed. At 1:00 A.M. I was called back to the ICU because my patient was fighting the respirator, trying to pull out the tubing. We were still not seeing significant improvement in his oxygen-saturation level. As a result, I tried to sedate him enough to keep him from fighting the respirator, but not enough to stop his own breathing. It was going to be touch and go through the night, trying to find the right balance and save this man's life.

I was writing new orders and still monitoring Mr. Adam's response to the sedative I had given him when I got another beep, this time from the medicine ward. Another of my patients, a Mr. McCreary, had just died. This wasn't unexpected, for he had terminal lung cancer and had been in the hospital hanging on to life by a thread for an entire week.

I hurried to Mr. McCreary's room and examined him to be sure his breathing had stopped and he had no pulse. His pupils were fixed and dilated. I made a note on the chart to pronounce him dead and jotted some orders as to what to do with the body. I then went out to speak with his relatives. By now it was 2:00 A.M., and the family was very distraught. Many of them had been without adequate sleep for a number of days.

Even though they had been expecting the news, my telling them he had finally died prompted a flood of tears. It's difficult to know how to be compassionate at 2:00 A.M., especially when you've just received another beep from the emergency room. But I sat down and began to explain to his family that Mr. McCreary, from all we could tell, had died peacefully in his sleep, and they could thank God for that. After a few more moments of encouragement and brief instructions as to what would happen next, I ran down to the ER to see a diabetic patient whose blood sugars had come back dangerously high.

The patient was breathing quickly and showing other symptoms of a life-threatening condition called diabetic ketoacidosis. I did an examination, checked the lab tests, and began to write the complex orders that were going to be needed to stabilize this patient.

This was my third admission to the ICU that night, and it didn't look as if I was going to get any sleep at all. After following the patient to the ICU and discussing the case with the nurse, I stood by as the first of a series of lab results started to come back and adjusted the insulin and fluid orders accordingly. It became clear in an hour or two that the patient was responding to treatment.

At 4:30 A.M., feeling totally exhausted, I headed for the house-staff unit, hoping to get at least an hour of sleep before running down to check on my diabetic patient again and pulling all of the information I would need for rounds at 6:30.

I dropped off as soon as I hit the sack. Minutes later the phone rang. ICU was calling: Mr. Adams had coded—that is, his heart had stopped. I went from fully asleep to fully awake in a split second as I grabbed my white coat and stethoscope and sprinted out the door, down the steps, through the long hallways of the hospital, and burst into the ICU. The nurses were already doing CPR as I checked the cardiac monitor for any sign of arrhythmia and simultaneously began drugs to try to get his heart started again.

An hour later I finished my note and a new batch of orders. We had successfully cardioverted his heart and his vital signs had stabilized. No more sleep tonight, for I had just enough time to check on my diabetic patient before rounds and another incredibly full day of work. The Lord willing, in another twelve hours I would get home.

Mr. Adams had coded—that is, his heart had stopped. I went from fully asleep to fully awake in a split second as I grabbed my white coat and stethoscope and sprinted out the door.

Being a resident on night call means the needs of others control your life. You have no rights to sleep or food or even to go to the bathroom. You are at the beck and call of patients, nurses, ER docs, senior residents, and any attending who admits to your hospital. You outrank the medical students, but you also have to answer all their questions, supervise their work, and provide any help they need. Being on call requires a total commitment to do whatever is needed, whenever it's needed, to get the job done. Indeed, while on call your life is not your own.

JESUS ON CALL

The Great Physician obviously knew what it meant to be on call. His healing skills were often in great demand. Mark 1:32–34 tells about one of the times he took night call: "That evening after the sun went down, they brought the sick and evil afflicted people to him, and the whole city was lined up at his door. He cured their sick and demented bodies" (*The Message*).

If you read Mark 1:21–31, you realize Christ's night call also began after an incredibly busy day. He had entered Capernaum on the Sabbath, which gave him an important opportunity to get his message out. He went to the synagogue and spent much of the day there teaching. The people who heard him were amazed that he was speaking to their needs. The crowd got larger and larger. Folks were probably leaning into the windows and doorways, trying to hear what he was saying. Everything was going well until the service was interrupted by a shouting and screaming man possessed by an evil spirit.

This reminds me of one thing I hated when I was on call, namely, carrying my beeper to church. As I got to be a third-year resident I had OB patients, so I was on call for them around the clock, not just every third or fourth night. It never failed; the pastor was always praying when the beeper went off (that was before they vibrated), and I would fumble around trying to get the thing turned down before I created a bigger disturbance.

But that's a minor disruption compared to what went on while Jesus was preaching. This man with an evil spirit began ranting and raving. Jesus dealt with the problem and healed the man right there in front of everyone. I rather doubt the people who saw what happened actually settled down again right away. Instead, as Jesus continued teaching in a hot, crowded room, they probably began yelling and calling out (or at least buzzing in amazement), hoping to be healed.

When Jesus finally did break away to eat a meal and spend a little time with his friends at Simon and Andrew's house, Jesus arrived to find his plans disrupted by illness. Simon Peter's mother-in-law lay sick in bed. After Jesus healed her, everyone finally got fed. I imagine they were beginning to settle down to some casual and quiet conversation. After a full day of public teaching and ministry, Jesus was worn out and probably thinking about getting a little sleep.

That's just about the time the sun went down, marking the end of the Sabbath. Now everyone felt free to travel, bring, or even carry all their sick or demented relatives and friends to Jesus for healing. Instead of turning them away and telling them the doctor's office was closed, Dr. Jesus began night call.

Can you imagine the impact that example must have made on his followers? The disciples were no doubt tired too. But Jesus was showing them what it was like to put others' needs ahead of his own. He could have taught them this lesson with words, but they probably weren't ready for that. At this point in their relationship with the Great Physician, his interns needed a real-life object lesson. He has provided it for us as well.

> *The Great Physician is saying to us all, "If you are going to be my interns, you are going to take night call."*

It wasn't until later in his ministry that he verbalized the concept this way: "If anyone would come after me, he must deny himself and take up his cross and follow me" (Matt. 16:24). Do you hear what he is saying to us? "You must be willing to do whatever I say, go wherever I go, imitate me. That's going to require you to deny yourself, your own needs, your own wants, your own concerns. That's what it means to sacrifice—to take up the cross and follow in my footsteps." In other words, the Great Physician is saying to us all, "If you are going to be my interns, you are going to take night call."

Let's now consider a few of the implications to that principle, because night call means a lot of different things to those of us who have done it.

Accepting Responsibility

First of all, taking night call means taking responsibility. When you are in residency, you take call for a particular service. The night I described at the beginning of this chapter involved night call for internal medicine; other residents were on call for pediatrics, OB, surgery, and the like. I was responsible for my section of the hospital, and I thought that was a heavy load.

But when I got to Africa, night call at Tenwek meant accepting responsibility for the entire hospital—for every patient. One time we had as many as 480 people in our 130 beds—though 150 to 200 percent occupancy was the norm.

Chapter 4 painted a picture of a normal day's challenges at Tenwek Hospital. We saw many of the same problems at night: dehydrated kids, patients needing immediate treatment for meningitis, emergency C-sections, and the like.

One major difference with night work, however, is that instead of dealing with the daily routine between crises, you were trying to get back to sleep. That took a while at Tenwek because it meant walking more than a quarter-mile down the hill through the compound to get home. Too often it seemed the very moment you climbed into bed and got comfortable, the phone began to ring (or before we got the phone system, someone knocked on the bedroom window). Then you would have another long hike uphill to handle another crisis.

When I left Tenwek after eleven years of service, during my very last night on call for the hospital, as a sort of gag gift, the other docs presented me with an "official" framed *Last Night on Call* certificate. I was only half kidding when I laughingly thanked my colleagues and assured them that their award would forever be one of my most prized possessions. For me it did have a deeper, significant meaning because of what it had meant to be on call and accept responsibility for the entire hospital. I felt an awesome weight in knowing others were dependent on me and on my skills and knowledge. Understanding this required a real commitment on my part, a willingness to accept the responsibility—to deny myself and do what needed to be done.

After all those years at Tenwek I felt a real sense of satisfaction in having done that, in part because I knew that such willingness hadn't always been there. There were times I really struggled over the sacrifice and the surrender of my own needs.

One of the biggest struggles took place before I even started my missionary career. I had graduated AOA from medical school. (Alpha Omega Alpha is the honorary science fraternity reserved for those among the top 5 percent of medical students around the country.) I had been further honored to be named chief resident in charge of the other forty residents at our residency hospital. While I considered that a privilege, it also carried responsibility for making up call schedules, helping handle any personnel and personal problems among the residents, and dealing with administration on the residents' behalf.

All these things looked good on my resume. Even though I had been planning on becoming a medical missionary since my senior year of high school, I realized as I approached the end of my training that my options were now wide open in terms of a medical career. I could teach in a residency program, open a private practice, or join a group.

The whole thing came to a head for me when I was invited to an all-expense-paid weekend at Calloway Gardens, a beautiful resort north of Columbus, Georgia. A number of my colleagues and other third-year residents from several residency programs around the state were invited there to meet with community representatives from Georgia and Alabama who were looking for physicians to come and practice in their communities. A number of these folks from small towns and rural counties had banded together and sponsored this extravagant weekend. They covered our hotel bill, fed us steak and lobster, and paid our green fees if we wanted to play golf. I shot skeet for the first time in my life. There was horseback riding along beautiful azalea-lined trails through the park. There were saunas and hot tubs, and swimming in the pool. You name it—and they picked up the whole tab.

Naturally, the real purpose of this weekend was to recruit you to come to their community. But Jody and I got this invitation—no strings attached. I thought, *Sure, I'm going as a missionary to Africa, but my mama didn't raise no fool. We'll go and enjoy this weekend with our friends. It'll be great.* And it was!

But that first night a business leader from a small community in Georgia walked up to me and introduced himself. He had obviously done his homework because he said, "Dr. Stevens, you are the chief resident?" When I told him I was, he said, "Well, let me tell you about our community; it may be something that you want to consider."

This gentleman was very polished, a real salesman. He told me all about their community and how badly they needed a doctor. Right now, he pointed out, they had to drive more than ten miles to the county seat just to see a physician. So they had put together a committee of prominent business, civic, and religious leaders to recruit a doctor to come to their community. He assured me they already had this nice office that they would let me use free of charge. "We'll even guarantee your salary for the first couple of years"—and he threw out a dollar figure that was more money than I ever dreamed of making.

"We know it'll take a little time to build your practice," he went on, "and we'll make sure you won't be taking any risk. Moreover, we'll give you a free membership to the country club." I could hardly believe I was hearing all this.

On and on he went. "You like to fish, don't you?" Sure. "Well, we have this wonderful lake just outside of town that has huge bass," and he put his hands out shoulder width as if to say that every bass in the lake would be that big, if only I came to be their doctor.

"I hear that you're religious," he said. You know that if people say it like that, it probably means they themselves are not. I had barely managed to say, "Yes, I . . ." before he was telling me about all the wonderful churches in their town.

The man went on for about ten or fifteen minutes before I finally managed to say, "You know, I'm planning on going as a missionary to Africa as soon as I finish my residency." You'd have thought I told the man I had contagious TB, he left so quickly. When I saw him cornering several other residents throughout the evening, I couldn't help smiling at the memory of his sudden reaction when he obviously decided he had been wasting his time with me.

But that conversation was the beginning of a time of real struggle for me. I began thinking how nice it would be to go to that small town and have that financial security. In medical school and residency you have denied yourself a lot and learned the meaning of delayed gratification. By this time many of my college friends had bought houses, drove nice cars, and had gotten a fast start on good careers. But here I was, still plugging away with my training almost seven years after college. We were renting a small house, driving a secondhand Volkswagen Beetle I had bought my first year of med school, and living on a shoestring with two small children.

And suddenly here was Shangri-la being offered to me if I would just be willing to say yes. I began to daydream about what it would be like to open a private practice of my very own, to be the town doctor in some idyllic community where the folks were friendly and the fishin' was fine. The more I thought about it, the better it sounded.

I didn't know then what I have come to understand since—that when God asks us to do something, when he wants us to be on call for him and we are committed to do that, the devil knows better than to try to get us to completely turn our backs and change our plans. But he does try to get us to alter our course just a little, maybe to get us to settle for second best.

I started thinking, *If I went to some nice little town, I could be the best family-practice doctor for miles around. What an impact I could make for Christ in my community by being a witness in my practice. I could be a lay leader in my church and teach Sunday school. I could help with the youth group and work with the schools. I could earn enough money to help support lots of missionaries and even pay my own way to go overseas on a short-term mission trip every summer. I wouldn't need to be a medical missionary in order to do a lot of things for the Lord right here at home.*

Whenever I speak to doctors today, I assure them that there's nothing wrong with practicing in the United States—*unless God's will for them is to be somewhere else*. I knew that God's perfect will in my life was to go to Africa, that doing anything else, for me, would mean settling for second

> *The devil knows better than to try to get us to completely turn our backs and change our plans. But he does try to get us to alter our course just a little, maybe to get us to settle for second best.*

best. But for a while there, second best looked pretty good. I really struggled with Jesus' call to deny myself, take up my cross, and follow him.

One night about 2:00 A.M., as I was tossing and turning, unable to get to sleep, I finally woke Jody up and said, "Honey, we really need to pray!" So we got down on our knees by the bed, and I told the Lord again that I was willing to answer what I knew was his call to serve him in Africa, "no matter what it means." I was ready to accept that responsibility, and so was Jody.

Giving up Control

In addition to accepting responsibility, one of the issues I was struggling with at this time of rethinking my commitment to Africa was the growing realization that being on call meant giving up control.

Like most doctors who not only have control-type personalities but are then taught to take charge and to make decisions, I realized I had some control issues to deal with. Surrendering control to God is hard enough for a controller. But turning my life and career over to a mission organization to make major decisions that would impact every facet of my professional career and my personal life went against my very nature. *I'd spent this many years in school to become a doctor only to let someone else decide my income, where I lived, and what kind of car I would drive?*

That involved a tremendous loss of control, which proved to be the biggest battle for me. It wasn't the fact that we would be halfway around the world, but that I was giving control over to the Lord and something outside of myself—to a mission organization.

Don't get me wrong. World Gospel Mission, the group we served with for eleven years, is a great mission agency. More than just an organization, it's a family of missionaries involved in highly effective ministry around the world. They do a fine job of meeting the needs of their missionaries. All the same, when we agreed to go "on call" with them, I had to give up a lot of control. That's not easy.

Making Yourself Available

Doctors aren't the only ones who struggle with control issues. I suspect that some people reading this book are struggling right now, perhaps with the fact that they know God wants them to accept some responsibility and to make themselves available to him. You see, when you go on call, not only do you accept responsibility but you make yourself available.

I noticed two types of residents in residency, and it doesn't take long before you know who are the good ones and who are the bad ones. The good ones aren't always the smartest ones (although intelligence is important, as are diligence and an ability to apply what one knows). The good residents are the ones that don't make excuses to try to avoid the work. The work is almost always demanding, but the good residents are there, and they are there with the right attitude and a spirit willing to help.

By contrast, a few residents aren't good. Again it's not a matter of intelligence, for nobody can make it that far without being bright. Their problem is a matter of attitude. The bad residents will do everything they can to avoid work. When the nurse pages them from the ER and says, "Dr. So-and-So, we need you in the ER," their first response often is, "Well, have you done this? Or have you tried that?" Then they go on to say, "Go do this or that, and then call me again." These residents don't want to answer the call, so they think up excuses not to examine the patient. They aren't making themselves available.

By not being available, they put the work back on the nurses. Nurses have a low tolerance for that because they know these same residents are the ones whose patients tend to get into trouble because the residents are trying to get some sleep and don't provide the care. When they do finally answer a call, they go with a bad attitude, which often shows through in their work. Patient care suffers; sometimes patients are even put at risk.

Ernie Steury made himself more available than anyone I knew. Imagine being the only doctor on call for hundreds of thousands of people. That was the situation he found himself in when he arrived at Tenwek in 1959—fresh from an internship in tropical medicine at Gorgas Hospital in Panama. Ernie had hoped to do a residency in surgery but instead answered a desperate call for help at this small hospital in the southwest corner of Kenya.

Tenwek had been open for a number of years as a cottage hospital, which meant they had nurses but no doctors. The hospital and mission staff had prayed since the 1940s that God would send a doctor. The Lord began speaking in Ernie Steury's heart when he was a college student at Asbury College planning on going into the ministry and had no interest in medicine.

When he completed his medical training and arrived at Tenwek, the makeshift OR was so small that the nurses had to crawl under the operating table to get from one side of the patient to the other. Ernie was there by himself taking call *for ten years.* I cannot imagine how difficult it must have been to be the only doctor who could bring health and healing to such a huge number of people. And not only was he the doctor, but he was mission mechanic, building designer, fund raiser, and much more—to take this little hospital and grow it to what God wanted it to be.

Ernie has told me there were days and nights when he didn't think he could go on. He would collapse into bed without enough energy to stand up. Then somebody with a lantern would knock on the window in the middle of the night and tell him of another emergency. He knew that if he did not take responsibility and go, someone would surely die. So he made himself available another day, another night.

Today Tenwek is one of the largest (three hundred beds) and most successful mission hospitals in the world. It is not just ministering to physical needs and improving the quality of life for hundreds of thousands of people, but it is making a spiritual impact through the hospital's medical and community-health programs, which have resulted in more than 10,000 Kenyans coming to Christ every year.

This all happened because one young Indiana farm boy heard God's call in his life and was willing to accept responsibility and make himself available to serve. Whenever I think about what has happened at Tenwek in the course of Ernie Steury's lifetime, I know there are at least two important considerations to think about. Certainly the Great Physician expects each of his interns to take call. At the same time, can you imagine what could be accomplished if all of us followed God's call in our lives?

You may be thinking there just aren't many Ernie Steurys. You are probably right— but there ought to be.

It's inconceivable to me that I as an intern or a resident would have ever turned to my attending doctor to say, "It's fine for other people to take call. But don't expect me to do it. I need a good night's sleep. I've got other plans. Maybe I'll take in a movie with my wife." My attending would have had a few words to say about that. He expected me to take responsibility and make myself available, unreservedly and without condition. That was my understood role. That was the essence of being a medical intern and a medical resident.

> *The Great Physician, by his example and through his Word, is asking us to assume responsibility, give up control of our own lives, and make ourselves available for whatever he wants us to do.*

That is the essence of our role in Christ's service. The Great Physician, by his example and through his Word, is asking us to assume responsibility, give up control of our own lives, and make ourselves available for whatever he wants us to do. That's the way he plans to get the job done. Amazing as it seems, he chooses to use us to relieve suffering and carry his healing message of life to those in danger of dying spiritually and facing eternity separated from God.

Maybe you already know what the Great Physician wants you to do. Perhaps your beeper's gone off. You have received the call about someone in the ER or a loved one that needs intensive care. Could it be that you won't accept responsibility? Maybe your problem is giving up control. Is God asking you to make yourself available?

Not everyone is called into medicine or overseas missions. Maybe God wants you to organize a Bible study in your home to reach out to your neighbors. Maybe he's calling you to be more responsible and make yourself more available as a parent. Perhaps he wants you to befriend and share your faith with a business associate, to serve on a committee at church, or to teach a certain Sunday school class. Maybe the Great Physician is asking you to volunteer to be on call caring for an aging parent or relative in your home. Maybe he wants you to answer the call to give of your wealth or use your influence for his kingdom.

Doing Difficult Things

I have no idea what God may be asking you to do right now. I certainly won't try to tell you it will be easy if you just do it, because there's another thing I've learned over the years about being on call: It often means doing difficult things.

When I got calls at night, especially at Tenwek, I knew I would be facing a difficult case. Had it been simple, the staff would have handled it without bothering me. So you know immediately when you're on call, you'll have to tackle the biggest problems.

The most common middle-of-the-night problems at Tenwek were OB calls. Not only did we have a high incidence of multiple births, with all the accompanying complications such as premature and breech deliveries, but one out of a hundred Kipsigis babies, for whatever reason, was born with some sort of neural-tube defect—the most common of which was an opening to the spinal cord in the lower back.

Thus, when I got called during the night, I was often taken to the limit of my skills and beyond my past experience. Sometimes it meant making difficult choices.

Just as my mentor Ernie Steury didn't build Tenwek into the premier mission hospital it is today all by himself, doctors are hardly the only ones who know that being on call means taking on difficult challenges. One of the people who epitomized this lesson for me was Edna

Borroff, one of the nurses that came to Tenwek in the 1940s. That was back in the days when patients and visitors often arrived by oxcart—the only transportation you could count on to make it through the muddy trails leading into that remote area of Kenya.

Edna, who had been raised (if you can accurately claim a woman less than five feet tall was "raised") on an Ohio farm, felt God calling her, and obeyed by going halfway around the world to Kenya, long before Tenwek ever had a physician to handle those difficult things. Edna had charge over the OB, where she became a legend in her own time. By the time she retired in the late 1980s, Edna had delivered almost 18,000 babies. That's probably twice as many as a *very* busy American obstetrician delivers in an entire career.

People loved Edna. By the time I got to Tenwek, women who had been delivered by Edna were now having their own babies delivered by Edna and were so honored they named their children after her—boys as well as girls. If you went with her anywhere in that part of Kenya—to a game park or a hotel—chances were good that Edna would get in free because the manager or someone else had been delivered by Edna or had a child she delivered. She was the honored guest wherever she went.

But when Edna first arrived in Tenwek, many of the old cultural taboos were still enforced, including the belief among the Kipsigis that whenever triplets were born, the second child was cursed and should be killed. So they would take the baby, put it outside, and let it die. Because of the high multiple birthrate among the tribe, triplets were not uncommon. But there wasn't a surviving set of triplets in the entire region.

When Edna learned about this custom, she faced a terrible dilemma the first time she delivered a set of triplets. She was handling nearly all the obstetrics at the hospital at the time, plus nursing on the wards and conducting the outpatient clinic. She was on call almost twenty-four hours a day, seven days a week. She felt constantly overwhelmed by more medical needs than she could ever hope to meet.

But when the first triplets she attended were born, she knew that if she let the mother take them home, one of them would surely be killed. What did Edna do? She solved the dilemma by keeping that set of triplets and caring for them herself in her own home. The Kipsigis were so convinced something terrible was going to happen as a result that Edna realized she had to take care of all three. So along with all her other duties and responsibilities, this single missionary nurse took care of those triplets for months—until she proved to everyone that one of the babies wasn't cursed and nothing bad was going to happen to her.

> *Is the Great Physician speaking to you about doing a difficult thing? Often he asks us to put that on the altar—to be willing to do the thing of all things we say we don't want to do.*

That was the first set of triplets known to have survived in the history of the tribe. Edna's intervention did away with the old tribal taboo once and for all. In fact, when I got to Kenya, those three triplets, grown and with families of their own by then, came back to Tenwek to have their photograph taken with Edna and to express their gratitude to the woman who took on a difficult challenge, was willing to surrender what little control she had left over her own life, made herself available, and assumed responsibility for three babies whose lives were threatened.

Is the Great Physician speaking to you about doing a difficult thing? Often he asks us to put that on the altar—to be willing to do the thing of all things we say we don't want to do. That's what being on call often requires.

What is God asking of you? Maybe he's calling you to leave your job, to move your family somewhere else, or to go into a second career at some point in your life. Maybe he wants you to become involved in some ministry or go back to school and get some extra education. Maybe it's finding a natural way to share your faith with your boss, befriend a neighbor who's been unpleasant to you, or get up earlier in the morning to spend time rounding with the Great Physician in Bible study and prayer.

Experiencing the Greatest Learning

I have learned from experience that if you are willing to be on call for the most difficult things, that's when you'll begin to see the blessings come through. At the same time, when you are on call, that's also when the greatest learning takes place.

Recently I saw a spokesman for ACGME (American College of Graduate Medical Education) make an appearance on the television show *Nightline*. The controversy under discussion was whether or not medical interns and residents should be required to be on call for thirty-six to forty-eight hours straight. The argument against the practice is that it results in the youngest, most inexperienced doctors being up for so long that they get tired and make mistakes that endanger patients unnecessarily.

After several of the other guests opposing the traditional system had all challenged him, the ACGME official turned to the moderator and said, "It's a lot like going to a movie."

The host's eyebrows raised in a quizzical expression while the man went on: "How much would you really understand of a movie if you only saw the first third or the middle third or the last third? If you walked into the theater late, or left early, or both? How much of the movie would you really understand?"

"Well," the moderator said, "not very much."

"It's the same for young doctors. If we have them in the hospital for just eight or ten hours a day, they are going to see only part of the picture, not the whole thing." He went on to argue the importance, during their years of training, of doctors being on call in the hospital to see how the disease presents itself, how it responds to your initial treatment, and what happens after the patient begins to turn the corner. Once you've been there for thirty-six to forty-eight hours to witness the whole course, later when you get into practice, you're more apt to understand and catch what's going on at whatever point you walk into "the movie." You know where you are in the course of an illness and what's likely to come next. Like a person who has seen *Star Wars* a hundred times, you know every nuance of the picture.

I thought this man's movie analogy brilliant. There are times when the on-call schedules that some training programs impose on young doctors can be excessive. Sometimes more consideration could be given to personal health and family relationships. But the long hours on call can indeed be beneficial to the learning process. And that's true not just in training, but throughout a person's medical career, because you often learn the most from the most difficult challenges you face—and you find a higher percentage of those when you are on call.

I think the same thing is true in a spiritual sense. When we are willing to be on call with God, we are apt to learn the most because we are out there on a limb of faith, swaying in the breeze, so to speak, facing new situations, and realizing that we're no longer in control. That's what stretches us, broadens our perspective, and deepens our experience so that we are better prepared to handle whatever we encounter in the future—both in our lives and the lives of those around us.

Developing the Deepest and Most Meaningful Relationships

I have also noticed that when you are on call, you develop the deepest and most meaningful relationships. Personal relationships are often forged and strengthened in the heat of a crisis shared.

> *Personal relationships are often forged and strengthened in the heat of a crisis shared.*

I remember when I delivered our third child, Stacy, who was born in Kenya. Ernie Steury was there with me to share the wonderful and emotional event and to take over if something went wrong. Jody had an abrupt and painful labor, and afterwards we did a tubal ligation. Jody was nauseated, so we gave her something that sedated her during this quick operation, and then we took her down to our house. I had already been on call and up all night the night before, so I really conked out.

When Jody finally awakened in the middle of the night, she wasn't sure what had happened. She wondered if she just dreamed it all until she felt the IV in her arm. Then she reached down to see if the baby was there. *No baby!* In a moment of panic she wondered what was going on. *Where is our baby?*

That's when Jody wakened me and I roused enough to stumble out into our living room. Ernie Steury's wife, Sue, had come down to our house to help. There she was now, lying on our couch with the baby sleeping warm and snugly on her chest, taking care of Stacy until Jody recovered enough to care for Stacy herself.

Lying on a couch and snuggling a helpless newborn seem like small things—unless it's your baby, unless you have been up almost forty-eight straight hours and your wife has just been through the ordeal of birth. Sue's gracious willingness to make herself available, to be on call for us, forged an even deeper bond with us, a meaningful bond that will never be broken.

It's interesting to me how many people use concern about relationships to justify their unwillingness to be on call. They worry that making themselves available to meet people's needs will somehow damage other relationships.

In fact, the disciple Peter brought up this very subject in Mark 10:28–30 when he complained to Jesus, "We've left everything to follow you." Jesus promised him that anyone who has left home and family to answer his call will be rewarded a hundredfold. And he was not just talking about eternal rewards, but in present relationships.

I can personally speak to the truth of that promise. As someone who took his family around the world to be on call, I know it wasn't easy to miss Christmas and birthdays and other such things with our parents, siblings, and extended families. But God helped make up for that by giving us closer relationships with our missionary family than the vast majority of people have with their own family. In Africa we were not only on call *with* each other (which builds relationships), we were on call *for* each other.

I cannot remember how many missionary babies I delivered. We took care of each other when we were sick and covered for each other on vacations. All the children called the other missionary parents aunt and uncle. In many ways they became closer than their aunts and uncles back in the States. To this day some of my family's dearest and closest friends are those missionaries who became our substitute family. It wasn't that our own family became less; it was that this extended missionary family became more.

Before we went to Africa, Jody and I worried about how the whole experience would impact our family. We soon found that despite the long hours spent dealing with the obvious and overwhelming needs all around us, we had more interaction time with our kids than ever. Unless an emergency arose at mealtime, we ate together as a family three times a day. With no television to distract us, we played games, read, or worked on hobbies together most evenings. The kids could come up to the hospital to see me just about anytime they were free. Being on call actually broadened and enriched our relationships in many ways.

I have seen the same thing happen in my life more recently. I do a lot of speaking at retreats and other getaway-type settings. It's often tempting after those public presentations to go off by myself, or with Jody, to go fishing, hiking, horseback riding, or some other fun thing a lot of others are doing.

But I have found that my most significant ministry often occurs when I announce, "If you want to talk, let me know. I'll be sitting out on the veranda afterward." Or, "I'll be down by the lake later if anyone wants to chat." Or even, "Stop by my cabin and we can take a walk." Those are the times I begin to understand what God is doing in people's lives, and I can have more ministry and impact. A doctor may sit down and begin sharing about marriage problems, his struggle with a bad habit, a difficulty with a partner, or anxiety over a malpractice suit.

Here, too, I've learned it's impossible to know about the whole course of what God is doing in people's lives and really to minister to them at their point of need unless I am willing to make myself available, learn what God is doing, and see the whole course of what is happening. It's not only being on call at crisis points that enriches relationships, it's not just emergency help and short timely platitudes, but it's standing by and letting them know you are with them for the long haul. It's our presence over time that makes the difference.

Receiving the Greatest Satisfaction and Rewards

I have also found in my experience that when I have been on call, I often receive the greatest satisfaction and rewards. As a doctor the most appreciative patients and their families are those I've gotten up in the middle of the night to care for—perhaps because they better recognize my effort when I've obviously sacrificed or inconvenienced myself to help them.

I am reminded of a Kipsigis couple who brought their firstborn son to the hospital with a fever at 2:00 A.M. I took the call and went up to the hospital in my scrub clothes, rubbing sleep out of my eyes. The moment I saw the infant I knew what was wrong. The spinal tap confirmed the diagnosis of meningitis and directed me as to what IV antibiotics we needed to start immediately. Fortunately we caught the problem in time. The antibiotics worked, and after a few days in the hospital, this family took home a perfectly healthy little baby.

A few weeks later a young man came to the hospital and asked to see me. I was busy but managed to break away to greet this man in the Kipsigis way.

"Chamege?"

"Chamege mising."

After a whole string of such pleasantries I finally learned that my visitor had been sent from the family of the baby with meningitis to offer a formal invitation for me to bring my entire family to visit their home the following Sunday.

I accepted the invitation, and after church Jody and I piled Jason and Jessica (this was before Stacy's birth) into our Subaru. Following the directions we'd been given, we bounced along the main road and then down a dirt path until we couldn't drive any farther. There we parked the car and began hiking up an even smaller trail through the beautiful green hills of Kenya. After asking directions a few times, we finally came to the right place.

This young family didn't have much in or around their mud hut, but the parents were so honored that we would come that they had killed a couple of chickens (which was significant for them), made gimet, and cooked up a pot of vegetables as well. They served us on an old mismatched set of metal dishes and invited the neighbors in to share the feast. After we ate, the young father stood and told the crowd the whole story about how they had taken their sick baby to the hospital in the middle of the night and I had gotten out of bed to save the life of his son, his firstborn—and as yet, his only son. He talked about how important their son was to them and how they didn't have anything they could give me to adequately express their gratitude. But they did have a presentation they wanted to make.

You can only imagine what the back of our car looked like when we got home with two scared chickens and one mad goat.

He gave me a Kipsigis *rungut* (roon-goot), a carved and polished wooden stick with a knob on one end that is a badge of honor and authority only tribal leaders carry. They presented Jody with a beautifully decorated mursik gourd with an artistic inscription burned into the side—the nicest gift you could give to a Kipsigis woman.

Then came the grand prize. Out from behind the hut they came leading a goat—not some little kid, but a full-grown billy goat. This stubborn animal was struggling and fighting at the end of the rope, which was now ceremoniously presented to me. I was afraid that at any moment the goat would decide to quit pulling and start butting me.

I knew what an honor this was. Giving away a goat like this was a huge sacrifice for this poor family. I didn't want him. I didn't know how we were going to get him home. I was thinking, *Oh, please keep your goat!* But I couldn't say that. It would have been a terrible insult to refuse the best they had to give.

So we headed off through the hills to our car, dragging that bleating and bucking goat behind us the whole way. Fortunately, the family accompanied us down the path, because I didn't know how I would have ever gotten the thing in the car by myself. It was kicking and butting its head even after they hogtied it and slid it into the back of our little station wagon, along with two live chickens they threw into the bargain. Off we went bouncing back to Tenwek.

You can only imagine what the back of our car looked like when we got home with two scared chickens and one mad goat. We took the goat out, and I tied it up at the back of our house thinking, *What in the world are we going to do with this thing?* I still hadn't decided by Monday afternoon, when I got a call at the hospital telling me the goat had chewed through his rope and was now terrorizing the neighborhood. By the time we finally caught him after chasing him all over the countryside, the final decision was easily made. We asked a Kenyan who worked for us to butcher tough old Billy. Then we ate a little for lunch the next day and gave the rest of the meat to Kipsigis friends who liked goat much more than we did.

Whenever I remember that thankful family, I'm reminded that whether it comes in the form of gifts, goats, or simple gratitude, being on call often brings the greatest rewards—not just in gratitude, but in what it does for our spirit and soul to give ourselves without reservations.

Making the Greatest Impact of All

Perhaps the greatest reward is that what you do on call often makes the greatest impact. As a doctor, when you're on call and an emergency arises, you can be the difference between life and death. If you're on call for a friend in crisis, you're the one who will make a difference.

When that happens, the effort seems to pale in comparison to the result as God turns our "cross" into blessing. Isn't that just what he did with Jesus? The Cross was the most horrible way imaginable for someone to die, and yet it has become our symbol of hope. It is now what we put on top of all of our churches or in front of the sanctuary. Its meaning has changed.

The meaning of being "on call" has changed for me over the years as well. I sleep better now that my current position no longer requires me to take night call for a whole hospital full of sick people. But I have to admit there are days (and nights) when I think about that *Last Night on Call* certificate. Sometimes I miss that opportunity of really making an immediate and concrete difference in people's lives.

> *The Great Physician's last night on call in the Garden of Gethsemane pushed him to his absolute limit. But that's when he told his attending Father, "Not what I will, but what you will" (Mark 14:36).*

The Great Physician's last night on call in the Garden of Gethsemane pushed him to his absolute limit. But that's when he told his attending Father, "Not what I will, but what you will" (Mark 14:36). He gave up control, made himself available, and willingly took responsibility not for a ward or a service or even an entire hospital. He volunteered to stay on call to save the entire world. If the Great Physician could do that for us, surely we can take our turn when he asks us to be on call with him.

THE GREAT
PHYSICIAN DIDN'T
REQUIRE AN APPOINTMENT

I WAS ASKED TO SPEAK AT ASBURY COLLEGE AS PART OF the twenty-fifth reunion of my graduating class. I felt more than a little pressure preparing to speak in front of my classmates and many of my former professors. I had grown up in Wilmore, Kentucky, where Asbury is located, so in that audience were many people I had known all my life. My mom and my in-laws were there, as were my brother and sister and their spouses.

Stepping up to the pulpit of Hughes Auditorium was a nostalgic moment for me. Three times a week, for four years of my life, I had come into that building for chapel services. God had done some wonderful things in my heart (and in the hearts of many others) in that place. Because it meant so much for me to be there, I had spent a long time thinking about and preparing what God wanted me to do and say on this special occasion.

I told the mandatory joke, had prayer, and launched into the sermon. I was into the flow of my

message, felt I was connecting with my audience, and was in the middle of a dramatic illustration that had hundreds of people on the edge of their seats, when all of a sudden . . . on the left side of the auditorium, about halfway back, an elderly woman stood up and in a loud voice announced, "This woman has collapsed! We need a doctor!" Sure enough, in the row beside her was another woman who had slumped to the floor.

What should I do? I never even stopped to consider. My medical training took over, and I instinctively started down off the platform to take care of this woman's emergency need. Fortunately, before I even reached the auditorium floor, I saw the campus nurse as well as my old mentor and friend, Dr. Ernie Steury (who was also there for reunion weekend), already converging on the woman. Knowing she was in excellent hands (she was taken to a nearby hospital, where it was determined she'd merely fainted and would be fine), I was able to return to the pulpit and continue speaking.

But it had been a big interruption. It gave me a fresh perspective on a similar interruption the Great Physician experienced when he was speaking to a large audience in the synagogue at Capernaum.

BIG-TIME DISTURBANCE

"Suddenly [Isn't that how interruptions always happen?], while still at the meeting place, he was interrupted by a man who was deeply disturbed and yelling out" (Mark 1:23, *The Message*).

This was a big day for Christ. He had been baptized by John the Baptist and been publicly announced from heaven as God's Son. He had been severely tempted by Satan in the desert. He had begun traveling around the countryside, calling his disciples as he encountered willing followers along the way. People were beginning to gather around him just to hear him. His public ministry was underway.

This was his first invitation to speak at a big church in one of the larger cities. No doubt he had prepared carefully to make sure this would be the right message. And the message was going great: "The people were amazed at his teaching, because he taught them as one who had authority" (Mark 1:22).

He was connecting with the congregation, and they were eating his words up. They had never heard preaching like this. God was obviously going to do a big thing in their lives. There would be a big altar call after that service, and exciting things were about to happen.

All of a sudden, in the middle of this service with the building packed, people hanging in the windows and riveted to what he had to say, a huge interruption took place. It wasn't a sudden heart attack. This wasn't just a listener silently passing out on the floor. Jesus was interrupted by a crazy, demon-possessed man, yelling out at the top of his voice.

In my experience as a doctor I have found the hardest people to deal with are the mentally disturbed. They not only interrupt, they usually disrupt. They are not easy to handle or quiet down. They usually require a lot of time and effort to get under control. But the Great Physician handled this man so effectively, ridding him of his demons, that the people again marveled. And Jesus' ministry went on.

Some days I think a doctor's life is little more than a long series of interruptions. No matter how well you plan your schedule, you will be interrupted.

I'm not used to major disruptions when I speak. That's one reason why my class-reunion experience sticks out in my memory. But as a doctor, I have constantly been forced to deal with interruptions. In fact, some days I think a doctor's life is little more than a long series of interruptions. No matter how well you plan your schedule, no matter how determined you are to see your patients in a timely manner, you will be interrupted. You are called to the hospital, someone walks in with an emergency problem, a new patient takes longer than planned, an associate wants to consult on a case, or a nurse hands you a lab report that requires an immediate phone call or a change in orders.

The Great Physician knew all about these sorts of interruptions. Read through the Gospels and you will see that his daily ministry was constantly interrupted. Look, for example, at Mark 5. Jesus went out to teach and preach. He had an agenda. He had a plan for the day that got interrupted by a man with an evil spirit living among the tombs. After Jesus cast out the spirit and revolutionized that man's life, his entourage tried to leave by boat. But the man interrupted again and begged to go with them.

When Jesus and his disciples finally reached the other side of the lake, a synagogue official wanted help for his sick daughter. So they all headed toward Jairus's house. On the way the woman with a hemorrhage problem interrupted them. By the time the Great Physician healed that lady, Jairus's friends showed up saying they needn't have bothered Jesus because the little sick girl had already died. Then he was interrupted yet again by the skeptical crowd around Jairus's house before he went in and raised the daughter from the dead.

This all happened in just one day. Like any busy doctor, the Great Physician's life was full of interruptions.

Waiting-Room Worries

I'll be honest with you, I have learned to accept interruptions. I have taught myself to cope with them by switching gears quickly. But I still hate interruptions.

In my time as a missionary doctor the daily routine at Tenwek was often like what I described in chapter 3. I would be making rounds on the wards, something that absolutely had to be done each day, when I would get the call about an outpatient child the nurses thought had meningitis. To start an IV, do a spinal tap, write the orders, and give the necessary antibiotics meant forty-five to sixty minutes before I could get back to the wards—if I wasn't interrupted again with a call to OB to take care of a woman who needed a C-section. Then a nurse would want me to see a postop patient who wasn't doing well, so I would be pulled away again. *Will those people on the ward ever be seen today?* I wondered.

You have probably experienced this same phenomenon from the opposite side of the stethoscope. You've sat in the waiting room of a doctor's office, stewing and fuming about all the time taken out of your own busy schedule and thinking, *Why can't this doctor be on time? Why am I having to waste an hour sitting here with my sick child? Why can't he just come take care of us?*

One reason is interruptions. If that's the case, your doctor too may be stewing. Chances are he's upset because he's behind and knows he is inconveniencing his patients. If he is at all like me, the fallout from those irritating interruptions can steal his joy, spoil his mood, make him abrupt or caustic, and damage relationships with everyone around him.

Aren't we all like that sometimes? Interruptions bug us. The kids come in while we're fixing supper and interrupt us. The phone rings when we're in the middle of something else. A friend drops by unexpectedly just as we're about to leave the house. A telemarketer calls in the middle of dinner. When you are deep in a high priority project, the boss walks in with a "higher" priority; he wants you to drop what you're doing and get this other thing done.

Or you come home with an agenda of things you want to get done in the evening when your middle-school child announces, "Oh my goodness, I've got to go to the library to get a book for my paper that's due tomorrow." You know she has had that assignment for two weeks, but she just kept putting it off. Now your plans for the evening are shot because someone's got to drive her to the library.

Again, you open the refrigerator and discover there's no milk because your son didn't pick it up as you asked him to last night. So instead of fixing supper you have to run to the grocery store.

Interruptions are the story of modern life. All of this adds significance to what the Great Physician's example can teach us on this subject. Our attitude toward interruptions and the manner in which we deal with them can have a great impact on our work, our ministry, our testimony, and our relationships with others. Let's compare and contrast our usual reactions to interruptions to those of the Great Physician.

IT'S A PEOPLE PROBLEM

I admit that, like most doctors, I'm one of those obsessive-compulsive people who always has a schedule, a well-thought-out plan to get the most work done in the least amount of time. That can be a valuable trait for anyone in the medical field. It's also helpful in my current administrative position.

> *Interruptions are the story of modern life. The manner in which we deal with them can have a great impact on our work, our ministry, our testimony, and our relationships with others.*

But I must confess that I will come home discouraged some days and complain to Jody: "I didn't get a thing done at the office today, honey. All I did was talk to people. They kept interrupting me with phone calls. People sent me I don't know how many e-mails. Then so-and-so stuck his head in the office and wanted my advice. I had a ton of correspondence I needed to get done and next week's conference to prepare for. I desperately wanted to outline my thoughts on that new program we're starting next year—but I didn't get any of that done. Too many people with too many problems."

Jody then gently reminds me what I should know from the Great Physician's example. I often make the mistake of seeing people (and their interruptions) as the *problem* with my job. Dr. Jesus never forgot that people and their concerns were the *purpose* of his life.

In John 5 we see a clear example of this. Jesus and all his associates have made a special trip "up to Jerusalem for a feast of the Jews." This was probably a long-scheduled trip for the holiday celebration. There must have been an agenda planned. Someone probably expected them at a specific time and place.

However, as Jesus approached the gates of the city, he walked by the pool of Bethesda, where he encountered a man who had been an invalid for thirty-eight years. Rather than hurry on to his appointment in town, Jesus interrupted his schedule to learn the man's problem. Determining that man wanted to be healed, Jesus cured him and sent him on his way with these words, "Get up! Pick up your mat and walk."

That was hardly the end of the incident because some Jewish officials took offense and challenged the man for carrying his mat (i.e., working) on the Sabbath. When they found out that Jesus was "doing these things on the Sabbath, the Jews persecuted him." So Jesus' schedule is interrupted again to answer his critics by explaining his mission on earth.

His enemies weren't ready to understand what he was trying to say. But looking at this chapter today we can see that despite his predetermined plans, he didn't see the man at the pool as an interruption, but as an opportunity. The man was in fact part of his reason for being on earth. Jesus never saw people as problems because he realized they were central to his purpose.

What a powerful challenge this lesson continues to impress on me. Maybe it's another outgrowth of an obsessive-compulsive personality, but I often think and plan in terms of priorities. So one of the biggest reasons I resent interruptions is because their urgency often interferes with *my* priorities. They keep me from getting my "more important" things done.

Jesus, by contrast, saw that interruptions could be opportunities for the "most important" work to be accomplished. Healing Peter's mother-in-law was more important than dinner (Luke 4:38–39). The story we just looked at—of the invalid by the Bethesda pool—is another example. An even stronger illustration of this point is in Luke 5:18–26, when Jesus is busy teaching inside a house. A group of men note the crowded waiting room, bypass the receptionist altogether, tear the roof off the building, and lower their sick friend down for Dr. Jesus to treat. That must have been some interruption.

But what does Jesus do? Surely what he was teaching was important. Yet does he scold the men for interrupting his lesson? Does he react as if they are interfering with his priorities? No! He heals the man and uses the entire incident as an object lesson about what is most important—not the healing of illness, but the forgiveness of sins.

Unexpected Visitor

I remember one particularly busy day at Tenwek in the early 1980s. The other doctors were both gone for some reason. I was thus the only doctor in the hospital with more than two hundred patients—and feeling absolutely swamped. Frantically trying to see the most urgent cases and having already given up hope of seeing even a quarter of the patients in the hospital that day, I seemed to be interrupted by one emergency after another. Sometime late in the afternoon as I was sewing up an Achilles tendon that had gotten sliced by a machete, one of the staff came to tell me, "Dr. Stevens, there's somebody who wants to see you down in the outpatient clinic."

My first thought was, *Are they dying? If they're not dying, I can't be bothered!* When I learned it wasn't a patient, I figured it must be some sort of drug rep. They even come way out in the middle of Kenya to try to sell us pharmaceutical products. I knew I didn't have any time to listen to somebody's sales pitch that day, so I told my messenger, "Tell them I'm too busy today. I can't be interrupted."

The attendant shook his head, "But it's a *musungu*" (that means an expatriate, non-Kenyan, white person).

I thought, *Who in the world is out here in the middle of nowhere to see me unannounced?* I wasn't expecting any friends from the States. No mission-agency folks had scheduled a visit. Tenwek wasn't exactly a scenic stop for tourists. We were so far off the beaten path that seldom did visitors simply happen by. My curiosity was piqued.

"Okay, okay, as soon as I finish this procedure I'll come up to the office. Tell him to wait for me there."

A few minutes later I was shaking hands with a man who introduced himself as Dr. Mark Jacobson. Mark's speciality was internal medicine, and he held a masters in public health from Johns Hopkins University Hospital in Baltimore, Maryland. Mark explained that he had been subcontracted by Johns Hopkins to come to Kenya and start three pilot programs for the community-based distribution of family-planning supplies. At that time Kenya had the highest population growth rate of any country in the world. It was difficult for any woman who wanted to space her children to get the things she needed to do that.

The plans for one of Mark's three pilot projects had fallen through at the last minute. He had heard through the grapevine that Tenwek was getting ready to start a community-health program.

I told Mark it had indeed been one of our dreams to start a community-health program to help educate the Kipsigis people in basic nutrition, clean drinking water, sanitation, and similar subjects in order to improve the region's quality of life and reduce the cases of preventable diseases such as gastroenteritis, malaria, and malnutrition—the treatment of which absorbed such an overwhelming proportion of our resources at Tenwek. But our plans for a program were still very much in the formative stage. We didn't have much money or a whole lot of expertise in community health. We were learning as we went.

Suddenly, here on our doorstep in rural Kenya was an expert from Johns Hopkins, arguably the best school for public health in the entire world. He already had funding through US AID, which ended up providing us with more than $150,000 for the first three years of our program. That money turbocharged Tenwek's community-based healthcare program, which became a model for similar programs around the world and helped revolutionize the people's health status in that entire region of Kenya by saving countless people from illness and death. The program is still going strong and now boasts over eight hundred Christian volunteer community-health helpers, teaching better health practices and introducing friends and neighbors to Christ.

That might never have happened except for an interruption that ended up being far more important than anything else I could have done that day, or in a month of days like it.

Despite such lessons, I still have a tendency to see interruptions as something like annoying speed bumps in my road of life. They slow me down. They divert my attention momentarily, and I often resent the way they delay the achievement of my goal. So let's take another look at Jesus' different attitude toward interruptions.

Jesus Interrupted

In Matthew 20 Jesus is traveling from Jericho to Jerusalem when two blind men keep calling out, trying to get his attention. The crowd keeps saying to them, "Be quiet. Don't bother the Teacher. He's too busy; he's got things to do." But Matthew 20:32 says that Jesus stopped. I love that: "Jesus stopped and called them. 'What do you want me to do for you?' he asked."

Of course, the Great Physician already had his day scheduled. In fact, he was on his way to Jerusalem, where thousands of people were waiting for him. This promised to be one of the biggest and most wonderful days of his life—which we now celebrate as Palm Sunday. He had important business to tend to, prophecies to fulfill, and just one more week of life on earth with his disciples. His mind must have been racing with plans—places he needed to go, people he longed to see, things he wanted to remember to say. So much to do and so little time! And yet . . .

Here are two disenfranchised blind men alongside the road. They have no power, no connections, no influence. And Jesus stops. He doesn't view them as a bothersome speed bump. He doesn't merely slow down and wave (though he could certainly have healed them that way). He stops, turns his attention from the road ahead, and refocuses on these men and their need.

Because doctors are interrupted so often, it's important for them to refocus quickly. The Great Physician certainly demonstrated that skill. You see it time and again throughout the Gospels, whether it's with these two blind men or when he stops under the sycamore tree, calls Zaccheus down, and then does lunch with the little man. Jesus had a knack for instantly turning his full attention to the person in front of him.

That's a key in handling interruptions effectively—as I have often seen in medical practice. When you walk out of one examining room and into the next, you have to shift gears and focus on the next patient and his or her problem. If you are thinking back over what the last patient said or what you were doing ten minutes ago, you are going to miss something. Every patient deserves your full attention, and if you try to do two things at once, both suffer. So I have to be sure to shut the door, set down the chart, look that person in the eye, and totally focus on him or her.

The same thing is required of us in daily life, isn't it? A colleague knocks on your door to give you a report on some meeting while you're poring over next year's budget. A child asks a question when you're reading the newspaper. A friend flags you down to ask if you've got a minute as you're rushing to your car in the parking lot after church. A teenage daughter sticks her head in the bedroom door to say good-night after a date.

Well, she usually wants to say a lot more than good-night—just as the friend wants more than a minute. And the colleague is hoping you will ask her to come in and sit down. Your child wants more than an answer to a simple question.

But it's easy to say to your daughter, "I'm tired and need to get some sleep. Let's talk about it in the morning." Or you tell your friend, "Let's have lunch some day this week." To the colleague you say, "I'm late for a committee meeting. Why don't you walk down to the conference room and tell me about it as we go." Or you keep on reading the newspaper and respond to your child with half-hearted uh-huhs, which send a clear message that your attention is not where it should be, that you really don't want to talk right now.

So what happens? The child shuts up, the colleague says she'll just catch you later, the friend promises to call about lunch but doesn't, and when you ask your daughter the next morning what she wanted to talk about, she says, "Nothing really." All because you were unable or unwilling to stop and refocus.

BREAKFAST SURPRISE

I see interruptions as obstacles forcing unwanted detours from my planned course. Dr. Jesus accepted interruptions as an integral part of God's plan and direction for his life.

Maybe one reason you and I struggle with this is because we cannot always see the amazing way God is working until much later. That was certainly true in the case of one of the most memorable interruptions of my life.

> *I see interruptions as obstacles forcing unwanted detours from my planned course. Dr. Jesus accepted interruptions as an integral part of God's plan and direction for his life.*

I have already written about the working conditions at Tenwek—how difficult it was to run a modern hospital when you only had electricity eleven hours a day, how more than a fourth of our budget went for fuel to run the generators, how patients died in the night because we couldn't run the equipment that might keep them alive.

What I haven't told you was that since the clinic was founded in 1933, Tenwek missionaries had long dreamed of building a small hydroelectric plant on the forty-foot waterfall just below the compound. But for all those years the goal of one day having a source of electricity for the hospital seemed an impossible dream.

By the time I finished my first term at Tenwek in 1984, our need for a reasonably priced and constant source of electricity had become desperate. Not only were patients dying, but the potential growth and ministry of the entire hospital was severely hampered by our lack of power and by the crippling cost of diesel fuel to run our generator a few hours a day. So as I was leaving to return to the States for a year of furlough, Dr. Steury said almost jokingly, "Dave, while you're home, why don't you see what you can do about building the power plant?"

I chuckled as I told Ernie I'd do what I could. He and I both knew I would have almost no spare time in my busy speaking schedule in churches all across America. Besides, neither Ernie nor I had any idea where to begin to do what seemed impossible.

But guess what? Jody and I were living in our hometown of Wilmore, Kentucky, that furlough year when early one morning I was interrupted by a knock on our front door. Opening the door, I saw Marilyn Kinlaw standing on our front step, in her housecoat, her hair in curlers, and a baby on her hip. Marilyn's husband, Denny, was a physician friend; they had been to Tenwek during his residency. She knew our needs.

"David," she said, "I was having my devotions this morning, and God told me to come over here and say something to you."

Now, I'm not exactly used to having people drop by with messages from God before eight o'clock in the morning. Actually, this was a first. Yet Marilyn had obviously disrupted her morning routine with her children because God had prompted her. So I said, "Come on in."

Marilyn stepped inside the door but declined to take a seat. "I'm in a hurry," she explained. "I've got to get back home and take care of the kids. But God told me to let you know that there's an engineer here in town today from World Radio Missionary Fellowship; they operate radio HCJB in Ecuador. I heard they built some sort of hydroelectric plant there. I thought maybe he could somehow help you in building the hydroelectric plant that Tenwek so desperately needs."

I said, "Let me get you a cup of coffee. Sit down a minute, Marilyn, and let's talk about this."

"No, I really can't, David. I've got to go." She told me the engineer's name and where in town he was staying. Then off she went back to her home.

The rest of this incredible story will have to be told later (see chapter 12). Here I will merely summarize by telling you that that morning interruption, by a harried mom who was herself willing to interrupt her morning routine to deliver a simple message, led that very day to a contact that started the ball rolling in a miraculous way on a dream that ended with an $850,000 hydroelectric dam, which is still providing 320 kilowatts of electricity twenty-four hours a day to the hospital. That power plant soon multiplied the hospital's ministry by letting us save enough money to start a nursing school and to expand and upgrade Tenwek into one of the premier mission hospitals in the world. It all started with a busy mom who interrupted her morning plans and responded to God's prompting.

We can't always see at the time how interruptions fit into the big picture. But God often works in and through the little and big interruptions of our lives to accomplish his greater purpose and plans—at least he wants to.

They may not be written on our calendars or in our Daytimers, but I have come to realize that God has divine appointments that he has set aside for us every day. Often the greatest opportunities to minister or see his plan unfold in our lives happen because of those interruptions.

It may be meeting a stranger on the plane when you really want to read and they want to talk. Or perhaps a phone call from your child who's away at school and seems overwhelmed. Or a neighbor who comes to your door after a fight with his spouse.

It's so easy to put these things off, to try to avoid them, and to think, "Boy, this is going to interrupt my schedule. I've got things I need to do. I've got to cut this short." But we need to think of these interruptions as divine appointments. And we must remember that this is often where real ministry takes place because when people are reaching out and seeking help, you often have the greatest influence and outreach. The same can be true in our families, if we learn to think of interruptions as divine appointments.

I don't know what God's asking you to do, but I do know he is asking you to be interruptible, as the Great Physician was.

HOW DO WE LEARN TO DO THAT?

I have discovered that learning to view interruptions as divine appointments starts with the right attitude. We have a choice in how we respond to interruptions. We can be perturbed and irritated, or we can welcome them, even eagerly look for the hidden opportunities in them.

When doctors regularly allow interruptions to irritate or upset them, it ultimately hurts them and their patients. Nurses become afraid to approach them. Staff members may put off discussing problems or asking questions until a patient is in a desperate state. Things that could be easily solved early on become bigger problems or even emergency situations. That not only endangers patients, it actually opens doctors up to liability and malpractice charges.

We need to think of these interruptions as divine appointments. And we must remember that this is often where real ministry takes place because when people are reaching out and seeking help, you often have the greatest influence and outreach.

Jesus did not have that problem. I have studied his example enough to see that he never became upset with the constant interruptions— whether they were large or small. He was always approachable. He naturally drew people to himself.

You probably know people like that, don't you? I do. You feel as if you want to snuggle up to them. They are approachable and open and willing to listen. In short, they are interruptible.

I want to be approachable for the people I work with. And I try to encourage my staff to do that with other people.

In our office we have a wonderful lady named Emma, who works in our Life and Health Resources Department. She talks to CMA members and other people on the phone all the time. Emma is a wonderful, saintly grandmother who has true approachability. People are so eager to confide in her and to have her pray with them because she always has such a welcoming attitude and is willing to be interrupted.

Divine Appointments

Emma is an inspirational example to me. But I'm afraid when it comes to being interruptible, I am not yet as consistent as she is. Not long ago my secretary buzzed me to say she had a doctor on the phone who wasn't a CMA member, but he wanted to talk to me about some problems in his life. I was having one of those pressure-filled days, so my first thought was, *Oh man, I've got too much to do. I don't have half an hour or more to talk to someone on the phone.*

So I put him off. "Tell him I'm busy right now. Can he call back?" I was rather hoping that he wouldn't.

My secretary came back and said, "He'll be glad to call back. What's a good time?"

I was cornered. I gave him a time and he did call later. He introduced himself as Sam and began telling me his story. He had been a highly successful family-practice doctor. He had built a large group practice. He became involved in politics first at the local level and at the state level with the governor. Quickly climbing high up the medical and political ladders, he wielded great influence and made a lot of money.

Then managed care came in and lowered his reimbursement levels. He became frustrated with the system. Here he was, working harder than ever before but making less, and struggling to support his big-time lifestyle. He was even more frustrated when Medicare lowered his reimbursement level further.

So he began overbilling. It was easy to do because doctors code every visit and every procedure they perform on a patient's chart. Sam would simply "upcode," that is, picking a higher level code indicating he did more than he actually did, or he marked down a ten-minute exam instead of a five-minute visit so he could get reimbursed more from

Medicare, a large part of his practice. He rationalized this by telling himself, *They're stealing all this money from me by reducing charges. I deserve it.*

Eventually Sam got caught. The authorities came in and audited his books. Even then he didn't think it was going to be any big deal—until he was charged with a felony. He was stripped of his license and lost his practice. He lost his house, and his wife left him. His entire life was in ruins.

Things got so bad that one night he found himself sitting on his bed with a gun in his hand, preparing to blow his brains out, when he remembered something a Christian friend had said to him. Instead of pulling the trigger, he called that friend. They talked, and Sam ultimately came to a relationship with Jesus Christ.

When he called me on the phone, he had already made this Christian commitment, but he was still working through what that would mean. He was still waiting for his sentencing and was sure he would be going to prison.

Sam phoned me because he had just heard about the Christian Medical Association and wanted to know more about us. He knew prison would be rough. But he was looking for resources and advice on how he might use his skills in ministry—perhaps with our organization or overseas as a missionary—once he got out of prison. He told me he now realized that God wanted him to do a whole new thing with his life.

This interruption that I'd wanted to avoid turned into a wonderful time of sharing, where I could encourage and pray with Sam. We became good friends. Later on he came to one of our meetings, and we got him involved with CMA. Sam is in prison now, but we write regularly and pray for each other. God is using this time "in the desert" to help make Sam more like his Son, Jesus Christ. My "interruption" has turned into a blessing and an opportunity for ministry. I'm excited to see what God will do with Sam when his prison term is finished.

So I am still learning to welcome interruptions with the right attitude. When I do—and sometimes even when I don't (as was the case when Sam called)—I am reminded again how God wants to work through the interruptions in our lives.

At CMA we are so convinced of this truth that we have been trying to teach it to our members. It's one of the lessons we have included for the more than six thousand doctors who have attended our Saline Solution conferences to learn how to make their Christian faith a more central part of their medical practice.

> *We want to know what we're doing and when we're doing it. But it's more important to ask, "What is God doing?" Our goal should be to become a part of his plan.*

Have you seen and heard about the WWJD fad? The bracelets, necklaces, and bumper stickers that stand for **W**hat **W**ould **J**esus **D**o? We have come up with our own variation of that. We suggest our docs print "WIGD" on a card that they can put in each examination room and over their desks where they will see it. These initials encourage them to ask themselves, "**W**hat **Is** **G**od **D**oing?" It is to remind them that the Great Physician is already doing something in their patient's life, and they should be eager to follow his agenda rather than their own. The card is to remind them to be interruptible and to be willing to turn a routine appointment into a divine one.

We all have plans and schedules we try to keep. We want to know what we're doing and when we're doing it. But it's more important to ask, "What is God doing?" Our goal should be to become a part of his plan.

If we can't post that question on our wall, we should at least keep it in our mind every day, at all times, in every encounter we make. Because God has a plan for our lives, and it just might interrupt our schedule.

We need to remember that the Great Physician doesn't require appointments. We ought to practice the same way.

THE GREAT PHYSICIAN WAS A SUPERB DIAGNOSTICIAN

DOCTOR JESUS WAS MAKING HIS ROUNDS THROUGH Jericho one day when he and his interns walked past a blind roadside beggar named Bartimaeus (Mark 10:46–52). When the man heard the commotion of the crowd and learned who was leading the passing throng, he called out, "Jesus, Son of David, have mercy on me!"

Some of the people tried to get him to quiet down, but they only made Bartimaeus more determined. He yelled even louder, "Son of David, have mercy on me!" You would have to call that a rather nonspecific request—a general complaint.

But Christ heard him and stopped. When he called Bartimaeus over, he went right to the crux of the matter by asking, "What do you want me to do for you?" Like any good doctor, the Great Physician wished to know his patient's chief complaint.

I find this to be an especially important question when trying to see crowds of people in relief situations or at a busy mission hospital. For every patient I see, I need to know as quickly as possible: What is your real problem, your chief complaint? Of all the things that you could talk to me about, what is the one thing that is bothering you the most? What brought you all the way over here to see the doctor? What do you want to make sure gets treated before you leave?

Often you can get to the root of the complaint with just a few questions and a physical exam. Then you know what treatment is called for. But I remember a case early in my missionary career of a seven-year-old boy in Kenya that was a real puzzler. The mother brought the child in because he was spitting up blood. I immediately suspected tuberculosis, a common disease among the Kipsigis that often causes its victims to cough up blood.

But when I listened to the boy's chest, I didn't hear any problems. I checked the underside of his eyelids and his tongue to see how pale they were and realized this boy was severely anemic. A blood test confirmed a hemoglobin count barely enough to keep him alive. He was obviously losing a lot of blood, a lot more than I would expect from TB.

Maybe he has some kind of GI problem, I thought. But he seemed awfully young to have bleeding ulcers, stomach cancer, or an esophageal carcinoma—which might have been my first concern if I had seen an adult male with his symptoms.

So I delved deeper into the history of this lad to determine just how much blood he was coughing up. The mother said it was a lot. I asked about her son's stools. She said they were black—indicating a lot of blood was going through the GI system. That led me to think it was something in the GI tract after all. I palpated his abdomen without finding any tenderness or any mass that suggested a tumor. I didn't know what to think. *Maybe we need to gastroscope this patient,* I surmised. But I wasn't sure we even had a scope small enough for a child this young.

I had seen a lot of kids anemic from worms, but they didn't cough up blood. Nothing made sense as I mentally went through a differential diagnosis. About that time the boy coughed and up came this blood.

But it was more of a choking, gagging kind of cough than something deep down in his lungs.

Finally, I sent one of the staff to get Dr. Steury. When he arrived, I shared about the case. Ernie smiled and the next thing he did was look at the boy's throat.

Of course, I had already done that. I had seen a little blood, but that was all. Ernie, however, took a sprayable anesthetic and coated the back of the boy's throat. When it was numb enough that the child wouldn't gag, Ernie took a tongue blade and lifted up the boy's soft palate so we could see up into the pharynx, where the nasal passage opens into the throat. Ernie took a quick look and stepped aside. Handing me the tongue blade he asked me, "What do you think that is?"

I saw something dark, about an inch and a half long and maybe a half inch wide. It didn't look like a blood clot or anything else I had ever seen. We didn't have time to play twenty questions, so Ernie enlightened me: "It's a leech."

I have to confess I hadn't studied much about leeches, certainly not leeches in the throat, during medical school. So Ernie explained that a leech doesn't actually suck the blood out of its host. Rather, it bites through the skin or mucosa. Its mouth secretion contains an anticoagulant that keeps the blood from clotting so that the bite wound continuously oozes blood, only some of which the leech injests. The remainder runs through the digestive system.

You can try to pull a leech off, but they are slick like a snail and hard to grab. Moreover, they can break and leave their head hooked in there. To treat this condition, we take a swab and paint the leech with 4 percent lidocaine gel. Its skin is so thin that the chemical is soon absorbed into its system and anesthetizes it. If the leech doesn't let go then, it will be easy to pull it off.

That's what we did with this young boy, who had almost bled to death from a little leech in the back of his throat. After we gave him a transfusion for his anemia and some iron, he made a quick and complete recovery.

I could have treated this boy for anemia to start with. I might have tried to track down the possible causes of his cough or done a GI workup. But it was by staying focused on the chief complaint—gagging and coughing up blood—that we finally found the source of the problem.

Asking the Right Question

Every doctor uses the chief complaint to know where to start with the history and the exam. The thing that usually makes the biggest impression on the patient is the exam—when a doctor listens to their heart, and so on. But the examination usually only confirms what you have gotten from the history. That's the key. The biggest reason for missed diagnoses is that a doctor doesn't ask the right questions to get a complete history. In other words, he doesn't get enough information pertaining to the chief complaint.

For example, suppose someone comes in with a cough and you don't bother to get a social history to find out that he is a farmer who has recently been working in a silo. You will probably fail to diagnose silo filler's disease, a fungal infection common to farm laborers working in silos breathing the dusty air. Based solely on symptoms, you might assume an ordinary case of the flu or maybe pneumonia. But you are not going to get to the real issue because you have not asked the key questions that need to be asked to arrive at the correct diagnosis.

The chief complaint is the main thing you are concerned about. It serves as your starting and reference point. Then you get to the next step by asking more in-depth questions that lead you to the diagnosis.

In this case, you ask a series of questions concerning the lungs. Are you short of breath? Do you have difficulty going up stairs? How often are you coughing? Are you wheezing at night? Are you bringing up any sputum? How much? What color? Do you have a temperature? Are you having any chest pain? Where are you hurting? What does it feel like? What makes it better? What makes it worse? What's the nature of your pain—sharp, dull? Does it ache? Does it vary when you breathe? If you have a fever, does it come in the morning or at night? How high does it go? Do you have chills with the fever? Do you also sweat? What seems to make it worse or better? What is your occupation? Are you exposed to any noxious fumes? Have you ever had anything like this before? Those are just some of the questions you ask for a lung complaint.

The more and better focused the doctor's questions, the more information is gathered with which to paint the picture and identify the disease. That's important because something that may seem inconsequential to the patient may lead a doctor to an accurate diagnosis.

And the Real Problem Is . . . ?

It's not always easy for a doctor to know what the chief complaint is. It probably will not be as plain as it was in the case of blind Bartimaeus. Occasionally there may be two, three, or even more bothersome symptoms, and the patient doesn't know which is the chief complaint.

Often a patient may be reluctant to even bring up the real reason for coming to see a doctor. Sometimes the chief complaint is the last thing mentioned. A patient may not broach the subject until the appointment is almost over and one of us is ready to walk out the door. Then she will say, "Oh, by the way, Doctor . . ." Or he will say, "There is just one more thing, Doc. . . ." Whenever I hear anything like that, my radar kicks in, because that usually signals the introduction of the chief complaint.

Often a patient may be reluctant to even bring up the real reason for coming to see a doctor. Sometimes the chief complaint is the last thing mentioned.

A man will come in with some simple, straightforward concern. "Doc, I've got this rash on my arm. Would you take a look at it?" So I give him an exam and determine that his rash is nothing but a little dry-skin problem. But as he's buttoning up his shirt and I'm heading out the door to my next patient, he says, "There is one more thing I was wondering about. I've been having a little trouble passing urine at night. Is that anything to be concerned about?"

That's the real reason he came in. That's his chief complaint. That's what I need to deal with. He may have prostate cancer or something else going on. The skin condition was just something he used as an excuse to come in.

I find that the more personal the problem, the more embarrassed people are to talk about it and the less likely they are to be up front about their chief complaint. Another reason patients are reluctant to open up is that they're afraid of what you are going to find. So a good doctor cannot afford to ignore these "by the way" or "one more thing" comments. You don't dare downplay it with an "It's no big deal" reaction or pass it off with an "I'll talk to you about it on your next visit." What you do is turn around, shut the door, sit down facing the patient, and say, "Tell me about it." If you are really going to help a patient, you must deal with the chief complaint.

When He Examines Us

I see a clear spiritual parallel here in our relationship with the Great Caregiver. When something personal is bothering us, we tend to be guarded with God. We may even avoid coming to him in prayer. There are a lot of issues we're glad to bring to him. But there are also other more personal, private, and often potentially serious subjects we're reluctant to open up about.

Our lives are like a big house where we invite people into the living room, maybe even the kitchen if it's clean. But there are definitely parts of the house we don't want to take guests because we know they aren't presentable.

It's often the same in our relationship with the Lord. We are happy to let the Great Physician examine and treat those areas of our lives we think are in pretty good shape. But we don't want to let him into those hidden areas where the real mess may be. We may be ready to let him examine some minor issue, but we do not want to discuss the chief complaint.

Until we open up, however, the Great Physician cannot help us the way he wants to. He cannot do his best work in our hearts and lives. Even though he already knows what our chief complaints really are, he waits for us to be like the patient who finally says, "Hey, God! There is one more thing. . . ." When we do that, when we are willing to confide anything and everything in him, he will be able to deal with our real problems.

> *We are happy to let the Great Physician examine and treat those areas of our lives we think are in pretty good shape. But we don't want to let him into those hidden areas where the real mess may be.*

I see another spiritual application of this chief-complaint idea. The Great Physician understands what's really important, what our chief complaints *should* be, even when we don't.

An example of this was a recent visit to my own doctor for a regular physical checkup. He took my blood pressure, checked my cholesterol, and listened to my heart. But he also made sure I took my shirt off so that he could look all over my skin. He knows that some little mole on my back may not be bothering me at all, if I even notice it. Yet one of those moles could be a melanoma, which could finish me off a lot quicker than chronic cardiovascular disease.

Like a good doctor, God wants us to allow him to examine our lives regularly for signs and symptoms of the most serious pathology. Perhaps it's something we haven't noticed or don't even understand that he wants to call our attention to—like our anger or some other character trait that concerns him, an old infected wound that needs to be cleaned out so it can heal, a damaged emotion to repair, an unhealthy relationship that needs work. Because he sees this as the real pathology, he wants to move it to the forefront, where he can deal with it and change our lives.

Like any good doctor, the Great Physician understands the connection between the chief complaint and our overall health. He not only listens to the chief complaint, he wants to do a review of systems to make sure nothing else is missed.

When you come in and say to me, "Dr. Stevens, I've got a cough," even if it's your only complaint, I will certainly look down your throat. But I am not going to stop there. I will also do a general overview of all the major systems of the body to look for indications that this little cough isn't a smokescreen for something more serious or significant.

I want to know if you have lost weight, how your appetite is, and whether you have noticed any lumps in your neck. Maybe this cough is only distantly related to the main problem or not related at all. But a "little cough" can mean a patient really has bone cancer. The pain in their leg has hardly registered on the radar screen, but now this stealth disease has mestasticized and is causing a cough.

God wants to do that sort of review of spiritual, emotional, and mental systems in our lives in order to expose the deeper issues we need to face and treat. We see this in the cases of several people who came to the Great Physician. Jesus had a way of getting down to the primary problem, the chief complaint.

Just a Checkup?

I get the idea the rich young ruler was coming to Jesus for a routine physical (Luke 18:18–30)—something like those cursory exams you might get when you need some signed medical release to run in the Jerusalem marathon, sign up for the Roman legion, or play ball for Mount Sinai High. He came to Jesus with a simple question and obviously expected a simple answer—a "You're okay" note from Dr. Jesus.

But the Great Physician immediately realized the real issue went a lot deeper than the man's initial concern. When the young man asked what he needed to do to ensure eternal life, he obviously expected to be told to just keep on doing what he'd been doing—keeping the Ten

Commandments and loving his neighbor. Instead, Jesus saw a young man with a serious heart problem about money, power, and position, who needed some major surgery. Unfortunately the young man refused to give consent. He was afraid to let the Great Physician cut though the obstructions between him and God.

I see another medical parallel. Whenever I'm examining someone, I know the area that is the most painful, the most in need of attention, is often the very part of the body the patient doesn't want me to touch. Yet it's the area I really need to examine the most.

If I suspect from a patient's history, for example, that he or she may have appendicitis, to get the best abdominal exam I always start the furthest away from where it hurts. That's because as soon as I do touch where it is, they'll flinch, tense up, and won't want me to touch anywhere on the abdomen again. So I have to work gently and slowly toward the problem spot, gathering important information as I go. I finally must touch that sensitive area to see if there is tenderness when I press in or when I let go (rebound), whether there is a mass or organ enlargement.

Don't Flinch

God is going to have to get to the sensitive spots in our lives if we expect help with our chief complaint, if we truly want him to make us whole. He often sends a sermon or portion of Scripture into our lives that lets him begin to palpate toward our point of pain.

Jesus had a knack for zeroing in on the sensitive spots. He quickly got to the heart of the problem with most of the people he encountered. Remember the paraplegic whose friends carried him to see Jesus (Matt. 9:2–8)? His chief complaint seemed obvious; the man couldn't walk. But Jesus quickly realized that this wasn't the most serious pathology.

We don't know many details of this story. Perhaps the man's condition was a direct result of something wrong he had done in the past. Whatever the background, Jesus focused on sin as his real problem, his chief complaint. He cut right to the chase and told him, "Son, I forgive your sin."

Jesus took much the same tack when confronted by the woman caught in adultery. He didn't say, "I'll treat your sexually transmitted disease." He said instead, "Go and sin no more!"

A physician who is not a good diagnostician can easily get so focused on treating the symptoms that he or she fails to deal with the underlying cause—the real problem. I remember encountering a Kipsigis woman sitting on the circular stone wall that enclosed a palm tree in the courtyard of Tenwek Hospital. Swaying back and forth, talking to herself, she was obviously delusional. Or, as the Kenyans colorfully describe anyone with psychiatric problems, she was "off mental." She also had a strange and serious-looking dermatological condition. A dry, scaly rash covered her arms, lower legs, and neck, but hadn't affected any skin shielded from the sun by her tattered cotton dress. As I got some history, her family told me she also had diarrhea all the time.

> *God is going to have to get to the sensitive spots in our lives if we expect help with our chief complaint, if we truly want him to make us whole.*

Diarrhea, a weird dermatosis, and mental problems. I had no idea what was going on with this woman. I could have treated the symptoms and put her on medication to try to restore her psychological equilibrium. I could have prescribed an antidiarrheal drug and/or antibiotics for her intestinal symptoms. Hydrocortisone ointment might have cleared her skin condition.

But none of that would have addressed the woman's real problem. Her underlying pathology was *pellagra*—the result of a simple vitamin deficiency. We rarely see this problem in the Western world because most of our food is fortified. But this condition is all too common in Kenya and other developing-world cultures if people don't eat vegetables with their maize diet. The classic symptoms, any one of which can seem like the chief complaint, are called "the three Ds" of pellagra—diarrhea, dermatitis, and dementia.

Once I knew the underlying problem, the treatment was simple enough. What this woman needed was vitamin supplements. When we addressed the real issue, all three symptoms went away. I had no need to treat them.

There's a lesson here for us, including for our secular culture. Remember the outcry after the tragic and senseless slaughter that took place at Columbine High School in Littleton, Colorado, in the spring of 1999? Lots of people had opinions on the best "treatment" for the obvious issues. Better security in the school, more gun control, punishment for parents who fail to supervise and control their kids. However the real problem—the underlying disease—was, as it so often is, sin. Sinful people do sinful things.

> *The Great Physician realized that the pathology in a lot of situations is sin. It's the illness that few want to talk about in our politically correct day.*

The Great Physician realized that the pathology in a lot of situations is sin. It's the illness that few want to talk about in our politically correct day.

HEART TROUBLE

I have a doctor friend named Bill who hasn't forgotten the Great Physician's regular encounters with patients whose problems were ultimately spiritual. Some time ago he told me about his own experience with a modern-day "woman at the well" (John 4:4–42).

This woman was unmarried with three children—each of them by a different father. She had been divorced twice and was on her third husband. The kids looked and acted neglected. She admitted a three-pack-a-day addiction to cigarettes. But she wanted a prescription for Valium because her nerves were killing her. That's why she was in to see Bill.

It would have been so easy for any doctor to just say no or to justify the prescription by telling himself, *This lady could obviously use a short course of Valium. She is a mess, and what else can I do for her anyway?*

But instead, Bill looked at her and said, "You know what your real problem is? Your life is all messed up because you don't know Jesus Christ. You need a personal relationship with God. He can transform your life and help you change these behaviors that are so destructive to you, your marriage, and your children." He went right past the symptoms to hone in on the underlying pathology.

I see another application here for most of our lives. I often want a quick fix, just as this patient did. Or I am hoping for easy answers like the rich young ruler. We all want someone to tell us how to raise our kids without raising our voices. We want a short book on how to preserve our marriage, a weekend seminar on how to decrease stress in our lives, and a twelve-step program guaranteed to rid ourselves of a lifelong bad habit.

All the while, the real issue in our lives is sin or a lack of obedience to do what God has already revealed in his Word. We are not living a Christlike life, and we are not in a right relationship with him. As a result, we are seeing a lot of these symptoms. Then we try to find a quick fix to make the symptoms go away without letting God treat the underlying disease. For instance, as parents we experience serious problems with our kids because we are not impacting them with Christ and are not spending time in family devotions or prayer. We haven't gotten them under the proper influences in school or church or whatever.

The same challenge faces us in our country, in our schools, and even in our churches. We must begin to develop a mind-set that looks beyond the symptoms to spot the real causative agents. Only then can we effectively deal with issues in our own lives and in the lives of the groups we relate to and work with.

Researchers have found, and the experience of American doctors confirms, that over 50 percent of the patients who enter a family-practice office have nothing organically wrong with them. Whatever their chief complaint is, the underlying problem is not physical. The reason they are there is usually because of an outside causative agent. It may make them depressed or stressed out, cause them to act out, or trigger an addiction to something.

Much of what American doctors see in medical practice is behavior oriented. People have inflicted health problems on themselves through smoking, alcohol abuse, illicit drug use, obesity, or promiscuity. That's one reason secular doctors here in the States are cynical and why many Christian doctors are beginning to find the most satisfaction in bringing people to the Great Physician, who can do surgery on people's hearts and lives that cuts out the cancer of sin.

CHANGING THE FACE OF MEDICINE

In Kenya physical health conditions were different. We were usually treating devastating acute problems where our care made a dramatic difference. We faced lots of infectious diseases or surgical problems where you knew the patient would get better as a direct result of an operation. The primary frustration there was the shortage of time, energy, and resources to provide for the overwhelming physical needs.

Spiritual issues did impact a patient's health, of course. But in Africa the doctors, nurses, or chaplains dealt with those head-on right at the bedside. For example, a patient who felt that he had been cursed by someone might literally waste away despite our medical care, unless there was spiritual intervention. Introducing patients to Jesus Christ gave them hope and healing.

The frustration I hear from so many North American doctors, however, is much different. They often struggle putting out the fires of their patients' behavior-related diseases but don't deal with the underlying source of the flame—a broken relationship with God. They are treating symptoms but not the disease. This is why at the Christian Medical Association we have been trying to train Christian doctors on how to better deal with patients' spiritual issues. Most doctors don't know how to take a spiritual history and have never prayed with a patient. We teach them to do both and, with permission, to gently point patients to the One who can heal their hearts as well as their bodies.

For too long in the Western world we have used a bio–psycho–social model of medicine that categorizes health problems and issues according to three types of causes—biological, psychological, or social. If the origin of an illness isn't organic, it's psychological or in some cases social. The spiritual dimension of humanity has been denied, or at least ignored.

Fortunately this is changing. Through the research, scholarship, and work of groups like the National Institute of Healthcare, headed by Dr. David Larson (a CMA member), and Duke University's Center for the Study of Religion and Health, directed by Dr. Harold Koenig, both the medical community and society as a whole are beginning to acknowledge the tremendous impact spirituality has on human health.

> For too long in the Western world we have used a bio-psycho-social model of medicine that categorizes health problems and issues according to three types of causes—biological, psychological, or social. The spiritual dimension of humanity has been denied, or at least ignored.

Research is showing that people who have a better spiritual life, who feel more spiritually fulfilled, who go to church regularly, who sense a close relationship with God, are more healthy. Studies also show they have better immune systems and recover faster from surgery, and when people are praying for them, patients actually have fewer complications in the ICU.

There's such a growing stockpile of evidence supporting a spiritual influence on health that it's impacting medical-school curricula. In the early 1990s there were only five med schools in America that offered courses dealing with the connection between religion/faith and health. By the year 2000 there were more than eighty.

Unfortunately most doctors still haven't learned how to address these issues in a practical way. In fact, when I was in medical school, I was taught (like most doctors) that I shouldn't talk about spiritual matters. Doing so would mean I was imposing my faith and personal beliefs on other people; this was not only considered wrong, but unprofessional and unethical.

Thus, even most Christian doctors have been cowered by our profession and persuaded to seldom discuss spiritual issues or problems we may recognize in our patients. Even when we see a direct connection between a health concern and a patient's deeper spiritual struggle, doctors have no idea how to raise spiritual issues or share about matters of faith. They are concerned that if they bring up spiritual issues, there will not be adequate time to deal with them in a ten-minute visit. Or perhaps the patient asks them a question they cannot answer. In other words, if the patient's real diagnosis is spiritual illness, even many Christian docs feel helpless to deal with it.

But frustrated at our inability to address so many patients' real problems, bolstered by research that backs our beliefs, and encouraged by a growing openness and acceptance of honest discussion of what seems (even to many unbelievers) an obvious connection between faith and health, the Christian Medical Association has accepted the challenge to help teach the medical profession how to address spiritual concerns.

THE SALINE SOLUTION

We have adopted as our motto, "Changing Hearts in Heath Care." One crucial part of our strategy for accomplishing that has been the establishment of a special professional training program we have dubbed the Saline Solution, since it is designed to help doctors to be salt in their patients' lives. More than six thousand doctors have already attended these weekend conferences, which we have held around the United States and Canada.

The primary goal of the Saline Solution program is to encourage and teach doctors how to address spiritually related health needs in an ethical and professional manner. How can they appropriately address spiritual issues? How can they take a spiritual history from a patient?

What questions should they ask, and how should they do it in a nonthreatening, non-embarrassing, and inoffensive way?

Much of what we have learned from and taught in these sessions with doctors about addressing spiritual issues can also be applied to other professionals and laypeople, as we all attempt to practice in partnership with the Great Physician.

> *Might we be guilty of malpractice, or at least short-changing our patients, if we ignore the spiritual dimension of human health and fail to address their chief complaints?*

I find it interesting, even amusing at times, when doctors act so concerned about not introducing spiritual topics in an awkward or threatening way. We feel perfectly free to inquire about menstrual periods, sexual habits, constipation, and any number of other very personal subjects. Yet we are afraid of, or feel inadequate, discussing spiritual beliefs and behavior that a growing body of scientific research shows can and does impact our patients' health.

How professional is that? Might we be guilty of malpractice, or at least shortchanging our patients, if we ignore the spiritual dimension of human health and fail to address their chief complaints? Saline Solution conferences teach doctors how to raise the subject by asking such questions as:

- When you are in a crisis, where do you find support or hope?
- Do you follow any organized religion?
- If so, how often do you attend services?
- Is prayer an important part of your life?

By drawing on this sort of faith history, we find that patients often begin to open up and feel comfortable talking about spiritual topics in spiritual terms. That enables us to treat and minister to patients in a more holistic and effective way.

Our organization wants to help Christian doctors realize that while evangelism is a gift not everyone has, for any of us (medical professionals and laypeople alike) who accept the Great Physician as our Master and model, witnessing is an obligation. Witnessing is nothing more than letting the people you encounter know that the Great Physician plays a significant role in your life.

We also teach that bringing people to Christ is a process. If you are a Christian, you know that many people have impacted you before you made a decision to accept Jesus as your personal Savior. So we encourage doctors not to push for decisions, but to just allow God to use them as part of their patient's spiritual journey.

To do this we teach doctors to raise faith flags. A faith flag is a short statement, perhaps no more than ten to fifteen seconds long, that falls naturally into their normal doctor-patient interaction. But it is something that lets the patient know that their doctor is comfortable talking about spiritual issues or that God and the Bible are important to him or her.

For example, a doctor may be dealing with someone just diagnosed with cancer. The patient is naturally devastated by the news. So in explaining the disease to them, the prognosis, and the treatment options, the doctor can also raise a faith flag by saying something like this: "Mary, I know this diagnosis of breast cancer is frightening for you. You know, I've had other patients dealing with a diagnosis like this who found enormous strength in their personal faith in God. If you would like, I can give you a prescription for Bible verses of hope and assurance." The doctor may just pause and wait to see if the person responds.

Or the doctor may throw out a general comment about how God has impacted his own life to see if the patient responds to that. It lets the patient know that if she wants to talk about spiritual topics, she can. If not, the doctor can go right on to whatever else needs to be covered medically. He or she may raise another faith flag on the patient's next visit.

Any of us can learn to use this faith-flag idea in our own appointments and conversations. At the Christian Medical Association we suggest repeated uses of this simple technique over the course of several appointments until a person expresses some interest. Then we propose following up with a thirty- to sixty-second faith story. That's when you briefly tell about a time God influenced your life, how God has impacted your marriage or your relationship with your children in raising them, or how faith has helped you or someone you know deal with loss, remorse, disease, or the like.

As medical professionals, however, I believe we must be more careful and more sensitive than the average layperson when we introduce spiritual subjects. Doctors do have a powerful influence in the patient-doctor relationship, and we never want to abuse that. At the same time we cannot ignore an entire dimension of human health that we know (and that all research shows) is important to a patient's well-being.

This is what the Saline Solution is all about. It helps doctors work through these issues by teaching them where to raise faith flags, when to tell faith stories, and even how to develop a network of pastors, Christian counselors, and capable Christian laypeople in their community to whom they can refer patients who have spiritual issues bigger than the doctors can deal with in the short amount of time they have for an appointment.

We have developed the Saline Solution because we are convinced that Christian doctors are in a unique position to minister to people in crisis situations—at times of birth, death, and disease—times that place great stress not only on individuals but on their marriages and families as well. What a wonderful platform doctors have for making a significant spiritual impact, not just on their patients but on the world.

Obviously, you don't have to be a doctor to encounter people in crisis. They may not call your office for an appointment to seek your help, but hurting people are all around you. The Saline Solution principles apply no matter what you do for a living. You can use them with the lady at the checkout line in the grocery store, on a golf course with business associates, after the death of a friend's mother, or over the backyard fence with a neighbor whose husband just left her.

God expects all believers to be faithful witnesses to what he has done in our lives. He wants us to raise faith flags, to share our own faith stories, and to point others to him. We must also remember, as the Great Physician did, that the best treatment for the most important diagnosis of many hurting people is spiritual.

We sometimes fail to realize that in our comfortable, materialistic, financially secure, sophisticated, and politically correct Western culture. But I once met a man whom I will never forget, and the memory of our interaction still convicts and inspires me.

> *God expects all believers to be faithful witnesses to what he has done in our lives. He wants us to raise faith flags, to share our own faith stories, and to point others to him.*

RICH LESSON IN A POOR COUNTRY

As a physician, even a Christian doctor, I admit I'm too often so focused on physical needs that I overlook the spiritual ones. I was never more aware of this than during a relief mission into Sudan during the early 1990s.

I served as the director of World Medical Missions at the time. We were the medical arm of Samaritan's Purse, the Christian relief organization founded by Franklin Graham, which is doing impressive work under the most devastating conditions in some of the world's most serious hot spots of danger and conflict.

We had already established a medical-relief outreach in the war-torn country of Somalia when U.N. officials informed us of a strange epidemic they had learned was killing thousands of people in the Sudan. They asked if we could do anything to help. So I took a medical team into yet another impoverished African nation that has been suffering through a long and brutal civil war.

We established a base in Ulang, a village of 2,500 people so close to the middle of nowhere I'm sure we were forty miles beyond the Great Commission. To reach Ulang we had taken a two-hour flight in the noisy cargo section of a United Nations C-130 from Chitokiloki in northwest Kenya to land on a remote dirt strip on the banks of a meandering river. We transferred tents, an outboard motor, fuel, food, and medical and camping supplies into the boat that had filled most of the plane's hold. Then we endured a four-hour trip up a snake- and crocodile-infested river in our fiberglass boat so overloaded that we only had a couple of inches of free board. We had to be extremely careful not to rock the boat or gun the motor and swamp our precarious craft.

There were no roads to Ulang because there were no vehicles that required roads. The people lived in abject poverty. Living conditions were like going back in Africa a hundred years. Yet there was a vibrant Christian church in Ulang because a national Christian had brought the Gospel to them years ago. It was an extra large hut with a grass roof and no walls; they had no other building materials. There was no microphone or PA system. They used makeshift pillars of crooked tree limbs to hold the roof up.

The day I was there a couple hundred people were packed under the roof. Maybe another 250 sat outside on the ground in the blinding sun and heat as the pastor preached.

Since we had just arrived the day before, I went up and met the pastor after the service. When we introduced ourselves through a translator, he invited us to his hut for a little bit of tea, a precious commodity in this remote, war-torn area. Once we were served, I inquired of this pastor through the interpreter, "I see you have so many needs here. How can we help you?"

He didn't even hesitate before he asked, "Could you please send us some Bibles?"

"How many Bibles do you have in your church?" I wanted to know.

"We have eight," he told me. "But we have seventy-eight evangelists who go out from here to preach in other villages each Sunday. We all have to share those eight Bibles. Do you think you could bring us some more Bibles?" His eyes seemed to light up at the prospect.

"I will do what I can," I promised, hoping I could find Bibles in their local language. "What else can we get you? What else do you need?"

He said, "I want you to know how much we appreciate your bringing the medical team to help us." He walked out with me behind the village to where there were four hundred fresh graves—people who had all died in the last month from an epidemic of relapsing fever. What a tragedy! Each person could have been cured by taking a single 250-milligram tetracycline tablet costing just pennies. "We need your medical help," he told me. Then he added, "And if it wouldn't be too much trouble, next time you come back to Ulang, could you bring us some cloth?"

That made me curious. Thinking maybe this pastor wanted to make something special for his church—perhaps choir robes or a cloth for covering a makeshift communion table—I asked, "What do you need cloth for?"

He smiled a little sadly and hung his head for a moment. "Well," he admitted, "it is just so embarrassing for our women to come to church on Sunday half-naked."

I began to think. Would I be at church next Sunday if I had absolutely nothing to wear? Would I be asking for Bibles before I thought to ask for clothes for my wife and daughters who were going to church topless? Would I be asking for Bibles before I asked for medicines to stop an epidemic that in a few short weeks had already wiped out 15 percent of my town?

In that moment it hit me that this simple, godly Sudanese pastor realized something about priorities that many of us still need to learn. He knew, as the Great Physician did, the importance of dealing with people's real pathology.

He knew the history. He had heard the chief complaint. He had seen the symptoms of war and disease. But he understood the real pathology. He knew the only effective, lasting treatment for his hurting people needed to be spiritual.

That's a lesson we too can learn from the Great Physician.

THE GREAT PHYSICIAN PRACTICED COMPASSION

EACH YEAR CMA PROVIDES SCHOLARSHIPS TO ENABLE thirty to forty medical students and another twenty-five to thirty residents to spend time working and learning on some overseas mission field. On our scholarship application form we ask a number of questions, including, "Why did you decide to go into medicine?"

The answer to that question is almost always the same. Students and residents alike invariably say they wanted to become doctors in order "to help people."

One of the saddest things I have noticed about medicine is that a lot of those who go into the profession with a deep and sincere desire to serve other people come out of their training with much of that altruism gone. Then over time our health-care system seems to drain compassion and caring out of many more doctors. I have often asked myself why.

One factor may be that a disproportionate percentage of patients we care for during our training experience come from the lowest socioeconomic strata of society, perhaps even indigent patients, whose most serious health problems are often the result of personal choices—such as smoking, alcohol, drug use, and other risky behavior. Thus, it becomes easy to shrug our shoulders and tell ourselves, *They are reaping the rewards of their own poor lifestyle choices.* We become unsympathetic, even cynical.

> *Then over time our health-care system seems to drain compassion and caring out of many more doctors.*

Or maybe our compassion is simply dulled by the constant demands of the job. There can be a sort of numbing effect that results from having to take care of so many sick people. We rub up against so much pain and heartache that calluses begin to form deep in the seat of our emotions.

For some of us it may be a defense mechanism, conscious or subconscious, we use to protect ourselves from feeling overwhelmed by the number of people who need help or to avoid feelings of pain or inadequacy when we encounter incurable suffering and death. Many young doctors are even warned by teachers and older colleagues that they need to be careful not to get too "emotionally involved" with their patients. *A good doctor cannot afford,* so they think, *to let sentiment or emotion cloud his or her objective expertise.*

> *We rub up against so much pain and heartache that calluses begin to form deep in the seat of our emotions.*

Much of the problem results from what we learn through example and medical socialization. If you aren't careful during training, you begin to talk about the "diabetic in room 136," and patients soon become diseases instead of persons. You can even begin to refer to patients in more derogatory terms as others refer to them that way.

Whatever the cause might be, whether the shortage of compassion in medicine is real or merely perceived by patients, this isn't good.

What every patient wants, often more than anything else, is a physician who cares.

Of course, there's much to be said for competence to go along with the caring. There is indeed the need for objectivity and professionalism that cannot be compromised by personal emotion. Critical spur-of-the-moment medical decisions require clear and dispassionate thinking.

The Kindest Cut of All?

I recall walking into a ward at Tenwek to encounter a woman in her fifties who had had uncontrolled diabetes for a number of years. In these sorts of cases many of the small blood vessels that nourish the distal extremities (especially the legs) become nonfunctional. This is why physicians routinely check the pulses in the feet of diabetics.

Unfortunately this woman had been working in the garden, cut her foot with a hoe, and neglected to get medical attention until it became badly infected. Because of the poor circulation, the infection had turned to gangrene.

The moment I started to examine the woman, I knew she had serious problems. The leg was extremely swollen and had turned black, and her skin was cold to the touch. The necrosis was already past her ankle and was clearly beginning to move up her leg—farther every hour. I had no choice but to inform her we needed to amputate the leg as soon as possible.

That's a serious thing to consider for any patient. But even more so in Kipsigis society, where a woman's worth is defined by her ability to work and to bear children. While this lady was past her child-bearing years, it was going to be difficult, if not impossible, for her with one leg to fulfill any of her regular family duties, such as gardening, carrying water, chopping wood, washing clothes, and working in the fields.

"*ACHICHICHICHA!*" she screamed. (The more *chis* in Kipsigis, the more emphatic the "No!") She was horrified by the idea. She clearly thought amputation was a fate as bad as death. So I calmly explained that if we didn't remove the leg she would definitely die—very soon and very unpleasantly. Even so it took all the persuasion I could muster to get her to finally agree to the operation.

It's never an easy thing for a doctor to cut someone's leg off. You cannot forget that the operation you are performing is actually maiming someone for life. Yet neither can you afford to dwell on that; instead, you have to remain cool-headed, objective, and deliberate in order to do what is best for the patient in the long run.

> *It's never an easy thing for a doctor to cut someone's leg off. You cannot forget that the operation you are performing is actually maiming someone for life.*

The same thing is true, though the feelings are less extreme, when you immunize a child. I have yet to meet a youngster who likes to receive injections. Yet we routinely have children restrained by a parent or one of our staff in order to give them shots we know cause temporary discomfort and pain. We know immunization will benefit them and save lives later on.

There are many other times in the practice of medicine when we cannot afford to let our patients' emotions or suffering dissuade us from the treatment they need. Being cool, calm, and objective is important for a doctor; I don't want to minimize that.

But at the same time, what patients are looking for, and what they also need, is someone who truly cares about them and demonstrates it. I would go so far as to say that, in my experience, the caring is ultimately more important than the curing—and often may have the greater therapeutic effect. This makes it all the more disturbing that so many doctors today are seen as impersonal, money-driven, harried, and just too busy to really care about their patients.

> *I would go so far as to say that, in my experience, the caring is ultimately more important than the curing—and often may have the greater therapeutic effect.*

Who Really Cares?

What does the Great Physician teach us on this score? We have already seen that Jesus knew what it was like to be hurried and harried. Yet he never appeared uncaring. In fact, we find a couple of specific cases where he was moved to tears, and in many other instances Jesus was obviously deeply affected by someone's suffering or pain.

Let's turn to Luke 7. Christ is walking near the village of Nain when he and his followers encounter a funeral procession leaving the town. This was a common occurrence at that time and remains a custom many places in the developing world today—including rural Kenya, where I lived and worked for years.

Often the funeral itself is held at the home of the deceased. Then the body is ceremoniously carried to a corner of the family plot or to a communal burial ground. Family members, friends, and acquaintances from the community walk along behind the coffin all the way to the grave site. Often there is great weeping and wailing among the mourners.

This funeral in Nain must have prompted more sadness than most because of the circumstances. The weeping woman walking behind the body of her son in this procession was already a widow. Having lost her husband, it was unlikely in that time, as in similar cultures today, that she would ever have the chance to remarry. She would not have anyone to provide for her or to protect her and would likely be economically destitute the rest of her days.

The only real hope a widow had for a better future was in her children. As they grew up, perhaps they would be able to care for her. The primary responsibility for this usually fell on the eldest son. Along with his birthright, he inherited a special obligation to care for an elderly parent.

The remnants of this custom survive even in our culture today. Ever since my own father died, I bear some of that responsibility as the eldest son in my family—to care for my widowed mother and make sure she has what she needs. But in New Testament days and in developing countries today, this role of sons is far more critical than in modern

American culture. Sons carry on the family name and thus have special significance. But they are also the ones who receive any inheritance and are always highly valued.

The fact that this woman of Nain had been widowed made her son, her only son, that much more important to her. When that son died, she not only lost a son she loved, but her only source of hope for the future had disappeared. She'd suffered tragedy upon tragedy. Christ saw all this and knew in a moment what the situation was. "When the Lord saw her, his heart went out to her and he said 'Don't cry'" (Luke 7:13).

Jesus' heart broke for this woman. He was deeply moved by her suffering and her circumstances. And it was that compassion that moved him to action. Because he cared, he restored the son to his mother.

EASY TEARS

It's easy to malign the medical profession for a lack of caring and concern about people's pain and suffering. But I think there are times when all of us could bear this blame.

It's so easy to be superficially compassionate, such as to send a card or flowers when someone dies. Perhaps we even show up for the funeral out of a sense of duty. But do we genuinely care? Perhaps not, unless it's someone we're close to. But that's not what God expects of us. It's not what Jesus did in his healing ministry.

Repeatedly in Christ's life as the Great Physician we are told that he really cared. One of my favorite passages in the New Testament is Matthew 9:36: "When he saw the crowds, he had compassion on them, because they were harassed and helpless like sheep without a shepherd." Similarly in Matthew 14:14 we read, "When Jesus . . . saw a large crowd, he had compassion on them and healed their sick."

I often remind the doctors I work with that for the Great Physician, the compassion came first and the healing came second. In fact, the healing came from a heart of genuine concern and caring for those he was going to touch. Compassion resulted in, and was demonstrated by, his actions.

SHOWING CARE

As I deal with Christian doctors, I find it helps to talk about practical ways for them to demonstrate compassion. Being compassionate means several things to me as a physician.

The first requirement in demonstrating compassion we have already analyzed in chapter 5—that is, *touch*. Whether it's placing a hand on a patient's shoulder or holding their hand as you talk with them, a kind and gentle touch says much more than words can ever say. Touch expresses a concern that connects you with the patient in a way better than any other I know. The Great Physician knew touch was extremely important for conveying compassion. He obviously believed that caring was as important as curing.

Second, being compassionate also requires a willingness to invest *time*, for it takes time to show compassion. In a hospital situation it means stopping on rounds to sit on the edge of the bed or to pull up a chair that actually gets you down closer to the level of the patient. In an exam room it means taking a seat and facing the patient eye to eye. That simple act of sitting down shows that you are willing to give of your time.

Too often doctors work standing up and look down from a superior position at a patient in a chair or a bed or on an examining table. Patients see the doctor looming over them with chart and pen in hand, ready to direct their lives. What a different picture is conveyed when a doctor takes the time to sit down and put himself or herself at the same level as the patient.

In fact, studies have shown that when doctors do this one simple thing, in posttreatment surveys their patients will rate the physicians as having spent more time with them than a doctor who actually stayed in the room the same amount of time but remained standing. People feel you have spent more time with them simply because you have demonstrated compassion in this manner.

Other simple ways to convey caring include setting down the patient's chart or laying down the pen and just listening—looking patients directly in the eye as they talk instead of jotting furiously on a chart. I often encourage doctors I train to wait and do their charting or dictation once they get outside the room, so they can be totally focused on the patient during the exam.

Though I have trained myself and other doctors to make these little indicators of compassion a regular part of one's professional practice, I constantly struggle to apply these same principles in my personal life. Yet I know my wife, my children, my neighbors, and the people I work with need my compassion just as much as my patients do. Whenever I honestly think about it, I'm both challenged and convicted.

I recently heard about some interesting psychological research conducted years ago in which subjects were shown pictures of human faces with a variety of expressions and asked to try to identify the emotion expressed in the picture. Most participants had little difficulty accurately recognizing a long list of emotions, such as anger, fear, sorrow, joy, surprise, and pain. But they found it almost impossible to distinguish between faces intended to depict intent listening and those expressing love. What should that say to doctors (and the rest of us) about one sure-fire way to demonstrate compassion for others?

The third *t* I use when I'm talking to doctors about demonstrating compassion—after touch and time—is *temperament*. Temperament covers a lot of territory. For example, how open and direct are we?

It's important to speak directly *to* the patient and not just *about* the patient. There's a temptation (especially when family is there) to end up talking to the family—explaining the diagnosis and talking about what's going to happen next, while totally ignoring the patient, as if he or she isn't even there. It's much better for doctors to address the patient directly the vast majority of the time and only bring the family members in at the end of the conversation.

A certain temperament is also conveyed by speaking calmly and directly using the patient's name. That communicates a tremendous sense of caring because everyone likes to hear his or her name—especially the first name.

Humor helps as well. Kidding, a joking comment, and a light-hearted demeanor can also convey warmth and caring. To an elderly woman who survived a near fatal case of pneumonia I might say, "Mrs. Jenkins, I know you want to stay here in the hospital, but I guess I'm going to be forced to discharge you today. The nurses have been complaining about you racing your bed up and down the hallway!" A comment like that is sure to bring a smile to her face.

> *Absolutely nothing demonstrates a caring temperament better than availability. As a physician, if you really want to let a patient know you care, simply say, "Here's my office number, and here's my home phone number."*

Absolutely nothing demonstrates a caring temperament better than availability. As a physician, if you really want to let a patient know you care, simply say, "Here's my office number, and here's my home phone number."

In residency, when one of my patients was in dire straits, I would say to him or to one of his family, "I'm not on call tonight, so I won't be here in the hospital. But if something happens, if there's a concern or a question, feel free to call me directly at home." More than almost anything else that statement says "I'm here for you; I care about you." Willingness to be available says so much and can play a critical role in helping a doctor demonstrate a caring and compassionate temperament.

These same principles can be applied to all our relationships with other people. Our touch, time, and temperament can communicate compassion and caring in our friendship, family, and business relationships alike.

Compassion in Action

If the Great Physician is truly our example, if we want to demonstrate the heart of God, we need to do more than voice words; our actions must show and communicate compassion. Jesus said as much when he told the parable of the good Samaritan as his answer to the question: How can we show love to our neighbors?

In Luke 10 the Samaritan "took pity" on the man waylaid in the ditch. But it wasn't enough that he felt compassion for the victim, nor was it enough for him to verbalize his concern. He didn't stand looking down in the ditch and make a speech saying how sad this made him or what a tragedy this was. He didn't make proposals about the need to educate people about travel dangers—maybe with an advertising campaign. He didn't suggest a sensitization program for would-be robbers to discourage the hassling of folks on the road between Jerusalem and Jericho. He didn't appeal to fellow travelers and take up a collection for the poor man in the ditch.

What did he do? Because he cared, he got down in that ditch with the man who needed help. He not only touched him, he cleaned and bound his wounds. He disrupted his own schedule; he took time. And he made not only himself but his resources available to the beaten man. He used his own oil and his own wine to minister as best he could to the man's immediate needs. Then he made arrangements at the nearest Holiday Inn for the man to stay until he recuperated, and the manager was instructed to put whatever was needed on the Samaritan's tab.

Jesus never told the final chapter of the actual story because he had already made his main point. We don't know what took place when the Samaritan came back later to check on the man. But can't you imagine how grateful the recovering man would have been? I can't help thinking that as these two men finally talked and got to know each other, it may have been the beginning of a long and wonderful friendship.

It's been my experience, both professionally and personally, that genuine compassion forges the richest relationships. I believe those deepest bonds are often tempered by the heat of crisis—at times of need or loss.

Doctors have an advantage here because people who come to us are already in need. What opportunities for rich relationships we can have if and when we demonstrate genuine compassion and show the love of Jesus Christ.

But doctors aren't the only ones with such opportunity. We all encounter people who are hurting and in need every day. We should also be particularly sensitive to any chance we have to reach out at times of loss.

I remember when Jody's mother died and we went back to my mother-in-law's funeral in Kentucky. How surprised we were to see two of my wife's cousins we hadn't seen for years and years. These busy and successful people in the banking industry in Toronto, Ontario, took the time and the expense to fly down and be there for the funeral. Their willing presence spoke highly to us of their caring and concern and helped us form a deeper bond, so that when we were in Toronto for a national meeting some weeks later, Jody and I went out of our way in the midst of a heavy schedule to spend more time with them.

Real compassion also means you are willing to come alongside and suffer with someone—to help bear their pain, to suffer together. There's tremendous power and ministry in that. The first step, often the only step required to accomplish that, is simply *being there*. That's why I always encourage younger physicians as I train them, whenever possible, to be at the bedside at the time of death.

Unfortunately in our day and time, that is seldom the place you find physicians. In fact, too many doctors will do everything they can to avoid a dying patient or the patient's family once they feel there is nothing else they can do to cure the patient. They have run out of options, and there is not another test to run or another treatment to try. They can't stand feeling helpless.

We forget the power of simple compassion. It seems like the least we can do when, in fact, it's often the most important, the most powerful care we can possibly provide. We need to just be there, to put an arm around a family member, and to say how sorry we are. Perhaps we can even attend the funeral. There is no better way I know for a doctor to amaze a patient's family than to go to their loved one's funeral or to send a personal letter to the family after a patient dies.

I know the tremendous impact it had when my mother-in-law's cardiologist took time out of his busy schedule to write a personal note after her death—to say how much my mother-in-law had meant to him, what a wonderful lady she was, and how sorry he was that she had passed on. He added that he felt he had done everything he could, but if we had any questions about her final course, he was available to answer them.

One physician friend whom I highly respect always calls and asks family members to come back into his office a few weeks after the death. There's no charge for this visit. But during that time he provides counseling and encouragement and answers any questions they might have about what had happened during the patient's final days. He knows families often wonder whether they made the right decisions or if something should have been done differently.

We forget the power of simple compassion. It seems like the least we can do when, in fact, it's often the most important, the most powerful care we can possibly provide. We need to just be there, to put an arm around a family member, and to say how sorry we are.

What a wonderful demonstration of care and compassion! And what a lasting impact that can have!

MEN OF COMPASSION

Below are stories about two men, one a doctor, the other a dentist, who have exemplified compassion for me.

Steve Furr, a family doctor who hailed from LA (that's Lower Alabama for you non-Southerners), traveled with me a few years ago as part of a CMA short-term medical mission in Zambian prisons. One day our team visited Lusaka Central Prison, a jam-packed facility in the capital city. It's an oppressive place with massive stone walls, constructed in colonial days and seldom repaired. When guards with guns hurried us through the gates that clanged shut behind us, I felt has if I had crossed the doorstep of hell. I vividly remember the hundred-degree heat, the sweat, the dirt, the smell.

Many of the prisoners wore nothing but tattered rags. They received one meal a day, consisting of a single helping of *nshima* (n-shee-ma—the same cornmeal mush the Kipsigis call *gimet*). Some days bits of cooked cabbage or beans mixed into the *nshima* provided added nutritional value.

Living conditions in Lusaka Central proved no more appealing than the cuisine. Built to house a few hundred colonial prisoners, somewhere between 1,500 and 2,000 are held there now. Eighty inmates sleep in cells built for twenty. Conditions are so cramped that many men don't have room to lie down at night; they have to sleep sitting up on concrete floors, leaning back on the prisoner behind them, with their feet and legs spread around the man in front of them.

> *Sammy was an orphan. One day, barefoot and cold, he stole a pair of tennis shoes from a street vendor and was caught. He had been in Lusaka Central Prison for three years, still awaiting trial.*

Steve Furr was one of our team of docs who saw over four hundred prisoners that day. Most of these prisoners hadn't had health care for years, so we saw many pathetic cases. The most disturbing case that day for Steve was a little boy about ten or eleven years old—we'll call him Sammy.

Sammy was a prisoner—a little boy among all those adult male prisoners. You can imagine what was going on.

Sammy was an orphan. After his mother and father had died, he had survived for a time on the streets because there was no orphanage to take care of him. He learned to fend for himself at an early age the best way he could, which sometimes meant stealing the food he needed to survive. One day, barefoot and cold, he stole a pair of tennis shoes from a street vendor and was caught. He had been in Lusaka Central Prison for three years, still awaiting trial.

Steve had examined this winsome little boy while holding him on his knee. There was an instant bond between them. When he heard Sammy's story, Steve's heart was just broken. He thought to himself, *What can I do?* If Steve could have put Sammy under his arm and taken him back to Alabama, I think he would have done it. But that wasn't possible.

Steve couldn't get Sammy out of his mind the rest of that day. He thought, *I know they won't let me take him home with me. And it will do no good to say anything to the prison officials. So what can I do to help that boy?*

Our clinic ended that day about 4:00 P.M. We packed up our things and went through another gate into the central courtyard of the prison. More than a thousand inmates, many of whom we had treated that day, crowded around and sat in the dirt as we conducted an evangelistic service.

After singing a few African hymns and choruses with our captive congregation, Steve was scheduled to speak. When he stepped to the front, he motioned for Sammy to join him. He put his arm around the boy and looked out at all those men in that prison. "I know a lot of bad things go on in this prison," he began. "But I want to tell you all a story I heard today . . . " and Steve began to relate Sammy's story. As he concluded the sad tale, with tears in his eyes, Steve said, "I want to tell you something, men. This boy needs a father in this prison. I wish I could take him home to America with me, but I can't. I can't be Sammy's father. But maybe some of you can. Maybe one of you can—to protect him like a father, to take care of him. Because there's nobody to care for him except one of you. This boy needs a father."

Steve went on to talk about how we all need a father and how we all have a heavenly Father who loves and cares for us. When he finished speaking and asked how many wanted to know God and accept his Son Jesus, whom he sent to show us the way to live for him and with him forever, hundreds of prisoners raised their hands—including Sammy.

With tears running down his face, Steve got down on his knees and prayed with Sammy, introducing him to a heavenly Father he knew would remain with the boy even after our team had to leave and the gates of that prison shut behind us.

Compassion. That's really all Steve Furr had to offer. But when he felt it that day, everyone in that prison saw it. And it made an impact on who-knows-how-many lives—an impact that will last an eternity.

A few weeks ago I received a phone call from the wife of a dentist in Bristol, Tennessee, where our organization's headquarters are located. She called to give me a word of encouragement and to let me know a little bit about a need in the community she thought we might be able to help with.

As we began to get acquainted over the phone, she told me her husband had practiced there for years. He was one of only a few dentists regularly taking patients who had no form of payment. Twenty-five percent of his practice was with indigents who came from the mountains around Bristol. They had no insurance and no way to pay for their dental care. Over the years, word had spread through the whole area: "If you have a serious dental problem and need help, Dr. So-and-so will see you even if you can't pay."

This dentist wasn't worried about Medicare or Medicaid or what dental plan he might collect from. Like the good Samaritan he knew what it was to be a neighbor. He felt compassion for the people in the ditch, and he was willing to get down and help them.

Whom do you guess the people of Bristol think of as the Christian dentist in town? What makes him stand out? This man has put his compassion into action. And this story could be retold a thousand times by citing the examples of other physicians and dentists who volunteer their skills and their time to take care of people in need—in this country and around the world.

That's what God is looking for all of us to do—whatever highway we're traveling, whatever our profession is or on whatever mission field he has placed us.

> *Compassion. That's really all Steve Furr had to offer. But when he felt it that day, everyone in that prison saw it.*

Buwale Heartbreak

Some years ago when I was medical director for Samaritan's Purse, on my first trip into Somalia during that country's civil war, I visited a place in Mogadishu called Buwale Camp. It wasn't really a camp, merely some open land behind an abandoned gas station that had been completely looted—the pumps ripped out, bullet holes everywhere. But it was where the Buwale people (a clan in Somalia) had congregated after they had fled starvation and clan warfare in their homelands and wandered into the city looking for food.

The people of Buwale Camp lived in hovels only a little bit higher than a table—flimsy "structures" pieced together out of sticks and covered with little scraps of plastic, paper, or whatever they found to keep the sun off. The temperature soared well over a hundred every day, and dust blew everywhere. If you stopped and listened, you could hear the constant buzzing of flies swarming all around what was a truly miserable situation.

I had left the States so quickly that the only medical equipment I had packed was a stethoscope. I didn't even bring any medicine to hand out since I was there on an initial scouting trip to see what the problems were and what our medical teams should bring when they came.

That's why I had gone down to Buwale Camp with my translator, merely to assess need. So I knelt down by the first hut I came to and looked through the door—which was not so much a door as a hole in that little hovel. There, sitting cross-legged on the ground, was a skin-and-bones woman. In her arms she held a tiny baby.

In all my years in Africa as a missionary doctor I had never seen a baby as starved as that little one was. You could literally count every bone in his body, which was nothing but a tiny skeleton shrink-wrapped with skin.

As she watched me and our eyes met, this mother tried to jiggle her baby to get him to nurse. But it was no use. Her breasts hadn't produced milk in weeks. She was in little better shape than her child.

I looked at the baby more closely and noticed the mother had him wrapped in a filthy, tattered rag. Immediately I surmised that this child had pneumonia. Respiratory rate looked to be forty to sixty. I had no medicine, but I told myself, *At least I can put my stethoscope on to listen to the chest. The mother will feel as if I've done something and it will confirm my diagnosis.* But as I placed my stethoscope against the baby's chest, the child gasped and died.

I couldn't believe what happened next. In her dazed and weakened state, that mother didn't immediately notice that her child had stopped breathing. Finally she did look down, and with no emotion registering on her gaunt face, she pulled the corner of that dirty cloth up over the child's head and patted it twice—almost like a benediction. Slowly she crawled out of the hut, stood up on legs as thin as twigs, and started walking away with her pitiful bundle.

Just across the street lay an empty lot with no building on it. As I looked in that direction for the first time, I noticed dozens of people, their bundles laid out beside them, digging in the ground with their bare hands, burying their loved ones. This mother trudged over among the others, knelt down, and with bony fingers began scratching out a grave for her baby.

> *I noticed dozens of people, their bundles laid out beside them, digging in the ground with their bare hands, burying their loved ones. This mother trudged over among the others, knelt down, and with bony fingers began scratching out a grave for her baby.*

I turned to my translator and said, "I've been in Africa for many years, but I don't understand this. When children die in Africa, the mother screams and runs and tears her clothes. She pulls out her hair; she wails. But she doesn't just get up without a word, without a tear, without any emotion, and walk over to start burying her baby."

The translator looked at me and said, "Doctor, you are right. You don't understand. This woman had eleven children, and that is her last one. She has no more tears."

So when I went to the next hovel, it was the same thing, and the next hovel and it was the same thing, I hurried back to our vehicle and drove back to where I was staying. I unzipped my bathroom kit and took out the little bottles of medicine I carry for myself on trips, and I rushed back to Buwale Camp. I started breaking open ampicillin capsules, crushing antibiotic tablets, and putting them into little babies' mouths with tears pouring down my face until I could hardly see. I was working as fast as I could until I finally ran out of medicines.

I had never, ever seen anything like that before.

I had never felt so helpless.

I will tell you something, this missionary doctor, who thought he had seen it all and whose heart had gotten a little bit callused, needed that. I needed to be reminded that the Great Physician was crying because people in that makeshift cemetery were going into eternity without ever having heard the Gospel—not once in this radically Muslim country with fewer than two hundred Christians in an underground church.

I needed to have my heart broken like Christ's heart was broken. I needed to see the world as he sees the world, because when I did, compassion welled up within me like never before.

We get so objective, so logical in what we do sometimes. We get desensitized by the latest disaster coming across to us in living and dying color on the evening news. What we really need is to round with Christ every day to see and to be broken by the pain and suffering all around us. We must see this world as Dr. Jesus sees it, to feel the suffering as he does. Then, and only then, can we practice compassion like the Great Physician. That kind of compassion changes our actions, changes our hearts, and changes other people's lives.

> *I started breaking open ampicillin capsules, crushing antibiotic tablets, and putting them into little babies' mouths with tears pouring down my face until I could hardly see. I was working as fast as I could until I finally ran out of medicines. I had never, ever seen anything like that before. I had never felt so helpless.*

THE GREAT PHYSICIAN KNEW HOW TO PROPERLY SCRUB

"DR. STEVENS, COME QUICKLY!"

My heart rate always goes up a bit when I hear those words. I heard them a lot during my time in Kenya. Whenever they came from one of our experienced nurse midwives, an extra shot of adrenaline automatically kicked in. Our veteran OB staff had seen everything and could handle all manner of problems without a doctor's help. So if they ever requested my presence in a hurry, I knew someone was facing serious problems.

On this particular day I sprinted to the delivery room to find a Kipsigis woman, eight months pregnant, bleeding profusely from the womb. I thought it likely she had an abruption of her placenta—in other words, a part of the placenta had prematurely separated from the wall of the uterus.

Such cases were among the most critical emergencies we faced at Tenwek because two lives were at stake. If the placenta separated much more, the baby would die from the lack of oxygen transfer from the mother's circulation. And the mother could easily die from blood loss because the large arteries in the uterus don't stop bleeding until the uterus contracts down. That will not happen as long as the baby is in there.

Every second counted, so we rushed the woman to the operating room. I figured that at eight months this baby should be mature enough that the best hope for mother and child was an emergency C-section. Once we got the baby out, we would remove the placenta, massage the uterus, and inject pitocin to get the uterus to clamp down and stop the mother's bleeding.

We started the woman on IVs and as soon as we got her blood type, we began a transfusion. We also put her on oxygen immediately so that whatever blood the baby was still getting would be well oxygenated. Already the old strap-style external fetal

> *Despite the urgency of a situation a surgeon always needs to scrub.*

monitor indicated some instability in the baby's heart rate. *Not a good sign. We've got to hurry!*

As the rest of the staff hurriedly prepared this woman and the OR for surgery, I stepped out to the scrub sink and began to thoroughly wash my hands. Despite the urgency of a situation a surgeon always needs to scrub.

Scrubbing means more than just washing your hands. We're not talking about sticking them under the faucet, rubbing on a little soap, and then giving them a quick rinse.

Scrubbing for surgery is something you do very, very methodically. In fact, there's a prescribed procedure you learn as a medical student and never forget for the rest of your life. You begin with a quick wash with liquid antiseptic soap, from your hands to your upper arms. Then you take a fingernail file (which in Kenya was hanging on a string at the sink) and you clean under your fingernails very carefully. Then you take a brush with fairly stiff bristles, coat it with antiseptic soap, and really begin to scrub. You meticulously go up your fingers, in between your fingers, all the way down into the webbed spaces. Then you work your way around your hands and go up your arm. When you're done with one arm, you repeat the process with the other hand and arm. You keep your hands higher than your elbows throughout the entire procedure so that all the dirty suds and water move down to where you haven't scrubbed yet.

At that point you rinse your hands using knee levers to turn on the water. You hold your hands under the faucet so that the dirty water always flows toward your elbows. You always want your cleanest area to be your hands.

After that you wash yet again because there are more than ten thousand bacteria per square inch of hand surface, and many are hidden in pores and at the base of hair follicles. That's why years ago, many surgeons would complete the process and then put alcohol on their arms—which burned a bit if they had any cuts. We don't use the alcohol so much anymore because we have much better antiseptic soaps today.

Once this entire washing procedure is complete, you then have to dry your hands in a certain way. You start with a sterile towel and using one half of it, you dry each finger, then the hand, and then down the forearm. Using the other clean half of the towel, you repeat the process with the other hand and arm. Then you drop the towel, still keeping your arms up, with your hands always above your elbows. You may wave your arms a little bit to get them dry enough so that when you slide into your gown and put on the gloves, your arms and hands are dry enough that they don't stick. That's why the gloves are powdered as well.

The scrubbing routine isn't finished yet. The scrub nurse helps you slip on a sterile gown with a carefully choreographed procedure that looks more like a ballet move than something you'd expect to pick up in med school. Then come the gloves, and here again there's a prescribed ritual. The scrub nurse holds the cuff of your gloves from underneath so that there's no way you can touch her sterile gloves with your hands as you put them into your gloves.

Even after that, whether you're just standing at the table or moving around the OR waiting for the surgery to begin, you take care not to raise your hands above your shoulders or lower them below your waist because those areas are considered to be nonsterile. The best way to ensure this is to fold your hands and hold them against your chest.

If an itchy nose needs scratching or a sweaty brow needs mopping, you have to ask someone else to do it. Otherwise you risk contamination, are no longer sterile, and have to repeat all or part of this time-consuming process.

When you're in a hurry, as with the case of this woman bleeding from the uterus, trying desperately to save the lives of a mother and a baby, there's a tendency to cut corners and do it quicker. But you must always maintain a balance—to weigh the immediate short-term needs of the patient(s) and what's required to save her against the long-term concerns of potential postoperative infection.

In this particular instance, we got the Kipsigis woman on the table, prepped her, and performed the emergency C-section. Fortunately we got the baby out in time; he survived just fine. We then stopped the mother's bleeding and she too fully recovered. One big reason for the successful outcome of this case was that we weren't in so much of a hurry that we didn't properly scrub.

WHAT'S THE BIG DEAL?

What's the big deal here? This just seems like further proof that doctors tend to be obsessive-compulsive types. Is scrubbing really that important?

Yes, it is! Indeed, the fact that successful surgery finally became routine in the 1800s was due primarily to the development of antiseptic and improved sterility in operating rooms. Until then, the greatest cause of postsurgical death was infection.

In those days doctors didn't have surgical gloves; they just used their bare hands. Thus, the growing practice of scrubbing with soap and utilizing antiseptic greatly reduced the number of those who contracted any number of infections that often proved fatal in the days before modern antibiotics.

But that was then. What about now, since surgeons wear sterile gloves? Why the continued emphasis on scrubbing? Because a certain percentage of the time you are going to get a torn glove. In Africa where we had trouble getting quality gloves, as many as one in ten times a defective glove might just rip. Other times you stick a needle through a glove, or you cut or tear it on some surgical instrument. Anytime that happens, it's the same as if you have your hands actually in the womb, in the abdomen, or wherever you're operating. Then any germs on your hands can cause potential infections.

But are infections really that big a deal today with all the antibiotics at our disposal? Yes. Consider the following evidence.

The *New York Times* recently quoted a Center for Disease Control study stating that 5 percent of people admitted to hospitals (1.8 million a year) will pick up an infection there, 20,000 of them will die as a direct result, and those acquired infections will contribute to the deaths of another 70,000 people. Just for comparison sake, only 17,171 people died of AIDS in 1998.

The Mayo Clinic sponsors regular Infection Awareness Week programs. One of their recent posters pictures a pair of hands with the caption "The Ten Most Common Causes of Infection." Another one of their posters reminded doctors and nurses, "A milligram of hand-washing is worth a kilogram of antibiotics." Yes, scrubbing before surgery and washing your hands between patients are still very important.

MALPRACTICE CHARGES

Did you know Dr. Jesus and his associates were accused of not scrubbing well? In Mark 7:1–15 the Pharisees came to him and complained that Jesus' disciples weren't doing the ritualistic hand washing prescribed at that time for Jewish people before they ate their meals.

Like many of the Old Testament laws God had given the Israelite people, the regulations about hand washing seem to have had a twofold purpose. On the surface they provided a guide to good health and higher community standards, which contributed directly to a better quality of life among the chosen people than what their neighbors experienced.

But a lot of these laws were also meant to convey meaningful spiritual symbolism. Those regulations concerning purification rites in particular were evidently intended as ritualistic reminders of the relationship between an imperfect people and a perfect and holy God.

Did you know Dr. Jesus and his associates were accused of not scrubbing well?

Over time, many people had confused the two dimensions of the law. They remembered the ritual, and the Pharisees even added to it. But in the process they had concentrated so much on the letter of the law (and all the possible applications of it) that they were completely ignoring the spirit of the law. As a result, Jesus scolded the Pharisees, telling them they were just going through the motions.

That's easy enough to do. Several decades ago now researchers conducted a study that has been cited as a warning for medical students ever since. This research proved that many medical people only thought they were scrubbing well. In this test, volunteer doctors, residents, and interns were instructed to coat their hands and arms with an unidentified liquid, let it dry, and then, "Just go about your usual routine." The subjects didn't know the purpose of the test, nor were they told that the liquid was an invisible, but scrubbable dye.

Only after the subjects scrubbed were they instructed to put their hands under ultraviolet light to see if they had gotten all the dye off. They hadn't. The most common spots missed in the scrubbing process were under the fingernails and down in the webs of the fingers. The subjects thought they had scrubbed sufficiently, but they really hadn't.

As a result of that study's findings, standard scrubbing protocols were revised with a much greater emphasis on the most common problem areas. The new and improved standards also specified more repetition, longer scrubbing, and the prescribed use of certain types of brushes in the scrubbing process. The intent was to force doctors to be more conscious of careful scrubbing.

The new protocols no doubt made a difference. But concern remains. A study reported in the *Annals of Internal Medicine* in January 1999 found that healthcare workers not only wash less frequently than they should, but many of them don't even wash for as much as ten seconds—though most protocols require at least thirty seconds of scrubbing. A Duke University study reported in November, 1999, found that only 17 percent of physicians treating ICU patients washed their hands appropriately.

It seems a lot of people in the medical field are still going through the motions today.

Master Dye Test

The Great Physician warned that the same sort of thing can happen spiritually. He had his own "dye test" and made it clear that the Pharisees were failing it. He told them their actions amounted to nothing more than superficial, outward scrubbing. They had become obsessed with peripheral things, while he was more concerned with a true, inner cleansing of the heart.

Luke 11:38–40 says, "The Pharisee, noticing that Jesus did not first wash before the meal, was surprised. [*Horrified* might be a more accurate word than *surprised*.] Then the Lord said to him, 'Now then, you Pharisees clean the outside of the cup and dish, but inside you are full of greed and wickedness. You foolish people! Did not the one who made the outside make the inside also?'"

In Mark's account of this incident Jesus goes on to say it's not what's on the outside of a person, or even what goes into a person's stomach (a reference to strict Jewish dietary laws), but "what comes out of a man is what makes him 'unclean.' For from within, out of men's hearts, come evil thoughts, sexual immorality, theft, murder, adultery, greed, malice, deceit, lewdness, envy, slander, arrogance and folly. All these evils come from inside and make a man 'unclean'" (Mark 7:20–23).

Dr. Jesus is saying that spiritually it's not enough to go through the motions. We also have to go farther than carefully scrubbing under the fingernails and down in the webs of the fingers. We must go deep enough to make sure even our inner heart is clean. And that standard of cleanliness isn't easy to achieve.

Simple hand washing sometimes presents a challenge. On a recent medical mission trip to minister in African prisons, our team saw hundreds of prisoners a day. We set up our clinic under a tent that local Prison Fellowship volunteers erected out in the prison yard, away from a regular water source.

With all the cases we saw it was impossible to take the time to scrub between patients. And with three or four docs working side by side, it wouldn't have been practical to set up a basin of water where we could wash with soap; any water would have been filthy in no time.

So we each carried a small dispenser of an antiseptic gel with us. We kept it in our pocket or set it out on the table in front of us so we'd see it. Then, after every case, before we greeted the next patient, we would pull it out and squirt some on our hands to kill the bacteria and keep from passing disease from one patient to another, or to ourselves. There are so many diseases running rampant through Africa's prisons that this was something we knew was necessary to stay healthy and to keep other people healthy.

In the same way, if we are going to maintain our spiritual health as a Christian in a world seriously contaminated by sin, we

> *If we are going to maintain our spiritual health, we have to do whatever it takes to keep our hearts scrubbed clean. But it's not like they dispense a gel that wipes out sin.*

have to do whatever it takes to keep our hearts scrubbed clean. But it's not like they dispense a gel that wipes out sin. So what do we need to do this?

A Sensitivity to the Dirt

It's so easy to deceive ourselves, to think, like the unwitting doctors who took the dye test, that our usual practice isn't a problem. In fact, however, we aren't scrubbing nearly as often as we think, and our haphazard routine leaves a lot to be desired. If that's the case, we run the risk of becoming the kind of people Proverbs 30:12 refers to as "those who are pure in their own eyes and yet are not cleansed of their filth."

In contrast, the most committed Christians I know have a real sensitivity to the dirt. They are conscious of any sin and deal with issues immediately as they arise.

For example, there's a staff member in my office for whom I have a great deal of respect as a Christian. Recently we were talking about a certain program we were going to have to bring to an end. This staffer made the comment, with two or three other people around: "You know, I really had my doubts whether this thing was going to work from the beginning."

The next day this person came to me and said, "Dave, I've really got to apologize."

"Apologize for what?" I wanted to know.

"Well, for that comment yesterday. I didn't want you to think that I was holding this in and for some reason not sharing with you how I really felt. And I didn't want to embarrass you in front of the other staff by sounding as if I was telling you so."

I said, "I didn't take it that way at all. I merely considered it an offhand comment."

Just that quickly and simply, the air was cleared between us. This person's heart was so sensitized to the potential for conflict and sin that he did not want to offend or come across in the wrong way. The mere possibility of harm had weighed so heavily on his mind that night that he thought about it, prayed about it, and the next day came and asked forgiveness. Now that's being sensitive to the dirt.

An Awareness of God's Purity

It's easier to develop such a sensitivity if we also have an awareness of God's purity. Jesus himself should serve as our dye test. When we hold ourselves up against his example, the dirt really shows. The trouble is, we don't do that often enough.

> *Jesus himself should serve as our dye test. When we hold ourselves up against his example, the dirt really shows.*

Too many of us routinely come into God's presence without preparing properly. We forget that God is holy, that he is perfectly pure. Yet we come before him just as if we were walking into an operating room without scrubbing—without first cleansing our hearts.

It's not surprising that in our feel-good society we try to forget or simply ignore sin. Even in our churches we sometimes talk more about the spiritual implications of a healthy self-image, dealing with issues, and solving relational problems than we do sin, its symptoms, and its ramifications.

We are encouraged to come before God anytime to ask that he: bless our children, provide us the finances we need, help me with my problem at work, heal Aunt Minnie who's been sick, and fulfill a long grocery list of requests. Yet we're seldom reminded that whenever we come before him we should first make sure our hearts are pure so that we can be in a right relationship with him. I don't think we really see the holiness of God, the purity of God.

We are too often like somebody walking into an operating room without knowing what's sterile and what's not. If you do that and accidentally bump up against someone, that person then becomes contaminated. If you touch the instrument table, it means ditching the instruments and having to get another sterilized set.

In the same way, if we come into God's presence or try to assist him in his work without proper preparation, without first scrubbing our hearts, we can contaminate the field and ruin what God wants to do in our lives or in the lives of others.

A Strategy for Dealing with the Dirt

Once we become sensitive to the dirt in our lives and see the glaring difference between us and the purity of the Great Physician himself, we need a protocol that enables us to deal with it. God spelled out the basic goals when through Isaiah he instructed his people to "wash and make yourselves clean. Take your evil deeds out of my sight! Stop doing wrong!" (Isa. 1:16). He presented it as a requirement, not merely a suggestion.

> *If we come into God's presence or try to assist him in his work without proper preparation, without first scrubbing our hearts, we contaminate the field and ruin what God wants to do in our lives or in the lives of others.*

Achieving those goals requires *confession* first of all—not just one time, but continuously. We are like little kids who are always getting dirty outside. We have a choice. We can stop, acknowledge our dirty state, and get cleaned up at the door, or we can ignore (or try to hide) our condition, walk on into the house, and make a huge mess.

We have that same choice in our relationship with other people and with God. Honest confession is our most productive course, yet this important part of prayer is often neglected—despite the fact that God has said that anyone wanting to enter into his presence needs to come with "clean hands and a pure heart" (Ps. 24:4).

Admitting the Problem

Confession is an essential step in effective inner scrubbing. We have no choice but to say, "God, this is dirt, it's wrong, it shouldn't be there, it's in my life, and I need to have it removed." Then we need to ask him, especially if there's sin involved, to forgive us for that.

Many times our offense is not just before God, but it is also an offense before others—our Christian brothers and sisters, or perhaps non-Christians—whether by words or actions or even attitudes. If we really hope to be near to God and draw others nearer to him, we need to deal with all those offenses and scrub ourselves by being willing to apologize, to confess, and to deal with the issues and their consequences.

This is a hard lesson to teach our children. But it may be even harder for us as adults because of our own pride and the fact that sometimes the dirt is deep down or has been there for a long time. It's really rubbed into us—way down into the pores of our skin.

I always hated to get called to surgery when I had been gardening or working on the car. I had to scrub forever. I could see grease way down deep under my fingernails, and it hurt to get it out. I had to dig down in there with the file and then get the brush bristles down in there and really scrub to get it all. And if I didn't do a good job, it was obvious, because I would still have these telltale black lines under my fingernails.

It's the same way with sin in our lives. Sometimes it runs so deep or has been there for so many years in relationships with other people that we know it's going to take some deep scrubbing to get it all out— scrubbing that hurts. And even then we may need to ask another person to examine us to make certain all the dirt is gone, after we've confessed our sin before them.

Who Do We Answer To?

A second valuable part of our strategy for dealing with the dirt is *accountability*. We often need help in coming and staying clean.

In an operating-room situation, part of the scrub nurse's and circulating nurse's job is to be watching for sources of contamination. Even though I'm the doctor and I may be in charge, the scrub nurse won't hesitate a second to tell me, "Doctor, you touched that! You've contaminated yourself." Or, "You're going to have to rescrub." "You'll need to reglove." "I will have to regown you."

There are many times in life when we might benefit from an alert scrub nurse. In areas where we are really struggling, we need someone to help hold us accountable—to call attention to a transgression we don't want to admit, perhaps something we didn't even realize we did, or a person we unintentionally hurt or offended.

> *It's not enough to say, "Hold me accountable," then not listen to what people say.*

Sometimes a spouse can do that for us. Or somebody in our Bible study group. A friend at church. A Christian colleague at work. We may need their help in dealing with our anger, our tendency to use unkind words, gossiping, or any number of other things that have been chronic bad habits—the ground-in stuff that can be so difficult to cleanse out of our lives. We need to have other people help hold us accountable, ask them to do that, *and* be willing to listen and take to heart what they say.

As a doctor in the operating room, I hold rank. I'm still in charge. I can just say to the scrub nurse, "No, my arm did not touch that wall. I am not going to rescrub!" But I'd be pretty stupid to do that, knowing somebody's going to suffer.

So there needs to be a willingness to be held accountable. It's not enough to say, "Hold me accountable," and then not listen to what people say. Listening and then submitting yourself to that accountability are essential requirements. A lot of Christians struggle with this, but I have found this a valuable part of the scrubbing process.

Developing a Habit

Finally, no strategy is going to work unless it becomes a *habit*. During the time I was working on this manuscript, I came across an interesting article in *U.S. News and World Report* about the building of a new Chicago hospital affiliated with Northwestern Medical School. Someone conducting yet another study of doctors' hygiene habits found that physicians on hospital rounds didn't routinely wash their hands before examining patients in their rooms. They claimed they washed after examining patients and clearly realized they should. Most of them fully intended to wash their hands. But the only sink in the hospital rooms were the ones in the bathroom, and doctors said they felt as if they were intruding to go into the patient's only private space.

So they would think, *I'll wash at the sink in the hallway before I go to the next room.* Then they would get paged, somebody would stop them in the hallway, a nurse would ask them a question, and they wouldn't get their hand-washing done. So to help facilitate the habit, planners put a second sink right inside the door of each patient room in the new hospital. That sink was for the doctor and the nurses and anyone else taking care of the patient to wash their hands before they left the room. The heart of their strategy for decreasing the hospital's infection rate was to make a habit out of better scrubbing.

As a doctor I know that no amount of scrubbing will ever make me completely sterile. As a Christian I also know that no amount of heart cleansing will make me completely pure spiritually; the Great Physician's standards are higher than our standards.

But we should never use our imperfection as an excuse. I am not going to get every germ off my hands when I scrub. Thus I know if a glove breaks, my hands are still going to contaminate the patient, but not nearly as much as they would if I hadn't scrubbed.

> *As a doctor I know that no amount of scrubbing will ever make me completely sterile. As a Christian I also know that no amount of heart cleansing will make me completely pure spiritually; the Great Physician's standards are higher than our standards.*

It's the same way in our lives. We are never going to be perfect Christians, but at the same time we must realize that we have an obligation to do the best we can in this area. Just as a doctor who is not careful can contaminate his patients, if we as Christians haven't scrubbed our hearts clean and confessed our own contamination before God, our sin is sure to infect the hearts and lives of all those around us.

Just as a major reason surgery failed throughout history was contamination, one of the biggest reasons Christians have failed in representing God and reaching the world with his message has also been contamination—in our churches and in our individual lives. We can revolutionize our lives, our churches, and our world if we take Jesus' teaching about inner scrubbing to heart.

James 4:8 elaborates on Jesus' idea and states it even more clearly: "Come near to God and he will come near to you. Wash your hands, you sinners, and purify your hearts, you double-minded." Proper scrubbing is a requirement of any closer walk with God. In other words, part of our reason to be properly scrubbed and sterile is not only to protect the patient and others, but to protect and benefit ourselves.

Sometimes when I put on gloves, it's not because I'm going to contaminate someone else but because they are going to contaminate me. Let's say I am doing a dirty procedure, such as lancing something that's already infected, like a big boil or an abscess. I don't necessarily walk over to the sink and go through a lengthy scrubbing process, but I am going to put on a pair of gloves. I know that if I don't and I get this contamination on me, it will be harder to get myself cleansed, and I also stand a good chance of contaminating others.

What Jesus said about inner cleansing applies here as well. Not only do we need our inner beings scrubbed, we also need to place *protections* around us to keep us from being contaminated. We need to glove so we don't contaminate our lives or our children. But how do we put a glove around our home? Around our loved ones? Around our own minds? Keeping our hearts and minds clean as Jesus prescribed is tougher than ever today. But it's just as important.

In the operating room everything that comes up to the table where the surgery is going to take place has to be sterile. The Mayo stand that contains the instruments has a sterile cover over the top of it to protect them and you from contamination. The electrocautery cord and handle are sterile. Even the operating-room light has a special handle you put on it that has been sterilized so that you can move the light without contaminating yourself. The patient too is draped with sterile drapes. Everything you touch you want to have clean so there's no contamination that comes to you or to the patient.

The Great Physician demands the same high standards in his operating room. If he's going to do his work in our lives and work through us on other people's lives, he expects us to not only scrub but also to protect ourselves from any type of contamination—not just in what we touch every day but from

> *Not only do we need our inner beings scrubbed, we also need to place protections around us to keep us from being contaminated. We need to glove so we don't contaminate our lives or our children.*

the television, movies, and videos we watch, the music we hear, and the like. If we are not careful, even the books we read can contaminate our worldview. If we want to remain spiritually healthy, we need to understand and apply what the Great Physician had to say about proper scrubbing.

One day a well-dressed Kenyan businessman we had never seen before arrived at Tenwek complaining of chronic abdominal pain. He had experienced that pain and had an intermittent fever for two years—ever since his surgery for appendicitis. The patient had lost weight because of loss of appetite. Because he was often too sick to work, his business had suffered. So had his relationships with friends and family. He said he had visited a number of doctors without any resolution. Now he was desperate.

His workup suggested infection, but his abdominal incision was well-healed. He complained of tenderness in the right lower quadrant, but his abdominal x-ray was not diagnostic.

We finally decided to do exploratory surgery. It revealed a chronic abscess in the right abdomen. The cause? His previous surgeon had left a plain gauze (with no radiopaque string in it to show up on an x-ray). We removed it and returned the patient to good health.

Many of us have a hidden sin or pain we haven't dealt with (sometimes for years), tucked away where we think no one will find it. Perhaps it's an addiction to pornography, an illicit affair, something stolen, an abortion at an early age—something we don't let anyone else know about, a concealed, unconfessed sin that is affecting our relationships and threatening our lives.

Just as surely as that patient with the abscess would have soon died without surgery, so these hidden sins contaminate our souls. Unless they are dealt with, they will destroy us.

It's almost impossible to deal with problems like these by ourselves. It may take painful surgery and exploration from the Great Physician and often one of his assistants, such as a trained Christian counselor or pastor. But once the problem is removed from our lives and we return to health, we will find that the pain and effort were worth it.

After my most recent trip to Africa to work in the prisons, I faced a thirty-six-hour trip back to the United States. I'd already been up all day when I left. So I got on the plane dirty, sweaty, and no doubt a little smelly. By the time I got off the plane I felt even worse. It seemed like the greatest feeling in the world to step into a shower and finally get clean.

The same sort of feeling is possible for us spiritually. Whenever our hearts and minds are dirty, God is waiting to scrub us clean.

The Great Physician knows how to properly scrub.

THE GREAT
PHYSICIAN ADVOCATED
A UNIQUE SAVING PLAN

DOCTORS ARE IN THE LIFE-SAVING BUSINESS. THAT'S why we went to school for all those years. It's why we take phone calls and get up in the middle of the night. Occasionally God actually gives us those dramatic moments when we literally pull someone back from death's door.

One such experience, among the most memorable cases of my medical-missionary career, took place at the very outset of our time in Africa. Jody and I spent our first six months in Kenya learning to speak Kipsigis. During that time we lived twenty-five miles south of Tenwek, a rough one- to two-hour drive away from the demands of the hospital. In this way we could concentrate on our daily language training supervised by a veteran missionary couple who lived on a small mission compound near the little town of Kaboson. Edwina (Eddie) Goff, the nurse who staffed the mission's small,

rather primitive two-room clinic in Kaboson, was under strict orders not to call me except for the most extreme emergencies. I was there to learn the language, not to practice medicine.

But one afternoon someone ran up to the tiny two-bedroom concrete blockhouse where we were living, shouting "Dr. Stevens! Dr. Stevens! Come quickly!"

I sprinted a quarter of a mile to the clinic, where the nurse had a woman in labor with a baby in fetal distress due to a prolapsed cord. That meant that the umbilical cord was down alongside the baby's head and actually protruding into the vagina. Thus everytime the woman's uterus contracted, it clamped down so hard around the infant's head that it pinched off the blood supply and threatened to asphyxiate the baby. A prolapsed cord is one of the direst emergencies in obstetrics and requires immediate delivery, usually by emergency C-section, if there is to be any chance of saving the baby.

> *While I'm literally locked in a life-or-death shoving match in the back-seat, there's a sweet middle-aged missionary nurse in the front, hunched over the steering wheel and driving like a maniac over some of the worst and ruttiest dirt roads in the world.*

The Kaboson clinic didn't have the instruments, much less the facilities, for a C-section. We had to get the woman to Tenwek. Meantime, the only way to keep this baby alive was to get its head up off the cord by actually pushing the baby back up into the uterus with my gloved hand. This wasn't an easy thing to do since the uterus is a terribly strong muscle, and every time this woman had a contraction we had a shoving match to see whether or not I was going to be able to hold that baby's head up off the cord.

The only vehicle at the clinic that day was Eddie Goff's 1968 Volkswagen Beetle. So Eddie pulled the car around by the clinic door. With my hand still inserted and with a sheet pulled over this poor lady for the sake of modesty, we loaded our patient into this VW Bug and laid her down on the backseat lengthwise (as if there is such a thing in the backseat of a Beetle). She had her knees as high in the air as she could get them. I knelt on the floor of the backseat with my arm stuck halfway to the elbow up this poor woman's birth canal trying desperately to keep that baby's head off the cord.

Picture the scene: Every time I feel a contraction starting I start yelling, *"Ma tagil! Ma tagil!"* ("Don't push! Don't push!" I hadn't learned a lot of Kipsigis yet, but I have never forgotten that phrase). And while I'm literally locked in a life-or-death shoving match in the backseat, there's a sweet middle-aged missionary nurse in the front, hunched over the steering wheel and driving like a maniac over some of the worst and ruttiest dirt roads in the world.

We hadn't gone very far at all before the constriction caused first my fingers, then my hand, and eventually part of my forearm to go numb because all the blood had been squeezed right out of it. This woman had a tight pelvis and the contractions only made it worse until I couldn't feel anything. After the first ten minutes I could no longer tell if the cord was pulsing or not, so I had no idea if the baby was still alive. All I could do was pray, yell, and push, even though I felt as if a giant anaconda had me in a vice grip.

After a wild hour-and-a-half ride we got to Tenwek. We rushed the woman straight into surgery, where Ernie did an immediate C-section. Incredibly, both mother and baby survived.

Immediately after I turned the patient over to our hospital staff, my hand began to swell until it was almost three times its normal size. It was blue and looked as if I had tightly wrapped a tourniquet on it for an hour and a half. For two whole days I had no feeling in the hand and seriously wondered if my surgical career had been ended because a laboring woman had squeezed my hand to death.

Only after my hand recovered could I finally look back on the whole experience and laugh. It had been much like something out of an old Laurel and Hardy movie. With Eddie at the wheel gunning that VW Bug (as much as you could gun a Beetle) like a wild woman, I knelt in the back screaming, *"Ma tagil! Ma tagil!"* In retrospect it must have looked and sounded absolutely hilarious.

> *This doctor propped himself up on the operating table, self-administered a local anesthetic, positioned a hand-held mirror so he could see what was going on, and gave step-by-step directions as his assistant took out the doctor's appendix.*

But it had been no laughing matter at the time. It was one of those occasional cases where I knew I had fought a touch-and-go battle with death—and won.

The Great Physician had his share of experiences successfully providing healing and treatment to a number of patients on the verge of death. He even brought some patients back to life after they had already died. No M.D. in history ever knew more than Dr. Jesus about saving lives. We would do well to take note of his unique perspective on the life-saving strategies he attempted to teach his disciples in Matthew 16:25: "For whoever wants to save his life will lose it, but whoever loses his life for me will find it."

That was one of the many lessons Dr. Jesus' interns didn't understand at first. In my mind I can see them puzzling over the words like a riddle. The application to us today may not be any more clear at first, for Jesus isn't talking about saving lives in a literal sense. Moreover, he's not talking about saving others' lives, but rather how we might save our own lives.

I heard the story some years ago about a missionary doctor in a remote area in North Africa who did just that when he developed appendicitis. He was the only physician at his hospital. The closest medical help was many days away over very rough roads. He knew he was in no condition to make the trip and couldn't wait days for treatment anyway.

So this doctor told his national assistant to come with him to the OR. He propped himself up on the operating table, self-administered a local anesthetic, positioned a handheld mirror so he could see what was going on, and gave step-by-step directions as his assistant took out the doctor's appendix. (I'd be giving directions too if I had someone without any formal surgical training operating on me.) This missionary doctor literally saved his own life with that operation.

But that's not what the Great Physician was talking about either; in fact, he wasn't even talking about saving lives in a physical sense. Perhaps we can begin to zero in on Jesus' meaning by looking in a dictionary and seeing that to *save* means "to secure, to keep from loss, to secure from injury."

SECURITY OR ETERNITY?

That's something most of us, whether we are doctors or not, know a lot about. I will go so far as to say a large percentage of Americans spend most of their time trying to make sure they are as secure as possible from possible future danger. We work hard at ensuring security.

If I came to your house and tripped on the rug as I walked in the door, you wouldn't worry about my filing a lawsuit because you have liability insurance. If you get sick and have to be hospitalized, you know your health insurance is going to pay the vast majority of your bill. If you are a doctor, you pay humongous premiums every year for malpractice insurance to keep your practice and profession secure. You have planned ahead; you want to make sure your family's physical and financial health are secure. As Americans we buy all sorts of insurance—dental, home, health, auto, unemployment, liability, and the like. But what insurance companies are really selling is security.

We spend billions of dollars every year in this country on home-security systems. We pay extra for warranties on our cars. We buy backup systems for our office and home computers—all in an attempt to have a sense of security in our everyday life.

And it doesn't end there. Most of us are even more concerned about securing our more distant futures. We plan and save carefully for our children's education or our own retirement. We invest in a variety of mutual funds. We don't want to be caught with an unbalanced portfolio, so we have large-cap, small-cap, international, balanced, sector, growth, and income funds. We also try to diversify with all types of bond funds. And maybe, just to be sure, we buy a REIT fund so that we can benefit from the real-estate game. We may dabble in some futures trading, but we keep a reasonable balance accessible in a money-market fund for unplanned emergencies. We try to make sure to fully fund our 401(k) plans or our SEPs or our pension plans. And, of course, we should remember the children's educational IRAs, our 403(b) plan, and perhaps a Roth IRA.

We all want to do everything we can to make sure that those last years of our lives are secure. (And we try not to get too stressed out remembering to do all that because stress isn't good for our long-term security.)

As Americans we work hard at being secure. We exercise to stay healthy. Are you watching your weight and is your cholesterol right? How are we going to enjoy that retirement that we are working so hard to prepare for if we don't take care of our health? Maybe you are trying a different diet, like the millions of other Americans spending billions on the latest "no effort, no pain" fad. We pay more so we can eat less. Or maybe you have bought another exercise machine you saw advertised on one of the cable networks, or purchased a membership in a local health club. Why? Because, we all want the security of knowing we are in the best shape possible for the days ahead.

We buy advice books on how to grow our gardens, train our pets, and raise our children. Why? Because we want to be more secure. Security is a basic human need. We also spend our spare time repairing and improving our houses, working on our yards, and making sure that our children get the best opportunities, because we want them to be secure as well. Then we go to church on Sunday morning without noticing the irony when we sing, as I often do, "My hope is built on nothing less, than Jesus' blood and righteousness."

Don't get me wrong. It's wise to be a good steward, to plan ahead, and to guard our family now and in the future. The problem arises when that becomes our primary focus and what we place our faith in.

We make that mistake when we fail either to see the application of Dr. Jesus' own life-saving prescription or to realize that most of the world can't even begin to think about security in our terms. Let me illustrate what I mean with a few quick word-picture postcards from some of the places I have been the last few years.

Postmark Russia

I visited the former Soviet Union several times in the early 1990s when World Medical Mission sent doctors in with desperately needed medical equipment and supplies, to teach cutting-edge medical procedures and to evangelize medical professionals. Outside Moscow I visited the historic town of Zgorsk, where the "Vatican" of the Russian Orthodox Church is located. The sun glistening off the gold minarets rising high above the town walls made it seem like we were entering some sort of magical, fairy-tale world as we approached.

As I walked through the gates into an ancient square containing Russia's most famous cathedral, however, my attention was forced from the ornate buildings above to the lines etched in the faces of the elderly crowd gathered along the street, each with a hand out. Each one was begging for just a little something, anything they might be able to use to put food on their table that night. To understand their predicament, imagine inflation so staggering that the price of Coca-Cola soared to $500 a can. That's what the Russian economy had been through over a three-year period. No retirement income or personal savings plan could withstand that. Thus, all these old pensioners on a fixed income were literally starving to death.

They had no security.

Imagine inflation so staggering that the price of Coca-Cola soared to $500 a can. That's what the Russian economy had been through over a three-year period.

Postmark Haiti

On another occasion, I was touring Hospital Luminaire in Haiti, a mission facility in a poor rural area of the country with a physician who graciously offered to take me on rounds to see some of the problems they were facing. In the pediatric ward we happened upon a beautiful ten-year-old girl. At least she looked beautiful until we went around to the opposite side of the bed and saw that the other side of her face was heavily bandaged. As the doctor removed her dressing I groaned inaudibly. Half of the right side of her face was gone. I asked the missionary physician, "What happened?"

He explained that economic conditions had become so bad that many soldiers were taking the law into their own hands. At night, once they were off duty, they would remove their uniforms but take their M-16s to rob the homes of local businesspeople. When they came to this girl's home, her father refused to open the door. They blasted the house with their automatic weapons, and a bullet took half the child's face off.

She didn't have any security.

Postmark Somalia

I had never before been anywhere like Mogadishu shortly after U.S. expeditionary forces landed there. I flew in several times to help start and supervise a medical-relief outreach in that war-torn land. When I got off the plane, there wasn't a soul there to meet me—no customs, no immigration, no police, no judges, no government. If you had any official problem or complaint, there was no one to go to. You were on your own, and so was everyone else.

Franklin Graham, head of the relief agency Samaritan's Purse, was my boss at the time and went with me on one trip. When we arrived in Mogadishu, he shook his head and said, "David, this is a picture of what the world is going to be like after the Rapture—total anarchy." Can you imagine practicing medicine where patients were so desperate to see you that people had to beat them away with sticks? That really happened in Somalia.

I began to realize how Jesus must have felt when the crowds pressed in on him demanding healing for themselves and their loved ones. We would no sooner set up our clinic at a refugee feeding center than a huge crowd gathered around, held back only by thin ropes strung around our perimeter. We were planning on seeing four hundred patients a day—working as fast as we could get them in. When I looked at my watch, we were seeing patients at an average of one every three to four minutes.

Most of these people had not seen a doctor in *years*, and they were there with their children or other loved ones. Scared to death that we were going to pack up and leave before we saw them all, they pressed closer, ever closer. Near the end of the day, the elders in the refugee feeding camp were literally cutting sticks down from the trees and beating the people back to keep us from being mobbed. I had to stand on my chair,

> *Can you imagine practicing medicine where patients were so desperate to see you that people had to beat them away with sticks? That really happened in Somalia.*

order the beatings to stop, and reassure everyone that we would be back the next day. There is no way I could fault these people. Their families not only didn't have health care, many of them had no health.

I remember one eleven-year-old boy. Hasad was nothing but skin and bones and had a badly infected sore on his leg that I feared might be extending down into the bone. Osteomyelitis is a serious condition and difficult to treat. The clinic was almost over for the day, so I took a few moments to talk with him as I debrided his wound. Through a translator I said, "Tell me what happened to you, Hasad."

He said, "My family lived outside of Baidoa. My father was a farmer. We had sheep and some goats. He wasn't a very wealthy man, but we got by. Then one day men came from another clan. They stole all our goats and all our sheep. Then they took my father out in front of our hut and shot him in front of the whole family.

"We tried to survive, but we had so little and the rains didn't come. Finally my mother died of starvation; she was working as hard as she could trying to keep us alive and gave us her portion of food. Then my brother died, and it was just my sister and me left. We heard there was food in Mogadishu. So even though it was more than three hundred kilometers [roughly two hundred miles] away, we began to walk. After many days my sister collapsed and died in a ditch by the side of the road." Then he concluded his story by matter-of-factly explaining how he pulled the sides of the ditch down over his sister's body and dragged himself into Mogadishu to the feeding camp.

There were too many stories like Hasad's in Somalia, and more in Sudan after that. In Rwanda a few years later. In Chechnya while I'm working on this manuscript. And I have no doubt there will be more in war zones we have yet to learn the names of in years to come.

Many people in this world, like Hasad, have no security at all.

The Great Physician knew that. He lived and practiced in an occupied land, torn by political conflict. Countless innocent people suffered and died because there was no health care to speak of and precious little justice to be had from the authorities. The people of Israel had little in the way of security in Jesus' day.

> *The Great Physician lived and practiced in an occupied land, torn by political conflict. Countless innocent people suffered and died because there was no health care to speak of. The people of Israel had little in the way of security in Jesus' day.*

Yet it was in that setting, like much of our world today, that Jesus said anyone who concentrates on securing his life will lose it. To *lose* the dictionary says means "to forfeit, to relinquish, to throw away." I think the words "to throw away" paint a vivid picture. Jesus was saying, "By trying to secure our lives, many of us end up throwing them away."

A Risky Investment

Isn't that true? Think about it. We invest so much of our time, energy, and money trying to make our lives more secure, and we make a bigger mess of things than ever. The unprecedented divorce rate in our society has made family less stable and secure than ever in history.

We spend so much to try to provide security for our children. Yet kids today face more and greater risks to their emotional and spiritual (not to mention physical) health than we did when we were growing up.

Stress-related illnesses have skyrocketed. We develop, market, and prescribe antidepressant drugs in record numbers. Yet suicide rates keep climbing. We are dissatisfied, unhappy, and burning out just trying to cope with it all. When it really boils down to it, so many of us remain miserable.

Here's where we need to take a closer look at Jesus' words. In essence he is saying: "Whoever relinquishes his life for me will secure it." My mother frequently quoted a saying as I was growing up that put this principle in a slightly different way: "Only one life, 'twill soon be past, only what's done for Christ will last."

The older I get, the more my experience bears that out. The closer I get to the end of life, the more I am reminded of how short life is and how only what I do for the kingdom of God will truly matter. I never understood that more clearly than when I was given . . .

Just Ten Minutes to Live

What would you do if you knew for certain you were going to die in the next few minutes? What would you think about?

I was in Zambia a few years ago when I had one of those "nearer, my God, to thee" experiences. I had been visiting a number of mission hospitals throughout central Africa and was flying in the oldest and smallest plane I had ever been in—a 1950-something Cessna 172. I had seen sewing machines with motors larger than that plane had.

When I expressed a measure of skepticism before the first leg of our flight, the pilot apologized that his usual plane was in for repairs. But this veteran missionary pilot assured me I needn't worry; the Cessna would get us where we were going. We landed at a tiny strip near Mukinge Hospital without any trouble. But when we took off the next morning, our wheels literally scraped the treetops at the end of the runway. Every stop after that we landed at larger strips in nearby towns, where we were met and driven by car out to the hospitals for visits.

My pilot assured me that after crash-landing three planes in the course of his flying career, he didn't believe in taking unnecessary chances. I sincerely appreciated his discretion but had mixed feelings about his reported flying record. It's a little disconcerting to know that the guy at the controls of your plane has already crashed three others. Still, there was something reassuring about his survival record.

We were on the last leg of that trip, about three hundred miles back to the capital city of Lusaka. We had been up for about an hour and a half and I was concentrating on the screen of my laptop computer. All of a sudden, a big clanking noise shot through the cabin. I knew we were in trouble when the pilot turned around to me and asked, "Did we hit a bird? What happened?"

> *It's a little disconcerting to know that the guy at the controls of your plane has already crashed three others. Still, there was something reassuring about his survival record.*

I looked up between him and the guy sitting in the copilot seat and I could see the altimeter; we were starting to lose altitude even though he still had the throttle wide open. Within a few seconds trickles of oil covered the windshield. Knowing that was a bad sign, I instinctively looked at the ground out my side window and saw we were flying over scrub desert. There wasn't a leaf, there wasn't a water hole, there wasn't a flat field, there wasn't a hut, there wasn't a road anywhere in sight. There was nothing in that whole area of Zambia—except rolling hills of brush, giant termite mounds, rocks, and ravines.

The pilot flipped on the radio and began calling, "Mayday! Mayday! Mayday! Do you copy?" and gave our call sign. No response. The old VHF radio in that plane only had a range of about forty miles. The pilot pulled his map out and looked, but there wasn't an airstrip closer than a hundred miles. All of a sudden we realized we weren't going home as we planned. In fact, we might be going home for good.

What do you think about in a situation like that? I had never really considered how I would react. My first thought was to wonder if it might help to throw out the suitcases, the seats, anything. But I quickly realized it wouldn't. There was nothing to be done. We were going down, and within minutes we would be on the ground, one way or another.

In those ten minutes I realized I was going to miss my family. I had dreamed of growing old with my wife; I was going to miss Jody. I had wanted to see my children grow up; I was going to miss my kids. But other than that, I realized I had no real regrets. If I was going to die, I was ready to go, for I knew I had invested my life in the right things.

We were only 150 feet from the ground when we cleared another long hilly ridge. The engine coughed and gave a big rattle that shook the plane. The pilot reached over and turned it off. That was it—no hope he could start it again.

I looked out the window again just in time to spot the grass roofs of two huts—the first signs of habitation we had seen for miles. Just past the huts the terrain flattened out, bare ground washed free of brush during the floods of the last rainy season. The pilot shouted for us to put our heads down as he pulled back on the control stick to set that little plane on its tail. Everything seemed like slow motion as we hit the ground at about forty miles per hour right between two termite mounds, bounced violently a few times, and jerked to a sudden stop with the nose only five feet from another twelve-foot-high termite mound, baked rock hard in the tropical sun.

We had barely climbed out of the plane and started breathing again before a Zambian man came running up from one of the huts we had just seen. He was a schoolteacher. Since they teach in English in Zambia, I will never forget his words as he looked at me in amazement and said, "Thank God! You were already dead!"

Not, "You could have been killed" or "You almost died." But a simple statement of fact, "You were already dead." That gave new meaning to Jesus' words for me. The Great Physician was saying only if we are "already dead" to ourselves for his sake can we find true life and the security we all long for.

Too many of us think about future security only in terms of our personal-savings and retirement plans. Jesus spelled out a very different personal-savings plan for his disciples as he himself was contemplating the end of his life. The wisdom of it became clearer to me that day after contemplating the end of mine.

> *He looked at me in amazement and said, "Thank God! You were already dead!"*

Every time I have thought about that experience since then, I have asked myself, "When my life is indeed finally over on this earth, when my last ten minutes are really up, how will I have invested my life? Have I invested in the most important things?"

I never consider those questions without thinking of something Charles Swindoll once said on this subject. When the final score is added up one day and we stand before the Lord, a lot of us are going to "wish we'd played a lot more Risk and a lot less Trivial Pursuit."

ONE SOUND INVESTMENT STRATEGY

I see a number of practical ways we can all apply Jesus' advice about losing our lives for him. Here are a few principles I have learned about the Master on how to invest your life rightly.

First, **it pays to invest early.** Every financial planner, every mutual-fund manager, will tell you the same thing. The sooner you put your money in, the greater the results in the end. As Christ's followers, as leaders in the church, as Christian parents, we have a responsibility to invest our lives in his service at the earliest opportunity. It's so easy to put it off.

We tell ourselves (and God):

- when the kids get a little older
- after we have a little bit more money

- once my career is a little better established
- when this takes place or after that happens

then I'll be able to do what I think God wants to have me do. We need to begin early to use Jesus' investment advice, if for no other reason than for the sake of our children. Do they see us investing in what's most important? More is always caught than taught. Examples speak louder than words.

How do our kids see us investing our lives? They will remember! Do you know what my fondest, most meaningful memories of my evangelist father are? Not of him playing baseball with me, not of fishing or any of the other fun things we did together. When I remember my dad best, I can still see him down on his knees at an altar, leading someone to Jesus Christ. I will never forget that picture or what it says to me about how he invested his life.

It wasn't easy for him or for Mom. When I was in grade school, he was gone two weeks out of three. In later years Dad told me he used to cry out of loneliness at night in his room because he missed his family so much. But he knew God had called him, and he didn't put it off until later.

You need to **choose where to invest**—not whether to invest. In our financial investments, we choose between putting our money into IRAs and TSAs and Keoughs and 401(k)s and mutual funds and money markets and whatever. We have even more choices in how and where we invest our lives.

Jesus calls each of us to our own mission fields. Some of them may be halfway around the world. Others may be in our own community, our own church, our own home. But they all have one thing in common. I understood it as my plane was going down in Zambia because my own father had told me again and again what I also saw him demonstrate with his life: "David, the most important thing you can do with your life is to invest it in the lives of other people."

Invest all you can. Good financial advisors will tell you that most people can afford to invest more than they think they can. The same thing is true of the Great Physician's investment advice. If we invest our whole lives as Jesus asks, it will require more than just an investment of money; it will also need an investment of energy, talent, and time.

Invest where you can realize the greatest gain. If you had an opportunity to invest at 3 percent or at 15 percent, which would you take? The 15 percent investment, of course. This principle seems so simple. Yet many of us fail to apply it when it comes to where and how we invest our lives. We suffer from tunnel vision that too often prevents our seeing, really seeing, beyond the narrow borders of our own interests, our own history, our own daily life experiences—to the greater needs and investment opportunities that are out there.

I once read a book by a physician who asked, "If there were ten people carrying a log with nine of them on one end and one on the other, which end should you help with?" The logical answer seems so simple here too.

But I often pose this question when I speak to other doctors because so many of our colleagues around the world are holding up their end of the log by themselves. I know this because I visit them regularly and see how overworked and stressed out they are, facing so many needs. They desperately wish someone would come down and help them carry their end of the load—for a month, or two months, or a few weeks, or a lifetime.

You don't have to be a doctor to make an investment in people. All of us need to be looking for people we can invest in, especially people who may be struggling and would welcome anyone who could help ease their load.

Invest regularly. When you do, it becomes a habit. Jim Teeter, a good friend of mine, is a surgeon in Pennsylvania. He has been to the mission field for two months every year since 1962. Every year! And almost every time he goes, he takes a resident and a medical student or two at his own expense so he can mentor them and influence their lives. I know the impact he makes because just seeing his regular, humble commitment has influenced my own life.

The rest of the year Jim lives in a modest home and works hard at his practice. But Jim has made a tremendous impact in missions and in young doctors' lives. Why? Because he has invested regularly in people.

It's never too late to start investing. Early retirement is a growing trend in our country, not limited to, but certainly including, the medical profession. I am meeting more and more early retirees all the time. It's happening in many occupations, and those opting for it all have similar reasons for their decision. They are tired of the rat race. The doctors tend to be fed up with managed care, malpractice, and all the rest. So at 55 or 58 or 60 or 62 they are packing it in and starting other careers. Some are going halfway around the world to serve in mission hospitals. Others, wanting to have impact for the kingdom of God, are volunteering with their local church or a stateside ministry.

Wherever I go to speak, I challenge people to think about how they will invest the remainder of their lives. The U.S. government even encourages you to think this way. You can go overseas and give your retirement income to the mission organization you are serving with. They can pay it to you as foreign-earned salary, which you can have tax-free up to $74,000 a year. Did you know that? It's a well-kept secret.

You can retire cheaper in Kenya or Zambia than you could ever retire in America. There are many places around the world where you can live well on $600 or $700 or $1,000 a month. Where can you do that here?

And it's not just doctors who are welcomed by mission boards today. Chances are some organization could utilize your skills to make a difference overseas. It's one invaluable way to invest the remaining years of your life.

Do you really want to secure your life? The Great Physician prescribed just one way to do that. At first glance it sounds like a tough course to take, but it's been field-tested for almost two thousand years. And his personal-savings plan comes with a *lifetime-plus* guarantee.

That's real security—now and for the future.

THE GREAT PHYSICIAN SPECIALIZED IN IMPOSSIBLE CASES

GET A GROUP OF DOCTORS TOGETHER ANYWHERE in the world and each of them will have a story of some patient who overcame what seemed like insurmountable odds. We have all had cases where we have had to shake our heads in amazement and say, "I can't explain it. I certainly never expected that. I would have said it was impossible! But it happened!"

Tenwek had one of those impossible cases that people were still talking about years later when I arrived. It took place when Don Mullen, a cardiovascular surgeon, was helping out at Tenwek for a month. A patient came in with stenosis of the mitral valve. His heart valve was scarred shut and wasn't allowing enough blood through the left atrium into the heart. We sometimes see this in patients after rheumatic fever.

This particular patient was about to die simply because he was out in the remote reaches of Africa

226

where there was no heart-lung machine to allow the blood flow to bypass the heart while surgeons performed cardiac surgery. Neither did the mission have the means to get this patient to any hospital where such surgery could take place.

So Dan Mullen attempted what seemed like an impossible operation for a mission hospital. He opened the patient's chest and sewed a purse-string suture, something like in a small draw bag, in the left atrium of the heart itself. Next he made a small incision through the wall of the heart inside the ring of the suture, quickly stuck his finger through the incision, and pulled the purse-string suture tight around his finger to keep the patient from bleeding to death. Then,

> *Using just the tip of his finger, which was now inside the man's heart, and operating totally by feel, Don opened the mitral valve by breaking the scars between the leaflets.*

using just the tip of his finger, which was now inside the man's heart, and operating totally by feel, Don opened the mitral valve by breaking the scars between the leaflets. When he finished, he loosened the suture just long enough to withdraw his finger, pulled it tight again, tied it off, and closed the patient up. The man fully recovered. In fact, because a bold doctor was willing to attempt an operation that should have been impossible in a bush hospital that didn't even have an anesthesiologist, let alone heart-bypass equipment, that patient is still alive today.

JESUS' IMPOSSIBLE CASES

One reason modern physicians remember and talk about the impossible cases they have seen or heard about is because they are so unusual. Most of us haven't seen that many in the course of our careers.

The Great Physician, on the other hand, seemed to specialize in impossible cases. If you read through the accounts of his career, you find one example after another. There are numerous references to whole towns that brought their sick to see Dr. Jesus, and he healed all manner of illness and infirmities. Matthew 9:35 says he "went through all the towns and villages . . . healing every disease and sickness." According to Luke 6:17–19, "a great number of people from all over Judea, from Jerusalem, and from the coast of Tyre and Sidon [came] to hear him and to be healed of their diseases . . . and the people all tried to touch him, because power was coming from him and healing them all."

No doubt in the course of seeing all those patients the Great Physician healed a lot of routine problems—runny noses, ear infections, chronic coughs. There's a good chance he treated an occasional ulcer, a sprained ankle here, a kidney stone there.

But virtually all the specific cases mentioned in the Gospels are a lot more dramatic—serious conditions that would have qualified as impossible cases in that day—the blind, the deaf, the mute, the lame, even leprosy, the most dreaded disease of the time. Many of the Great Physician's patients had suffered for years: the woman who had been hemorrhaging for twelve years, the paralytic who had been at the pool of Bethesda for thirty-eight years, the grown man blind since birth, the demon-possessed Gerasene living alone in the local cemetery for much of his life.

> *Lazarus had been dead and buried for so long before Jesus made it to Bethany that people were worried about the stench when the tomb was opened. He wasn't just dead; he was decomposing. Now that's an impossible case for a doctor if ever I heard one!*

In addition there were those patients Jesus actually brought back to life after they had died. I think they would be classified as impossible cases in anyone's book—Jairus's daughter (Matt. 9; Mark 5) and the widow of Nain's son (Luke 7).

But the Great Physician's most impossible case had to have been Lazarus (John 11). Unlike Jairus's daughter, who had just died while Jesus was on the way to see her, or the widow's son, who was in the funeral procession on the way to be buried, Lazarus had been dead and buried for so long before Jesus made it to Bethany that people were worried about the stench when the tomb was opened. He wasn't just dead; he was decomposing. Now that's an impossible case for a doctor if ever I heard one!

Yet this was evidently just the kind of case Jesus was looking for to demonstrate God's power. After all, he had heard his friend was sick but actually delayed his trip and timed his arrival to be there four days after Lazarus's burial.

So what did he do when Lazarus's sister complained that he hadn't been on call when her brother needed him? Jesus made this astounding claim: "He who believes in me will live, even though he dies; and whoever lives and believes in me will never die." Then he challenged Martha's faith by asking her, "Do you believe this?" (John 11:25–26).

After also being confronted by Martha's sister, Mary, and sensing the great sadness of all those who had loved Lazarus, the Great Physician finally took action. He went to the tomb and ordered the stone that sealed the grave to be removed. When Martha expressed concern about the smell, Jesus challenged her faith again saying (John 11:40–45):

> "Did I not tell you that if you believed, you would see the glory of God?"
>
> So they took away the stone. Then Jesus looked up and said, "Father, I thank you that you have heard me. I knew that you always hear me, but I said this for the benefit of the people standing here, that they may believe that you sent me."
>
> When he had said this, Jesus called in a loud voice, "Lazarus, come out!" The dead man came out, his hands and feet wrapped with strips of linen, and a cloth around his face.
>
> Jesus said to them, "Take off the grave clothes and let him go."
>
> Therefore many of the Jews who had come to visit Mary, and had seen what Jesus did, put their faith in him.

People have been talking about that impossible case ever since.

WE CAN DO GREATER

We seem to have forgotten, or at least we don't seriously consider, what the Great Physician told his interns just a short time after he raised Lazarus. This rather astounding claim of Jesus appears in John 14:12: "I tell you the truth, anyone who has faith in me will do what I have been doing. He will do even greater things than these."

If Jesus really expects us to do "even greater things" than he did, then why don't we see a lot more impossible things being done today?

When I read that verse, it prompts two different reactions. First, I start looking for proof that the promise is true, and I am reminded of "impossible" cases I have seen or heard about. I think Don Mullen's mitral-valve story could qualify as one of the "even greater things" Jesus was talking about. The Great Physician never performed open-heart surgery where he had to stick his finger inside the patient's heart to heal him. There are any number of procedures Christian doctors routinely perform today that would have seemed mind-boggling fifty years ago, let alone in Jesus' day.

But my second reaction to Jesus' promise is to wonder, "If that's true, if Jesus really expects us to do 'even greater things' than he did, then why don't we see a lot more impossible things being done today? Why don't more of the Great Physician's followers specialize in impossible cases?" If we believe that promise, if we truly believe in Jesus and see him as a model for our lives, then why aren't we out looking for more impossible cases to take on?

I can only answer that from my own limited experience. So I would like to tell you the first story that leaps to mind when I think of attempting the impossible. I have already included a snippet from this tale in chapter 7. But before I give the entire account here, you need a little background.

IMPOSSIBLE BEGINNING

In the last years of the nineteenth century an extraordinary man by the name of Willis Hotchkiss left the United States, boarded a ship, and traveled for over three months to reach Africa. He landed in Mombassa and spent a number of weeks in that Indian Ocean port, purchasing supplies and equipment he thought he and his colleagues would need to head into the unexplored interior of Kenya. Hotchkiss and his party pushed past the small settlement of Nairobi and into the hinterland. It took them almost six weeks to make a trip that can now be made by car in less than eight hours.

Willis Hotchkiss and seven other missionary pioneers faced what seemed an impossible task. They were taking the Gospel to a tribal group that had never heard it before. But their ministry did not start well. Within six months, five of the missionaries died of malaria. Two others were so sick with blackwater fever that Hotchkiss hired litter bearers to carry them back to the coast. Only one of them made it out.

Willis Hotchkiss stayed. When he suffered recurring bouts of malaria, there was no one to take care of him. He didn't yet speak the language very well, and the local chief of the tribe forbade anyone to help this outsider.

Hotchkiss finally became so sick that he could no longer crawl out of the crude shelter he had made for himself. His supplies ran out and he almost starved to death before one of the tribal women took pity on him. Every morning she walked past his shelter with a basket of fruit on her head, and every morning when she got right in front of the door to his hut, she would shake her head to the right and a banana, or a couple of oranges, or a papaya would drop off and roll where Hotchkiss could grab it.

Hotchkiss eventually recovered. And he stayed, because he had a burden to reach this tribe called the Kipsigis. They were a people who worshiped the sun. They had many cruel beliefs. They did hurtful things to their children, like knocking out their lower incisor teeth and creating "beautification" scars on their skin with knife cuts or burning pieces of wood. Many young girls died during female circumcision rites.

The Kipsigis practiced all sorts of witchcraft. If someone became sick, they would lay them on the ground, take knives, and cut over the area where the pain was felt. Then they would make hundreds of shallow knife cuts to let the evil spirits out and then rub herbs and charcoal into the cuts to keep the spirits from getting back in.

Willis Hotchkiss poured out his life for the Kipsigis people—preaching and teaching among them for over thirty years. He eventually won some of them over to Christ and started a fledgling church. But he remained a lone missionary with a handful of national helpers.

In the 1930s a group called World Gospel Mission came looking for a new field of outreach in Africa. When they heard of Willis Hotchkiss's work, they sent a team of missionaries over there to meet him, work with him, and eventually take over and continue his ministry.

Willis knew the area well by then; he had been working in Kenya for most of his life. So he led this group of young missionaries up to an area in the southwestern highlands of the country where he recommended they begin their work. He knew good land was precious because there wasn't much soil in Kenya good for growing crops. The particular area he showed them was fertile, yet no one lived there because it had been a traditional female circumcision site. Many years before, during annual circumcision rites, two girls bled to death on this spot, and the tribe considered the ground cursed ever since.

So Willis Hotchkiss, after long discussions, talked the tribe into giving the mission this land where no Kipsigis wanted to live anyway. This place of death the Kipsigis called Tenwek.

Willis Hotchkiss was elated because he had had his eye on this location for a long time. On a river just below the site was a forty-foot waterfall. This pioneer missionary had a vision, as impossible as it seemed at the time, that someday someone would build a hydroelectric plant there. He believed that World Gospel Mission, in its effort to reach out to the Kipsigis people, could get all the power it needed from that waterfall.

The first missionaries found people at their door daily seeking medical help. A call went out to the mission board. They sent out a nurse, who was soon overwhelmed with medical needs. More nurses came. The first clinic was built, and then a small ward for patients too sick to return home. This became a cottage hospital by the late 1940s, and people began to pray for a doctor. In 1959, after eleven years of faithful prayers, God answered those prayers with the arrival of Ernie Steury, Tenwek's first residing doctor. The medical ministry of Tenwek continued to grow.

POWER SHORTAGE

As I noted in chapter 7, by the time I arrived on the scene in 1981, the cost of generating enough power for the 135-bed hospital to have electricity less than half a day had become a tremendous financial burden. The lack of a consistent power source severely limited the care we could offer our patients. Patients were dying for the lack of electricity. I told the tragic story of one earlier—the little girl who died when her mother failed to stay awake to manually suction her daughter's trach after we had to turn the electric suction machine off for the night.

We did have a little 5,000-watt gasoline-powered generator we could afford to run at night, but it only put out enough power to run one or two incubators. Some nights we would have three premature babies in each incubator. That obviously created a problem in spreading disease. Moreover, we had to worry about what to do when a another preemie was delivered. How do you decide which baby should live and which one is going to die?

How do you decide which baby should live and which one is going to die?

For more than fifty years that goal of one day having an adequate source of electricity for the hospital seemed an impossible dream. Back in the early 1960s somebody actually donated a used turbine generator set to the mission. They shipped it all the way to Kenya at great expense and even sent a missionary engineer out to install it. But the local people opposed the idea. They were afraid if you put water through that machine, the turbine would eat it, and their cows would have no water to drink.

Demonstrations were held to show tribal leaders where the water went in and where the same water came out. But they couldn't understand how you could make power without consuming something. So the whole plan fell apart.

In the 1970s the mission tried to revive the idea. By then, many of the Kipsigis had become a little more sophisticated. More of them had been to the city and seen what electricity could do. They were now agreeable to building a small power plant, but only if we would provide everybody in the area with a ten-watt light bulb in their hut. The logistics and cost for that were impossible, so the plan once again failed to get approval.

The next part of this story I told in chapter 7. At the end of our first term, as our family left to come back to the States for a year of furlough, Dr. Steury said almost jokingly, "Dave, while you're home, why don't you see what you can do about building the power plant?"

I told Ernie I would do what I could. But the whole thing seemed so impossible that I pretty much dismissed the idea from my mind. There were too many other things I had to do while we were home, things I thought I could do.

ENVISIONING THE IMPOSSIBLE

Here is where the rest of this story illustrates the first of three main reasons why we don't see God doing impossible things through us: We limit ourselves to the probable because we avoid even asking God what impossible things he wants us to attempt. We have no vision simply because we don't take God's promises seriously enough to ask.

That was my problem. I had forgotten, or at least failed to apply to this situation, the lesson Jesus tried to get across to some of his slow-learning followers when he said in Luke 18:27: "What is impossible with men is possible with God." I had a lot to learn, which must have been one reason God spoke to Marilyn Kinlaw early one morning and sent her to interrupt me on that August morning back in 1984 (see chapter 7).

Soon after Marilyn left that day, I headed across town to meet this engineer she thought had something to do with building a dam in Ecuador. It seemed the least I could do after someone knocked on my door at 7:30 A.M. to tell me God wanted her to pass along a message.

We limit ourselves to the probable because we avoid even asking God what impossible things he wants us to attempt.

I found the man Marilyn referred to. After I introduced myself to Bruce Rydbeck and told him briefly about our need for a hydroelectric dam in Kenya, he smiled oddly and said, "David, I was having my devotions this morning and praying to God saying, 'Lord, it would be great if you would give me a chance to work on another hydroelectric project like we did down in Ecuador.' I just can't believe there would be another opportunity like this! Boy, am I excited!"

I could see that excitement on his face and hear it in his voice as he said, "I tell you whom we need to get hold of right away. Where can we get a couple of phones where we can both get on the line?"

We jumped in the car and drove to my parents' house. Bruce got on one phone to place the call and I picked up an extension. We were telephoning a civil engineer with Duke Power Company in North Carolina, which Bruce told me was one of only three power companies in the U.S. that built their own hydroelectric projects. This man had helped Bruce and provided expert advice when HCJB had built their hydro project high in the mountains of Ecuador.

Hugh McKay answered the phone. Bruce greeted him warmly, then introduced me, and I briefly explained our desire to build a hydro plant for our hospital in rural Kenya. There was a long pause before Hugh said, "Dave, I was just sitting here at my desk, leaning back in chair, enjoying a good cup of coffee. [It was about 10 A.M. by this time.] And I was praying, 'Oh God, give me another chance to do what we did down in Ecuador.' Then the phone rings, and it's you and Bruce!"

Hugh too was now excited. Both he and Bruce had already grabbed on to this vision of a hydroelectric plant for Tenwek. I could hardly believe it! But I could feel it—something incredible was going on here. I got this spine-tingling sense that God was definitely at work.

BELIEVING THE IMPOSSIBLE

It's only in looking back at that morning that I see that what was going on was an illustration of the second common reason we don't see God doing more impossible things in our lives today: We lack faith, so that when God suggests the impossible, we look only to our own resources. We think, as I had been doing, *I sure don't have what it takes to do that!* But we forget who does. We don't even stop long enough to look and see he's already working.

> *When God suggests the impossible, we look only to our own resources. We think,* I sure don't have what it takes to do that! *But we forget who does.*

I was a prime example. In focusing on the obstacles and my own lack of resources, I had made a mountain out of a hydro plant. I had forgotten all about Matthew 17:20, where Jesus said, "You're not taking God seriously; the simple truth is that if you had a mere kernel of faith, a poppy seed, say, you would tell this mountain, 'Move!' and it would move. There is nothing you wouldn't be able to tackle" (*The Message*).

If Jesus would have just mentioned waterfalls instead of mountains, I like to think I might have made the connection a little quicker.

But then again, maybe not.

"Dave, have you got a piece of paper?" Hugh asked over the phone that morning.

"Sure," I told him.

"Then take this down. Here's what we need to know," and he began rattling off a bunch of info he wanted me to gather for him. Exactly how high was the waterfall? How much water flowed over it per minute? How much did the flow change from season to season through the year? And a whole lot more.

I was practically reeling from the speed of all that was happening. Part of me was wanting to stop and say, "Whoa! This idea is still impossible. We don't have the funding. No one at our mission has any expertise in this at all." But Bruce and Hugh were excitedly talking about this possibility and that option—how this would be just like, or how that might be different from, what they had done in South America.

Most of us lack experience in doing the impossible.

EXPERIENCING THE IMPOSSIBLE

What was happening that morning is a perfect illustration of the third reason so many of us don't see God doing impossible things in our lives: Most of us lack experience in doing the impossible. That hydro dam still seemed to me an impossible dream. But Hugh and Bruce, because they had built one before, were ready and raring to do it again.

I had yet to learn what they had already experienced. There is no greater excitement for a Christian than to see God working in and through us to accomplish impossible things. Such experience actually strengthens our faith for accepting more and bigger challenges.

To put it another way: We need to exercise our faith. It's a lot like working out physically. We need to do frequent reps with increasing weights to build our faith muscles. A lot of us have weak faith because we simply haven't exercised it enough with small things and worked our way up.

One of the things I miss about Africa now that I'm back living in the States is that I find I don't have to be nearly as dependent on God here on a daily basis. For example, if my car breaks down here, I call AAA on my cell phone. In Kenya every trip was an adventure. If we were out on the road and something broke down, you never knew when or from where help would arrive. You learned to trust God even in the small things, and that practice steadily increased your faith for dealing with the bigger crises.

I had only had one term on the mission field before that morning I was introduced to Bruce Rydbeck and Hugh McKay. I hadn't worked my way up to "impossible" exercises yet. This missionary doctor's faith still needed a lot more training. What I didn't know that morning was that I was about to begin a workout regimen that would challenge my faith as nothing I ever imagined before. In the process I would learn some valuable training lessons I've been able to apply many times since.

So here's the rest of the story about Tenwek's impossible hydro-electric project—including some of the most important faith-training tips and techniques I picked up in the process. Added to that is an effective prescription for anyone seriously interested in accomplishing the impossible for God.

Looking back at this experience from today's perspective, I can see how important it is to have a vision if you want to do the impossible. Lots of people had the vision of a hydro plant for years, but I hadn't yet latched onto it. Anyone who wants to do the impossible must first have the vision.

I challenge you to ask God to stir your heart, to give you a vision for what he wants to do in you and through you for his kingdom. If you want to do the impossible, ask God what impossible thing he would like you to do. The Bible tells us that without a vision people perish (Prov. 29:18, KJV).

PLANNING THE IMPOSSIBLE

I took that checklist of requested information Hugh McKay gave me over the phone that morning and sent it over to Tenwek. The folks in Kenya took a few weeks to collect all the data and send it back.

The next thing we needed was a feasibility study. Could the idea work or not? How could it be done? What was it going to take? I knew just coming up with a plan would cost a lot of money we didn't have.

But Hugh McKay said, "Dave, don't you worry about that. Leave that to me." Three weeks later he sent me a sixty-page feasibility study—complete with diagrams, pictures, graphs—based on our data. The report looked great. By the time I finished reading it, I finally believed it could be done. Hugh had spelled it out plain and simple, step by step. I was beginning to believe the vision was possible.

What is your personal plan for the impossible case the Great Physician wants to refer to you?

I was also beginning to learn another important lesson about doing impossible things. You not only need a vision, you also need a plan—a practical plan, a personal plan. Once we have a plan, we know where we're headed. Then we can even see how we might be able to get there. What is your personal plan for the impossible case the Great Physician wants to refer to you? Keep reading and I'll prescribe a few more exercises.

BEGINNING THE IMPOSSIBLE

As I was saying, in reading that feasibility study I began to believe the impossible might happen, that the vision could come true. That is, until I got to the bottom line, where Hugh said all I needed to do was raise approximately $600,000. That was his rough estimate of the cost.

My immediate reaction was a discouraged, *Oh, man! How many churches am I going to have to go to, to raise that kind of money?* That really seemed impossible.

So I sat down and I tried to think of any and every possible alternative source of money. I knew or had heard of people in eight different foundations, so I decided to write each of them a formal proposal letter. I worked hard on that letter, got input from a number of people, and sent it off about the end of September.

October went by and nothing happened. November came, and I still hadn't heard from anybody. Hugh McKay and a couple of other engineers wanted to go over and check out the actual site. But they needed money for airfare; they had already ordered their tickets.

They planned to go the third week in November. They had already requested time off from work. They needed to see the waterfall in order to examine its location and determine for certain if everything we had put in our formal proposal was actually going to work. But two days before the engineering team was scheduled to take off, we still didn't have money for their tickets.

That's the day I got a phone call from Joe Luce, whose family-owned Blue Bird Bus company manufactured a large percentage of the buses used by schools and transportation departments around the country. I had sent him a copy of the feasibility study and the formal proposal.

He told me later, "David, when I called you that day I told myself, *There is absolutely no way they can do this at Tenwek. It's impossible. It's too expensive. No one at Tenwek knows how to build a hydroelectric plant. They don't have the resources or the manpower.* But you seemed so sure you could do it. So I thought, *I'll give him $20,000. If that's gone, it's gone. But at least he can try.*"

So Joe Luce sent us the first $20,000. The engineering team went. When they came back, they told me they were absolutely convinced the plan would work.

December went by. Nobody sent us any more money. January was almost over—still no funds. I spoke at a mission conference with someone from World Vision, the large Christian relief and development agency that works all over the world. I hadn't sent our proposal to them, so as we were each setting up our displays in the back of the church, I walked over to ask the World Vision rep if his organization ever got involved in projects like ours. He said he didn't think they did, but suggested I write their U.S. headquarters. So I contacted a World Vision vice president my dad happened to know and sent them a proposal. My contact got back to me right away to say, "Sorry, we don't do this sort of thing here. Why don't you contact our Kenyan World Vision office in Nairobi."

Five months later we went back to Kenya to begin our second term. Our year of furlough, which had begun with Ernie's challenge and gotten off to such a memorable start—with Marilyn Kinlaw's interruption, the subsequent connection with Bruce Rydbeck and Hugh McKay, the plans, the proposal, the seed money from Joe Luce, and the confirmation that our plan

> *I reminded myself that if you want God to do an impossible thing, you may have to take the first step out of the boat, as Peter did.*

would in fact work—ended on a rather discouraging note. Nothing else had happened. We still didn't have any money for the project.

We did have faith, however. Bruce had asked his mission organization, World Radio Missionary Fellowship, if he could help us build our hydroelectric plant. I thought that too was impossible because that organization had plenty of use for Bruce's skills in their own effective television, radio, and medical ministry in South America.

When WRMF generously gave Bruce permission to join us, we took most of the remaining seed money to buy tickets for him and his family to move to Kenya. That seemed a huge (perhaps even reckless) step of faith with no more money coming in. I couldn't help thinking, *Maybe it really is impossible.* We kept on pushing ahead. I reminded myself that if you want God to do an impossible thing, you may have to take the first step out of the boat, as Peter did.

I had little hope World Vision would be able to help, but I stopped at their office in Nairobi when I arrived back in Kenya. They told me,

"We don't do this type of project. But thanks anyway. We wish you the best."

We also didn't yet have official government permission to even build a hydroelectric dam on the river. Ernie had been trying to get permission but to no avail. He had been told it would take two years to get the paperwork approved before we could even begin construction on any hydroelectric plant. There would be forms to sign, reports to be filed, studies to be conducted, inspections to be made, committees to meet. It sounded like bureaucracy at its best.

So we went to another office—and another office. Then we went back to each of them again. The discouraging word never changed: "It will take two years to get an answer. And the likely answer will be no. No private organization has ever built a hydro plant the size you propose. We think it is impossible for you to do."

Finally, somebody had a brainstorm. We already had an official government license to generate power for the hospital from a diesel generator. What if we stop asking approval for constructing a hydroelectric dam and just asked permission to change our source of power? So we went to a different government office, showed them the license Tenwek already had giving us the right to generate our own electrical power, and asked if we could get their official okay to switch from our old and inefficient diesel generator to a hydroelectric power source.

We were told, "No problem. If you want to change your power source, that's fine!" We didn't bother to mention that the hydroelectric power source didn't exist yet. An official signed a simple form. We then took that form back to the government office that had denied us permission to build and told them, "Look! The power board has given us permission. Why can't you?" And in less than a week, they did.

DOING THE IMPOSSIBLE

By this time we had little of Joe Luce's seed money left. Since the next step was to build an access road down to the falls, we began hiring local men to do that arduous job. Without dynamite or even a bulldozer, they began to widen the footpath that ran along a narrow ledge high above the river. On one side was a drop-off, and on the other, solid rock.

We bought picks and shovels. The men built fires to heat the rock and then poured cold river water on the hot stone to crack it. Slowly a road wide enough to get construction equipment and materials down to the falls began to take shape. We had begun work on the project as if we were going full-speed ahead, even though we didn't yet have any resources to do it.

Two days before the money ran out and we were going to shut down the work, I received a phone call from the director of World Vision in Nairobi. He said, "Dr. Stevens, after you were here, I decided to send your proposal to our head office in the States anyway. Lo and behold, they have approved it. I've got a check for $50,000. I want to fly out tomorrow and give it to you."

Just like that we had the money we needed to keep construction going. The whole project was going to end up costing over $800,000. So I sent proposals to forty more foundations—none of whom gave us anything. But the Lord provided the funds. You know from whom we received it? From the first eight foundations I had contacted. And every bit of that $800,000 came in just when we needed it to keep the construction on track!

I learned a couple important lessons from that. One key to doing impossible things is to ask yourself, *If the project were possible, what's the first thing I would need to do?* Then do it. Then do the next thing, and the next. Eventually, one step at a time, the impossible gets done.

> *One key to doing impossible things is to ask yourself,* If it were possible, what's the first thing I would need to do? *Then do it.*

Vision, faith, and plans are essential. But none of them do any good unless we put the plan into action. Accomplishing the impossible always takes work—sometimes a lot of work.

Thus, I learned another lesson: If we want to achieve the impossible, we need to work as if success depends entirely on us, yet trust and believe that the results all depend on God. If we do our part, God will always do his. Even if all we think we can manage is a mustard seed worth of faith, effort, or talent, once God pitches in, mountains will move. Dams will rise.

GROUNDED FOR THE IMPOSSIBLE

We began our work on the dam itself above the falls in the dry season. The engineers told me the timing was perfect because the dry season is the best time to lay a firm foundation. It made sense to me because I have found that true in life as well as in dams. God has always taught me more lessons during difficulties than when things are going well. It's the tough work we have to do in the dry seasons that give us the strength to attempt the impossible. As the apostle Paul reminds us concerning his thorn in the flesh, "When I am weak, then I am strong" (2 Cor. 12:10). That's how it turned out with our dam when we got down in the river.

God brought people from all over the world to do this project. For example, an engineer came from Australia to build the powerhouse. A specialist in heavy equipment volunteered from Canada. When they started working down in the river, I expected them to start pouring cement right away. But no. Instead, they hired a hundred Kipsigis men who were down there with chisels and hammers chipping at the riverbed—for weeks.

What these men were doing was digging an eighteen-inch-deep trench into the bedrock all the way across the river. When I questioned the engineers about it, they said, "Oh, David, this is the most important step in the entire project. If you don't get down into the bedrock, it won't matter how much concrete you pour. They dam will move when the waters come. We need a firm foundation."

From this I learned another lesson I offer as one more prescription for anyone wanting to attempt the impossible: We first need to be grounded and growing in our personal faith. We cannot lay a foundation alone. You must plan for it. You must seek God's help. And you must give him time to make it happen.

Each of us has a personal responsibility to cut down through the rock and lay a firm foundation. We must create depth in our own lives. Richard Foster said it this way: "Superficiality is the curse of our age. The doctrine of instant satisfaction is a primary spiritual problem. What we desperately need today is not for a great number of intelligent people or gifted people but deep people."

THE IMPOSSIBLE REQUIRES PURITY

All the labor needed for building the dam at Tenwek was local. Transportation prices were so high and the roads so bad that it was actually more cost effective not to truck materials in but to pay hundreds of local Kipsigis workers with hammers to sit on the hillside, patiently making tons of gravel by breaking the rocks they had hauled up from the riverbed. There were always a lot of people and a variety of activities going on down at our construction site.

We had capable engineers and construction people supervising the on-site work. I was keeping the books on my home computer in the evening and trying to raise the funds we needed while still practicing medicine and serving as the hospital's medical superintendent. Life became even more hectic than it had been during our first term.

Yet every day or two I found the time to get down to the river. It was like building your first house—you want to see what's happening. One day down on the riverbank I noticed something that struck me as odd. A crew of Kipsigis men getting rocks out of the river were carefully washing each one off before they put it up on the bank.

I turned to Billy Wayne Fuller, our missionary in charge of construction, and asked, "Why are you washing those rocks?"

He replied, "Because they are going to be mixed into the concrete, and anything that goes into the concrete has to be washed first—even

If we are ever going to be strong enough to accomplish impossible things for God, we are going to have to be careful about our own purity—whether it's purity of motive, mind, or heart.

the sand we use. If there's any dirt in this cement, it won't bond; instead, it will crumble. The water will soon penetrate it and the dam will collapse. When you're making cement, all the ingredients need to be clean and pure."

Do you see the parallel? If we are ever going to be strong enough to accomplish impossible things for God, we are going to have to be careful about our own purity— whether it's purity of motive, mind, or heart. As the person in charge of a Christian organization, I have learned that the quickest means for Satan to weaken us as individuals, as a Christian group, even as a church, is to cause dissension. Common ordinary things like damaged relationships, pride, and selfishness can break our unity, prevent us from fellowship with God and each other, and keep us from becoming strong enough to achieve the impossible things he wants us to do.

As executive director of CMA I travel a good bit and speak to many groups of people in churches and conferences across North America. Many Christians confide in me. These are good people, spiritual people who want to be godly but are struggling with money, sex, power, and relationships. These things are keeping them from forming a rock-solid bond with God.

Just as it would be foolish and disastrous for us to build a dam, a bridge, or a skyscraper with poorly bonded concrete, God cannot use us to do impossible things for him unless we are well bonded to him. For that to happen, we need to guard our purity.

THE IMPOSSIBLE DEMANDS A GROUP EFFORT

Believe it or not, we made every bit of the concrete for our hydroelectric project in a half-cubic-yard cement mixer. If you know anything at all about construction, you realize that that's the size mixer you would use to pour a patio or a new step up to your porch. But that's all we had to build a 150-foot-long dam that was forty feet high and more than twenty feet thick at the base.

Impossible? No. But it helped me imagine what it must have been like to build the pyramids.

We had three lines of men at once converging on that mixer. One line brought sand, another rock, the third cement. They each dumped their load in the mixer, another man added water, someone else counted the minimum turns before dumping the contents of the mixer into one of the wheelbarrows waiting in yet another line. Then the finished cement was wheeled on the run out onto the dam and poured into wooden forms. At crucial points of the dam's construction, crews poured cement like that for twenty-four to forty-eight hours straight. It took everybody working together to make it happen.

Accomplishing the impossible usually requires a carefully synchronized effort. This may help explain why we don't see God doing more impossible things today. Independence is a big part of our American heritage. We pride ourselves in our self-sufficiency, our personal responsibility. Our society so much admires and honors individual achievement. Somebody one-upped John Donne by saying, "While it may be true that no man is an island, some of us make pretty good peninsulas." That seems true of many Americans.

So a lot more of us *think* we can do the impossible by ourselves than ever actually succeed. If we are going to accomplish the impossible things God would like to see us do, Christians today need to do a much better job of working together in our accountability groups, in our communities, in our

> *A lot more of us think we can do the impossible by ourselves than ever actually succeed. If we are going to accomplish the impossible things God would like to see us do, Christians today need to do a much better job of working together.*

churches, and with other Christians around the world. Doing the impossible almost always requires cooperative effort.

Power for the Impossible

If we want to find the strength to do the impossible, we also need to tap into the power of prayer. I thought a lot about this while we were building the dam because we were doing a lot of praying throughout those months.

One of the challenges we faced in developing our hydro plant and trying to decide on the most efficient turbine was the seasonal fluctuations of the river. During the rainy season there was often enough water flow to generate a couple of megawatts of electricity. But there were times during the dry season that the river had only enough water to generate fifty kilowatts. Most turbine generator sets require a full water flow all the time to work efficiently. So it took a lot of research before we found a German system that could operate efficiently with widely varying flows and could be synchronized to work in tandem with our diesel generators during the dry season.

The fact that the perfect set to meet our needs came from Germany influenced a German charity to pay the $225,000 that the generator cost. Impossible? I would have thought so a year before because I didn't know a soul in Germany. Why would a German group decide to donate the best generator set in the world for our particular hydroelectric plant? By this time, seeing God do the impossible was becoming routine. So many more "impossible" things happened that it would take another book to tell them all.

We started building the road in September, and by the next August construction on the dam was finished. So was the powerhouse. The turbine generator arrived before the end of the year. Just eighteen months after we began, the whole project was finished—the penstock in place, the turbine set, the powerhouse, the computer controls. Everything was beautiful and gleaming like new.

But nothing was happening. Absolutely nothing.

Do you know why? Because we hadn't opened the gates to let the water through. You can have the biggest and best hydroelectric power plant in the world, but you won't get a bit of power until you open the gates and let the water flow.

In the same way, prayer is the key to generating power in our lives, in our ministry, in our Christian organizations, and in our churches. Prayer opens the gates of heaven and the power flows down.

If you want to see impossible things happen, you need to start praying now. Pray for yourself, pray for your family, pray for your colleagues, pray for your church, pray for your country. Paul said, "Brothers, pray for us." If Paul needed prayer, I know I do. I know you do.

I consider it one of the great privileges of my life that as a freshman at Asbury College in 1970 I witnessed what came to be called the great Asbury Revival. The revival broke out in a regularly scheduled chapel service, and so many people responded to the Spirit of God that that service continued nonstop, day and night, for over a week. People came to the campus from hundreds of miles around. And when Asbury students visited other schools to tell what was happening, revival spread to campuses all across the country.

There are thousands of people today whose lives were impacted by that revival. The spark that ignited it was a small group of premed and predental students who regularly gathered in a college dorm room to pray together consistently and fervently that God would send revival. One morning the gates opened and the power poured down.

I remember the day we opened the gates and turned on the hydroelectric power at Tenwek. All of a sudden we could do things we had never done before. Prior to this moment the lights always blinked a warning about 8:55 every night; five minutes later, after giving you just enough time to light your candles or switch on a battery light, the power went off until morning. The first night that the lights didn't blink at 9:00 P.M. seemed such a novelty that Jody and I were up until 1:00 A.M. Nobody told us to go to bed.

Our newfound source of power definitely took some getting used to. It seemed almost too good to be true. The impossible had happened.

REMEMBER THE IMPOSSIBLE

The last lesson I learned from the many impossible things God did in this project, and the last prescription I have to offer here, is actually illustrated by this entire story. If we want to see God accomplish more impossible things through us, we need to remember what God has already done in our lives. Like the Hebrew people in the Old Testament who built a stone altar to mark the important places on their journey where they had seen God work, we need to establish our own remembrances wherever and whenever we have seen the impossible happen.

> *Like the Hebrew people in the Old Testament who built a stone altar to mark the important places on their journey where they had seen God work, we need to establish our own remembrances wherever and whenever we have seen the impossible happen.*

I can't tell you how many times since, when I am facing what seems like yet another impossible task, I look back in my mind at an altar constructed with countless answered prayers, anchored in the bedrock in the bottom of a deep and beautiful little river valley running through the highlands of southwestern Kenya. And every time I picture that dam in my mind, I am reminded again that with God's help, impossible things can still be done.

If I was looking for a quote to place on that mental altar, I would certainly consider what Hudson Taylor, the great missionary doctor to China, once said: "Many Christians estimate difficulties in light of their own resources and thus attempt little and often fail. All of God's giants have been weak men who did great things for God because they reckoned on his power and his presence being with them."

In other words, with the Great Physician's help, we too can tackle the impossible cases.

THE GREAT PHYSICIAN IS LOOKING FOR PARTNERS

MY FATHER HAD BEEN IN THE MEDICAL CORPS IN the army during World War II. Although he was just an orderly whose duties were limited to changing bedpans and making up beds in hospital wards, his experience inspired in him a lifelong fascination with medicine.

As an evangelist he was particularly excited about and supportive of my decision to go into medical missions. Realizing his interest in medicine, whenever he came to visit me at Tenwek, I would take him on hospital rounds with me. Sometimes I would let him observe my work or even help by handing me an instrument during a minor procedure. And he loved it.

I remember one time I had him hold the legs of a patient while I removed a thorn from a man's heel. The next time I came home to the States I learned he had a three-point sermon built around that case, telling of his thinking during the operation about all the places that man's feet had been. He had preached that sermon all across the country.

Another time I let him come in and watch me do a C-section, and he talked about that for weeks. One day while he was with me in Africa, I thought to myself, *You know what would really be neat? To have my father deliver a baby.* So I approached him and asked, "How would you like to deliver a baby, Dad?"

He got this alarmed look on his face and said, "There's no way I can do that! Are you crazy, Son? I don't know anything about delivering babies. They didn't even let me in the delivery room when you kids were born."

I had to work on him for three days. I twisted his arm and kept promising, "Dad, I'll be right there with you. I'll help you out." He finally agreed.

Since we delivered several babies a day, I knew we could find him an easy one. So I instructed the staff, "When you get a grand multip, give me a call." What I was looking for was a woman who had already had ten or more babies and could deliver another one with a single grunt.

The phone in my office rang during lunchtime. I had gotten tied up with some paperwork, and Dad had already hiked down the hill to our house to eat with my family. The OB nurse told me, "Dr. Stevens, you'd better get your father up here quick. This patient isn't going to wait much longer. The baby is going to come out any moment."

So I got on the phone and called the house. When Jody put my father on the line, I said, "Dad, you've got to get up here quick. We don't have much time." Then I hung up and hurried over to the delivery room to ask the patient's permission to let my father help with delivery. She happily agreed, knowing I would be there.

At 7,000 feet altitude, Tenwek is much higher than Denver. And my sixty-three-year-old father ran more than a quarter mile up the hill. I thought he was going to die right there. When he reached the hospital, he was panting so hard for breath he couldn't gasp out more than one or two words at a time. "Son . . . I can't . . . do this . . . it's too . . . much."

I grabbed his arm and insisted, "Dad, come on." And I led him over to get scrubbed and masked and to put on a plastic apron to protect his clothes. After I gloved him, I quickly scrubbed and got ready myself.

I knew we had cut the time close. The patient's loud "OOOEEE"s were getting closer together, and the midwife was telling the woman not to push yet. "Now, Dad, we don't have much time."

But he kept saying, "I can't do it, David. I can't do it. I'm still out of breath and I just don't know how."

I insisted, "Dad, come on, the head's starting to crown. You better hurry." He rushed over to the delivery table, and I said, "Now put your left hand on top of the baby's head." The baby's head was halfway out.

He said, "But, David I don't know how!"

I was out of time to encourage and teach. So in a tone he had occasionally used on me as a child, I said, "Put your hand in my hand."

He put his hand in mine, and I guided it to the right position. Reaching over his arms I said, "Give me your other hand." I moved it so he had the baby's head cupped in his two hands. Then I said, "Here comes the head. Let it come slowly and support it. Now you are going to feel the head begin to rotate to the side."

I could feel Dad's hands trembling. I moved them to get his fingers under the baby's chin and around the back of the neck. "Now, Dad, we need to pull down on the head gently to get the baby's shoulder under the pubic bone." It really didn't take much pulling. A lot of babies had already traveled this way.

"It's going to come quickly now, Dad. And it's gonna be slippery. You hang on tight. Don't drop this baby, Dad!"

The baby slipped out in an instant. But I could feel with my hand that Dad had a good grip as I showed him how to swing the baby around and support it with his arm.

"I've got it, David! I've got it! It's okay!"

Then I said, "Now get a clamp and clamp the cord. Here's the other clamp. Put it just a little ways from the first one. There are the scissors; now cut between the clamps. Do you hear me, Dad? Between the clamps." (If he cut on either side, we would have blood everywhere. His hands were shaking so badly, I wasn't sure he was thinking straight.)

"Okay, Dave, between the clamps."

"Now grab that baby by the heels and give it a slap on the buttocks." He smacked that baby on the rump, and it gave the most beautiful cry you ever heard.

My dad was smiling so big you could see it out the sides of his mask. That grin nearly passed his ears. He had never experienced anything like that in his life. He had helped bring a baby into the world.

That was a magic moment for my father, and for me, as he gently laid the baby in the mother's arms.

After Dad died just two years later, I realized that of all the experiences he and I ever shared, that day will always stand out as one of the most memorable and meaningful. Perhaps it was his willingness to finally trust me and reach out despite his feelings of inadequacy. Maybe it was the rare privilege of guiding him with my own experience and training and seeing the joy it brought him. Or possibly, it was merely the thrill of bringing new life into the world, hand in hand with the man who gave me life.

I cannot think of that day with Dad in the delivery room without being reminded that we all have times like that in our lives as Christians. God gets all of us at times into some situation where we feel just like my dad. God will be asking us to do something so much bigger than we had ever imagined that we will be scared and trembling inside. We'll be saying, "Ohhh, Lord, not me, not me. I can't do that. I don't know how."

I want to tell you something. If my father were still alive today, I wouldn't advise any woman in the world to go to him to have her baby delivered. Because, like Scarlett's maid said in *Gone with the Wind,* he "don't know nothin' 'bout birthin' no babies."

Yet I have learned that whatever God calls us to do, whatever cases he asks us to accept, whatever procedures he asks us to perform, he's going to be right there beside us, saying, "Put your hand right here in my hand, and put your other hand right there and let me speak through you. Let me use your actions and your experience and your abilities. Let me fill you and use you and mold you and make you into what I want you to be."

If we let God do that, we too may be smiling from ear to ear as we discover the kind of satisfying happiness that results from rounding with Jesus. God then will be able to take us to new heights of trust and faith in him. He will make us partners with the Great Physician and will be able to use us to help in his practice—to reach out and heal a hurt and dying world.

Christian Medical Association
Resources

Medically reliable . . . biblically sound. That's the rock-solid promise of this dynamic new series offered by Zondervan and the Christian Medical Association. Because when your health is at stake, you can't settle for anything less than the whole truth.

Finally, people of faith can draw from both the knowledge of science and the wisdom of God's Word in addressing health care and medical ethics issues. This series allows you to benefit from cutting-edge knowledge of experienced, trusted, and respected medical scientists and practitioners. Now you can gain their insights into the vital interconnection of health and spirituality—a critical unity largely overlooked by secular science.

While integrating your faith and health can actually improve your physical well-being and even extend your life, it can also help you make health care decisions consistent with your beliefs. A sound biblical analysis of emerging treatments and technologies is essential to protecting yourself from seemingly harmless—yet spiritually, ethically, or medically unsound—options.

Founded in 1931, the Christian Medical Association helps thousands of doctors minister to their patients by imitating the Great Physician, Jesus Christ. Christian Medical Association members provide a Christian voice on medical ethics to policy makers and the media . . . minister to needy patients on medical missions around the world . . . evangelize and disciple students on more than 90 percent of the nation's medical school campuses . . . and provide educational and inspirational resources to the church.

To learn more about Christian Medical Association ministries and resources on health care and ethical issues, browse the Web site at www.christianmedicalassociation.org or call Christian Medical Association Life & Health Resources toll free at 888-231-2637.

"Dear friend, I pray that you may enjoy good health and that all may go well with you, even as your soul is getting along well."

(3 John 2 NIV)